THE POETRY OF
EDMUND SPENSER

The Poetry of
EDMUND SPENSER

A STUDY

By WILLIAM NELSON

COLUMBIA UNIVERSITY PRESS

NEW YORK AND LONDON

Copyright © 1963 Columbia University Press
Third printing and Columbia Paperback edition 1965
Printed in the United States of America

To
Elsa, Susan, and
William

Preface

IN SIR PHILIP SIDNEY's judgment, Spenser's *Shepheardes Calender* is one of the few English poems with "poeticall sinnewes," and Milton calls its author "our sage and serious poet." But in a verse epistle to Charles Cowden Clarke, Keats describes the reader of Spenser's poetry as

> one who had by Mulla's stream
> Fondled the maidens with the breasts of cream.

Between these poles critical evaluation oscillates: for some Spenser is an elfin voluptuary, for others he is a learned moralist and an eloquent, highly sophisticated artist. I have come slowly to accept the latter characterization.

The governing principle of Spenser's poems is intellectual and thematic rather than narrative, dramatic, or symbolic. The poet himself says as much in the letter to Sir Walter Ralegh which accompanied the first publication of *The Faerie Queene:* he begins with the statement of an abstract "general intention" and proceeds to justify the method by which that intention is expressed. This does not mean that *The Faerie Queene* is a philosophical discourse in verse like Lucretius' *De rerum natura,* for the process of the latter is logical demonstration, that of the former exposition or "fashioning," to use the poet's own word. But it does mean that Spenser's overriding concern is with the moral nature of man rather than with happenings or people. In poetry of this kind the resources of literary expression stand as servants. Stories, characters, symbols, figures of speech, and the whole range of rhetorical devices constitute the medium by which the poet tries to convey his meaning vividly, beautifully, and movingly. In a sense, the distinction between rhetorical means and conceptual end is artificial, for either must shape the other and in the poems themselves they are one. But in the interpretation of Spenser's poetry the distinction is necessary, for only when the theme of his discourse is grasped does the means by which it is stated become relevant and significant. In this book, therefore, I direct attention first of all to the intellectual core of the poems and then to the techniques by which their meaning is given shape, precision, and power.

The task of working into and out from the themes of Spenser's poems is beset with hazards. Although the poet is, I think, at pains to point the reader to the heart of his meaning, his signs may be ignored or misread, particularly if one begins by thinking that the path should lead in another direction. Furthermore, since fashions in literary communication have changed much more radically than language itself, the means by which the poet develops and refines his ideas may be misconstrued and the ideas themselves distorted. In either case, the interpreter forces his conception of subject or method upon an unwilling poem. But if Spenser is indeed constantly led by the intention to delineate the moral nature of man, misinterpretation of his meaning, however difficult to avoid, is neither undetectable nor unavoidable. The text stands as the test. Every part of the poem should contribute in one way or another to the conception which gives it life. If it apparently does not, either the poet has lost his hold or, as I incline to think more likely, the reader has gone astray.

In choosing to deal primarily with the conceptual structure of Spenser's poems I have necessarily treated only at a tangent subjects which have concerned other writers: the genesis and chronology of his compositions, the identification of his sources, his political and personal allusions, the techniques of his versification, the classification of his imagery, the relation of his work to that of his contemporaries and predecessors. I begin with an account of the poet's life, stripped as far as may be of the mass of conjecture that has accumulated about it and designed to discover what the scarce and scattered materials available tell of his career and his aspirations. The poems other than *The Faerie Queene* are examined in part because of their intrinsic interest and in part because they provide examples in little of the preoccupations and techniques which determine the nature of the great poem. Since I find no clearly marked change or development in Spenser's style or thought and since the dates of many of the poems are uncertain I have chosen to discuss them by kind rather than in chronological order: first the pastorals *The Shepheardes Calender* and *Colin Clouts Come Home Againe;* next the "complaints," elegies, and satires; then the love sonnets, the *Epithalamion,* and the hymns to love and beauty. The subject of *The Faerie Queene* is introduced by a chapter defining its principal literary model, its intention, and its method. The several books of the poem are treated severally in the conviction that Spenser organized them as units dealing with logical subdivisions of his moral theme, not arbitrarily to provide convenient resting places in a continued narrative. A concluding chapter on the Cantos of Mutabilitie serves to recapitulate the conclusions of this book about the plan and philosophy of the poem. The whole is therefore a study of all of the major poems, though from a special point of view.

Readers who are familiar with the body of Spenser scholarship will recognize at once my profound indebtedness to it. That debt I cannot properly acknowledge here, nor have I tried to recognize it in the Notes. Indeed, after so many years of immersion in the study of the poet and the literature of his time I can no more assign a source for this or that idea about his work than I can claim originality for such insights as I have had. Certainly, everyone who writes on this subject must rely upon the scholarship and long labor of the editors of the great Johns Hopkins edition and upon the contributions made by Professor Osgood's *Concordance* and Professor Carpenter's *Reference Guide*. An immense amount of learning and critical acumen has been brought to bear upon Spenser's poems from the eighteenth-century studies of Jortin, Warton, and Upton to our own day. If I have been able to contribute in some measure to the understanding and therefore to the appreciation of Spenser's poetry it is largely because of the instruction and stimulation provided by the scholarly and critical literature.

A more personal kind of debt I gladly pay. During the years in which this book was being written I have thrust half-formed notions and raw drafts at friends and colleagues whose learning, taste, and judgment have led me to enrich some conclusions and to modify or abandon others. Among those who have read and commented on the work in one or another of its stages are Marjorie Hope Nicolson, Eleanor Rosenberg, S. F. Johnson, Edward Tayler, Maurice Valency, and Carl Woodring—Professor Woodring I thank particularly for the quotation from Keats in the first paragraph of this preface. I have sought and found help for my deficiencies as a scholar from Josephine Waters Bennett, Rosalie Colie, Elizabeth Donno, and Isabel Rathborne; from Jerome H. Buckley, Moses Hadas, W. T. H. Jackson, Paul O. Kristeller, Joseph Mazzeo, Howard Schless, and Earl Wasserman. Professor Donno graciously undertook to read the final proof. The generosity of the John Simon Guggenheim Memorial Foundation and the Columbia University Fund for Research in the Humanities has allowed me some respite from my duties as teacher. My wife and my children have not only helped with the reading of proof but have even tolerated my long preoccupation with the subtle and sensitive poet who is the subject of this book.

Quotations from Spenser's writings are from *The Works of Edmund Spenser, a Variorum Edition,* ed. Edwin Greenlaw, Charles Grosvenor Osgood, Frederick Morgan Padelford, Ray Heffner, and others (Baltimore, The Johns Hopkins Press, 1932–57), cited in the Notes as *Works.* Vols. I–V include the first five books of *The Faerie Queene,* Vol. VI Book VI and the Cantos of Mutabilitie, Vols. VII and VIII the minor poems, Vol. IX the prose works, and Vol. X the Index. The availability of the Index makes it unnecessary to weigh down these notes with documentation which may now readily be found in the *Works.* For biblical passages I have used the Geneva version. When possible, quotations from foreign sources are given in sixteenth- or seventeenth-century translations. In the cases of Vergil and Ovid, however, I have preferred modern translations since they are closer to the originals which Spenser often reflects literally. I have regularly followed modern practice in the use of *u* and *v, i* and *j,* and italics.

Columbia University   WILLIAM NELSON
New York
September, 1962

Contents

THE POETRY OF
EDMUND SPENSER

Prince of Poets

IN THE LONG LIST of English poets whose works are remembered there are a very few who devoted their lives to their art inspired by the idea that it was the most powerful for good within human reach. That Edmund Spenser was one of this number we learn from the spirit of his works rather than from the bits of information about his life that have survived. For one described on his funeral monument as "the Prince of Poets in his tyme" there remains remarkably little material that the biographer can rely on; the inscription itself is wrong both in the date of his birth and in the date of his death. What we have is a scattering of official records, a few letters exchanged with his friend Gabriel Harvey, chance references in the writings of his contemporaries, and such information as can be drawn from his poems and their dedications.[1] Yet even these details suggest the career which his poems make manifest, a career conforming to that humanist ideal which called upon learned eloquence to be at once the servant and the guide of the commonwealth.

Spenser tells us in one way or another that he was born in London in 1554 or a year or two before, that his mother's name was Elizabeth, and that he was kin to the Spencers of Wormleighton in Warwickshire and Althorp in Northamptonshire, a family grown noble and rich in the time of Henry VII. He attended the Merchant Taylors

School in London, and in 1569 received a gown and a shilling for
representing the school at the funeral of Robert Nowell, a wealthy
London citizen. The Nowell family contributed to his support after
his entrance into Pembroke Hall in Cambridge later in the same
year.[2] His status at Pembroke Hall was that of sizar, or poor student,
but this did not mean that he was indigent. At about that time there
were 13 sizars at Pembroke and 36 pensioners, students who paid
their way. Spenser proceeded bachelor in 1573 and master of arts
in 1576. Nothing more is recorded except that he was granted al-
lowances, ostensibly for illness, several times in the academic year
1573–74. By the practice of the time, illness was not a necessary
condition for such payments. In the year of his arrival at Cambridge
his first work appeared in print, an unsigned contribution of verse,
most of it translated from the French, to a volume of godly monition
and anti-Catholic propaganda set forth by John van der Noot, a
refugee from the Low Countries.

When John Young, master of Pembroke Hall during Spenser's
residence, became bishop of Rochester in 1578, he made the poet his
secretary. An exchange of letters between Spenser and Harvey
throws some light on the events of the years immediately following.
His secretarial duties did not keep him pent up in the bishop's
palace, for he was several times in London, in the summer of 1579
bearing the appearance of "a young Italianate signor and French
monsieur," Harvey jocularly remarks. By October 5, Spenser had
become a servant of the great Earl of Leicester and wrote to his
friend from Leicester House about his imminent departure for
France, "which will be, (I hope, I feare, I thinke) the next weeke,
if I can be dispatched of my Lorde. I goe thither, as sent by him,
and maintained most what of him: and there am to employ my
time, my body, my minde, to his Honours service." This letter is
enclosed with another dated October 16 which makes no mention of
the intended mission, nor does Spenser refer to it in subsequent

correspondence. But he is now in "some use of familiarity" with Leicester's nephew, Philip Sidney, and with Sidney's friend Edward Dyer, and has been talking with them about the techniques of English poetry. He does not tell Harvey about another matter that must have occupied him at the time, his marriage to one Machabyas Childe, then about twenty years old, on October 27 at St. Margaret's, Westminster.[3]

It may have been even before the beginning of his service to the Earl of Leicester that Spenser, under the pen name "Immerito," dedicated his *Shepheardes Calender* to Leicester's nephew, Philip Sidney.[4] The prefatory letter signed by E. K., a friend of Spenser and Harvey, is dated April 10, 1579; the book was entered in the register of the Stationers' Company on December 5. Although the Colin Clout of the poem in some sense stands for Spenser, he is a fictional character in an imagined pastoral setting and the attempt to read Colin's life as autobiography has led to little but confusion. We may indeed confirm what we already know: Colin professes himself a poet, he is "the Southerne shepheardes boye" (that is, a servant of the bishop of Rochester), and he is a close friend of Hobbinol, otherwise Gabriel Harvey. E. K. and the Harvey correspondence tell of other works which Spenser had completed or was writing at about this time: the *Stemmata Dudleiana*, the *Epithalamion Thamesis*, *The Dying Pellicane*, *My Slomber*, *The Court* of *Cupide*, the *Dreames* (to appear with annotations by E. K. and illustrations), *Nine English Comoedies*, *Pageaunts*, *The English Poete*, and *The Faerie Queene*. Some part of the last Spenser had sent to Harvey by April, 1580. None of the other poems remains. The correspondence with Harvey was published in 1580 in a two-part volume entitled *Three Proper, and Wittie, Familiar Letters: Lately Passed betwene Two Universitie Men* and *Two Other Very Commendable Letters, of the Same Mens Writing*. It is not clear who was responsible for this publication; if it was Harvey he was very ill

advised, for some of his comments, whether indiscreet or misin-
terpreted, brought upon him a storm of criticism and the threat of
imprisonment. Spenser appears not to have been touched by the
affair, however.

Most of the remainder of the poet's life was spent in Ireland.
He was appointed secretary to the new governor of that troubled
and rebellious land, Arthur Lord Grey de Wilton, and probably
arrived with him at his post on August 12, 1580.[5] His office was no
sinecure, and there are extant many official letters in his hand written
from Dublin and the places throughout Ireland to which Grey's
military expeditions carried him. Grey was recalled in 1582, but
in the meantime Spenser had established himself in his new home.
For seven years beginning in March, 1581, he held the post of
Clerk of the Chancery for Faculties, an office entrusted with the
issuing and recording of dispensations granted by the Archbishop
of Dublin, not a time-consuming appointment since the work was
done by a deputy. He was involved in a number of real estate trans-
actions, and in 1582 he was able to lease at a low rental a property
known as New Abbey, formerly a Franciscan friary, about twenty-
five miles from Dublin. He made this his residence, so becoming
albeit modestly a member of the landed gentry. In 1584 or 1585 he
was appointed deputy to Lodowick Bryskett, a gentleman who had
accompanied Sidney on his tour of Europe, as clerk of the council
of Munster. The two became friends: Spenser addresses him as
"my Lodwick" in one of his sonnets, and Bryskett makes Spenser
an interlocutor in his *Discourse of Civill Life,* a treatise on moral
philosophy which he adapted from the Italian. Benefits followed
the Munster appointment. In 1585 Spenser became prebendary of
Limerick Cathedral, an office not always restricted to members of
the clergy and one which required few duties. And in late 1588
or early 1589 he took up residence on the estate of Kilcolman. Although it had been assigned to him in 1586, he did not receive the

formal grant until October 26, 1590. Over three thousand acres in extent, it was part of the war- and famine-ravaged country which had belonged to the rebel Earl of Desmond; Spenser describes it as naturally rich and plentiful. Kilcolman was one of the estates granted by the government to reliable Englishmen who would undertake to find English tenants to farm and improve them. Despite legal and extralegal quarrels about boundaries with his neighbor, Lord Roche, Spenser made it his home until very near the end of his life when he was forced from it by a new Irish revolt. Features of its landscape recur in his poetry, like the river Bregog of which the poet sings in *Colin Clouts Come Home Againe.*

If the account in that poem be taken as historically true, Spenser's tale of the love of Bregog for Mulla (his name for the river Awbeg) was sung in friendly rivalry with "the Shepherd of the Ocean," Sir Walter Ralegh, who was the possessor of a huge tract of land some thirty miles distant from Kilcolman. Colin is said to have accompanied the Shepherd to the royal court (Ralegh arrived in October, 1589) where the goddess queen deigned to listen at timely hours to his oaten pipe. The poem from which he read to her was presumably *The Faerie Queene,* the first part of which, Books I, II, and III, was entered by the publisher Ponsonby on December 1, 1589, and appeared in print the following year. Spenser had been working on it, no doubt, ever since 1580 when he sent some piece of it to Harvey. Part of the three books, if not the whole of them, had been read in England before Spenser presented the poem to the Queen. Abraham Fraunce's *Arcadian Rhetorike,* which was entered for publication in June, 1588, quotes a stanza from Canto iv of Book II, giving the reference to book and canto as it appears in later printed editions. Perhaps Fraunce had the manuscript from Sidney's sister, the Countess of Pembroke, of whose literary coterie he was a member. Another bit of evidence suggesting circulation of the manuscript in England before its printing is Marlowe's borrowing of an extended simile from Book I (vii.32) in the Second Part of *Tamburlaine*,[6] for that play may have been written as early as 1587 though it was not published until 1590.

Spenser dedicated *The Faerie Queene* "to the most mightie and magnificent empresse" Queen Elizabeth. In addition, he presented the poem to nine great nobles of the realm, addressing a sonnet to each and an additional one to "all the gratious and beautifull Ladies in the Court." While the book was being printed he inserted seven new dedicatory sonnets to other noble persons, among them William Cecil, Lord Burghley; Sir John Norris, Lord President of Munster; and the Countess of Pembroke. There is no convenient explanation for this change of plan. It has been suggested that the original omission of Burghley had to do with the antagonism between the peer and the poet (about which I will have something to say later) and that the decision to include him showed Spenser's desire to placate the great man, or at least to avoid offending him further. But it is hard to imagine that Spenser was also at odds with the other six for whom new sonnets were written, or that they were added merely to make the sonnet to Burghley less conspicuously an afterthought.

The formal grant of Kilcolman in October, 1590, may have been part of Spenser's reward for the presentation of *The Faerie Queene* to Elizabeth. And on February 25, 1591, the Queen bestowed upon him a pension for life of £50 annually to be paid in quarterly installments by her and by her successors:

> my sovereigne Queene most kind,
> that honour and large richesse to me lent.[a]   (*Amoretti*, LXXIV)

There is no ready way of interpreting this sum in terms of a modern currency. It was probably rather less in value than the £200 Dryden received as poet laureate a century later. But Spenser's pension should also be compared with the £20 per annum salary he received

[a] lent: granted.

as secretary to Lord Grey and with the rental of £22 he paid for his estate of Kilcolman. An income of £50 a year was required by the College of Heralds of those who would bear a coat of arms and boast the name of gentleman. I know of no other poet so honored by Queen Elizabeth.

In the wake of *The Faerie Queene* its publisher, Ponsonby, produced a collection of Spenser's poems under the title *Complaints. Containing Sundrie Small Poemes of the Worlds Vanitie* (entered on the Register December 29, 1590), which includes verse written years earlier as well as some of recent composition. The *Visions of Bellay* and the *Visions of Petrarch* are reworkings of the translations Spenser had made for Van der Noot's book in 1569. *Mother Hubberds Tale,* according to the author's note, was written "in the raw conceipt of my youth" and *Virgils Gnat* was "long since dedicated to the most noble and excellent Lord, the Earle of Leicester, late deceased" (Leicester had died in 1588). *The Ruines of Time,* however, which opens the volume, was conceived "sithens my late cumming into England." Ponsonby accepts responsibility for the collection since the author has departed "over Sea." He hopes that he will be able to publish other of Spenser's poems of which he has heard: "*Ecclesiastes* and *Canticum canticorum* translated, *A senights slumber, The hell of lovers, his Purgatorie,* being all dedicated to Ladies; so as it may seeme he ment them all to one volume. Besides some other Pamphlets looselie scattered abroad: as *The dying Pellican, The howers of the Lord, The sacrifice of a sinner, The seven Psalmes,* &c." Some of these are mentioned by E. K. and in the Harvey correspondence; none has survived.

In spite of Ponsonby's statement that Spenser had gone "over Sea" it is not clear when he did return to Ireland.[7] He was certainly there, squabbling with Lord Roche, in 1593, and in the year following he served as Justice of the County of Cork. And he married again. In a letter introducing the volume *Amoretti and Epithalamion* (entered November 19, 1594) Ponsonby expresses gratitude for the conveyance of these poems across the seas and regrets the long absence of Spenser's gentle muse. The *Epithalamion* celebrates the poet's wedding on the day of "Barnaby the bright" or Midsummer Day—though of what year we do not know—to Elizabeth Boyle, of a family distantly related to the Spencers, the poet's noble connections. She brought with her a marriage portion of £250, some of which was involved in a legal dispute. Spenser's first marriage had given him two children, Sylvanus and Katherine; the second brought him a son whom he named Peregrine.

Spenser was in England again perhaps in 1595 and surely in 1596. These years saw the publication of a considerable number of his poems. *Colin Clouts Come Home Againe,* bearing marks of revision which postdate its dedication to Ralegh in 1591, was printed for the first time in 1595. Included in the same volume was *Astrophel,* a collection of elegies on Sir Philip Sidney by various writers (among them Lodowick Bryskett) to which Spenser contributed the framework and introductory poem and also, in the opinion of some scholars, the "doleful lay" of "Clorinda," Sidney's sister Mary. The *Fowre Hymnes,* the first two of them said to have been written "in the greener times" of his youth, was dedicated from Greenwich, September 1, 1596, to two noble ladies of the Spencer family. Most important of all the publications of this period was the second installment of *The Faerie Queene,* Books IV, V, and VI, registered on January 20, 1596.[8] In November of that year King James of Scotland transmitted into England a sense of his indignation at Spenser's treatment in Book V of his mother, Queen Mary, under the guise of Duessa, together with a demand that the poet be tried and punished. James was not yet king of England and his message appears to have been ignored. Yet Spenser surely must have expected a reward of some kind for the presentation of the three new books of his great poem, and none is recorded, unless, perhaps, it was his nomination to be sheriff of Cork two years later.

It may be to the disappointment of his expectations that the complaint recorded in the *Prothalamion* refers. The occasion and principal subject of this poem was the betrothal of the daughters of the Earl of Worcester to two noble gentlemen, and it must have been written shortly before the double marriage which took place at Essex House (formerly Leicester House) on November 8, 1596. To begin this joyful celebration with a sad account of the poet's

> long fruitlesse stay
> In Princes Court, and expectation vayne
> Of idle hopes, which still doe fly away,
> Like empty shaddowes   (ll. 6–9)

is an offense against decorum, as Spenser himself declares:

> But Ah here fits not well
> Olde woes but joyes to tell   (ll. 141–42)

The offense is obviously deliberate. Against the happy promise of the marriage bed, its pleasures, and its fruitful issue, the poet sets the barren defeat of his own hopes. The sight of Essex House, soon to be the scene of the wedding, reminds Spenser that there his stay had not been fruitless. Once the Earl of Leicester had befriended him:

> oft I gayned giftes and goodly grace
> Of that great Lord, which therein wont to dwell,
> Whose want too well, now feeles my freendles case   (ll. 138–40)

The contrasting motifs are resolved by the appearance of Essex himself, "Great Englands glory and the Worlds wide wonder," who comes with his train to greet the two fair brides. His victory over the Spaniards at Cadiz promises the freeing of England from foreign threat and opens the great poetic opportunity:

great Elisaes glorious name may ring
Through al the world, fil'd with thy wide Alarmes,
Which some brave muse may sing
To ages following   (ll. 157–60)

The prophecy proved false. Two years later Essex paid the costs of the poet's funeral, and two years after that he died a traitor to Eliza.

Except for the Cantos of Mutabilitie, published for the first time in the 1609 edition of *The Faerie Queene,* and a sonnet commending a translated description of Venice, these are the last of Spenser's poems to appear in print. In April, 1598, his prose *Vewe of the Present State of Irelande,* a description of that country and recommendations for its government, probably written in England in 1596, was entered on the Stationers' Register, but it was not published until 1633. Manuscript copies of it, however, came to the hands of the privy council. On September 30, 1598, the council recommended that Spenser be made sheriff of Cork, "being a man endowed with good knowledge in learning and not unskilful or without experience in the service of the wars." He did not long enjoy that important and lucrative office. In October Irish rebels swept into Munster and sacked Kilcolman. On Christmas Eve, Spenser arrived at Whitehall to deliver dispatches from Sir John Norris, governor of Munster, to the privy council. He was paid £8 for his labor by a bill signed by Robert Cecil. On January 13 following, the poet died. He was buried, according to the historian Camden, "at Westminster, neere to Chaucer, at the charges of the Earle of Essex, his Hearse being carried by Poets, and mournfull Verses and Pomes throwne into his Tombe." [9]

These are the records of Spenser's life. The documents themselves may be unreliable or we may be misled in drawing inferences from them. Nevertheless, the bare recital of events sounds like a success story. Although his rise was not meteoric, the more-or-less poor boy at Merchant Taylors School came to be a landed gentleman, sheriff-designate of Cork, and recipient of a substantial annuity granted by the Queen. Though his goods were destroyed, the estate of Kilcolman was not lost, nor is it likely that Spenser would have thought it was—reinforcements to suppress the rebellion had arrived even before he left Ireland. His son Sylvanus inherited Kilcolman, and Peregrine, after his mother's death, enjoyed the castle and lands of Renny in which the poet had at some time invested £200.

Nevertheless, there is a strong tradition that Spenser died impoverished and neglected. Ben Jonson told Drummond of Hawthornden the sensational story that beggared by his poetry Spenser died "for lack of bread." But it is conventional for poets to think of poets as ill-treated, and the tale of starvation is obvious hyperbole. It is less easy to dismiss the account of Camden whom the poet honored highly in his *Ruines of Time:*

By a fate peculiar to Poets, hee alwaies strugled with poverty, though he were Secretary to the Lord Grey, Lord Deputy of Ireland. For scarce had hee there gotten a solitary place and leasure to write, when hee was by the Rebels cast out of his dwelling, despoyled of his goods, and returned into England a poore man, where shortly after hee died.[10]

If by the "solitary place" from which Spenser was cast out Camden means Kilcolman, his residence there lasted ten years. Of course, the loss of his goods may have seemed irreparable in 1599, and he may have incurred debts that ate up his pension.[11] But it is reasonable to conclude with most of Spenser's modern biographers that his reputed poverty can be understood only to mean that he was not wealthy.

Three years after Spenser's death a diarist noted the following anecdote:

When hir Majestie had given order that Spenser should have a reward for his poems, but Spenser could have nothing, he presented hir with these verses:

> It pleased your Grace upon a tyme
> To graunt me reason for my ryme,
> But from that tyme untill this season
> I heard of neither ryme nor reason.[12]

A letter dated 1593 ascribes the doggerel with much more likelihood to the hack writer Thomas Churchyard,[13] but the association of the lines with Spenser by a contemporary suggests that stories of this kind were told about him. In fact, more than a year elapsed between the presentation of the first part of *The Faerie Queene* to Elizabeth and the recording of her grant of the annuity. The interval is not excessive by modern standards of government efficiency; perhaps it was excessive in Elizabethan times. Whatever the case, Spenser is the author of a passionate and powerful exclamation against those who delay the fulfillment of promised rewards:

> Full little knowest thou that hast not tride,
> What hell it is, in suing long to bide:
> To loose good dayes, that might be better spent;
> To wast long nights in pensive discontent;
> To speed to day, to be put back to morrow;
> To feed on hope, to pine with feare and sorrow;
> To have thy Princes grace, yet want her Peeres;
> To have thy asking, yet waite manie yeeres;
> To fret thy soule with crosses and with cares;
> To eate thy heart through comfortlesse dispaires;
> To fawne, to crowche, to waite, to ride, to ronne,
> To spend, to give, to want, to be undonne.

The passage occurs in *Mother Hubberds Tale* (ll. 895-906), part of the *Complaints* volume published in 1591. Although Spenser says that the *Tale* was written in his youth, the lines quoted appear to be an interpolation. Just before the section of which they form part (ll. 891-918), Mother Hubberd has been telling how the false Fox mulcts poor suitors at court by pretending to have power which he lacks; just after, we learn that his trickery is brought to light and that he is punished by the administrators of justice. The passage between is not about the Fox at all and really an irrelevance, breaking the connection between crime and punishment. Since the suitor has won the favor of a female Prince—Elizabeth, of course, and not prince-in-general—the lines demand to be read autobiographically, and they must have been composed after the Queen had granted Spenser "reason" for his rhyme.

The Peer whose grace the suitor lacks must be Elizabeth's chief minister, William Cecil, Lord Burghley. No recorded act or statement of Cecil's demonstrates his antagonism to Spenser, but the poet's writings reflect it clearly enough. The sonnet addressed to Cecil, one of the late additions to the group dedicating *The Faerie Queene,* speaks in tones of respect and awe:

> To you right noble Lord, whose carefull brest
>   To menage of most grave affaires is bent,
>   And on whose mightie shoulders most doth rest
>   The burdein of this kingdomes governement,
> As the wide compasse of the firmament,
>   On Atlas mighty shoulders is upstayd;
>   Unfitly I these ydle rimes present,
>   The labor of lost time, and wit unstayd:
> Yet if their deeper sence be inly wayd,
>   And the dim vele, with which from comune vew
>   Their fairer parts are hid, aside be layd.
>   Perhaps not vaine they may appeare to you.
> Such as they be, vouchsafe them to receave,
>   And wipe their faults out of your censure grave.

None of the other dedicatory sonnets has quite this character. The poet is not merely making a conventional apology, he is on the defensive, as though he had some intimation that Lord Burghley's censure would be adverse. Six years later, in the prologue which stands at the head of the second installment of *The Faerie Queene,*

Spenser comments bitterly on the judgment of his poetry by what
seems to be the same grave and powerful statesman:

> The rugged forhead that with grave foresight
>   Welds kingdomes causes, and affaires of state,
>   My looser rimes (I wote) doth sharply wite,[b]
>   For praising love, as I have done of late
>
>   . . .
>
> Such ones ill judge of love, that cannot love,
>   Ne in their frosen hearts feele kindly [c] flame:
>   For thy [d] they ought not thing unknowne reprove,
>   Ne naturall affection faultlesse blame

With something like contempt the poet turns from him to rest
his hopes in the Queen herself:

> To such therefore I do not sing at all,
>   But to that sacred Saint my soveraigne Queene,
>   In whose chast breast all bounty naturall,
>   And treasures of true love enlocked beene

There are passages in Spenser's other poems that have been
read as attacks on Lord Burghley, notably an invective against a
niggardly noble in *The Ruines of Time*. The poet remembers that
Solomon had said (in Ecclesiasticus 26:28) that two things grieved
his heart, "a man of warre that suffereth poverty: and men of
understanding that are not set by."

> But now his wisedome is disprooved quite;
>   For he that now welds all things at his will,
>   Scorns th'one and th'other in his deeper skill.
>
> O griefe of griefes, O gall of all good heartes,
>   To see that vertue should dispised bee
>   Of him, that first was raisde for vertuous parts,
>   And now broad spreading like an aged tree,
>   Lets none shoot up, that nigh him planted bee:

[b] wite: blame.   [c] kindly: natural.   [d] For thy: therefore.

O let the man, of whom the Muse is scorned,
Nor alive, nor dead be of the Muse adorned. (ll. 446–55)

He who "welds all things at his will," like the loveless statesman of the prologue to Book IV, strongly suggests the Cecil of Spenser's sonnet "whose carefull brest/ To menage of most grave affaires is bent." If these are what they appear to be, attacks on the greatest man in the realm, they could scarcely have been published without drawing counterfire. In 1592, Gabriel Harvey remarks "with the good leave of unspotted friendshipp" on Spenser's rashness in *Mother Hubberds Tale:* "Mother Hubbard in heat of choller, forgetting the pure sanguine of her sweete Feary Queene, wilfully over-shot her malcontented selfe." Later in the same year, Thomas Nashe adverts to this comment in an attack upon Harvey: "Who publikely accusde or of late brought *Mother Hubbard* into question, that thou shouldst by rehearsall rekindle against him [i.e., Spenser] the sparkes of displeasure that were quenched?" An epigrammatist writing in 1599, after Spenser's death, remembers that *The Ruines of Time* was "called in" or suppressed.[14]

Both *The Ruines of Time* and *Mother Hubberds Tale* appeared for the first time in the *Complaints* volume of 1591. There is no clear sign of an attack upon Lord Burghley in poems published before this. But because Spenser says that *Mother Hubberds Tale* was written in his youth, it has been argued that the quarrel arose more than a decade earlier as a consequence of the poet's attachment to the Earl of Leicester, Burghley's rival for political power, and that his Irish "exile" was made necessary by his overeager partisanship of his master's cause.[15] This elaborate and ingenious hypothesis requires that the secretaryship to the governor-general of Ireland be counted a punishment or at least a refuge, and that *Mother Hubberds Tale* be dated before August, 1580, and read as a propaganda pamphlet attacking Cecil. But the Irish post seems a step up rather than a step down for a young man who had recently been secretary to the bishop of Rochester. The *Tale* is not one of the poems mentioned by E. K. or in the Harvey correspondence, nor, as I shall try to show later, is its interpretation as topical satire (apart from the inserted passage quoted above and another very obscure one) either necessary or probable.

On the basis of the documents as they stand, the most economical hypothesis is that Cecil did not like *The Faerie Queene,* as Spenser had feared, and that he interfered with the fulfillment of the reward the Queen had promised. Spenser was rash enough to attack him in *The Ruines of Time* and also in lines which he interpolated into *Mother Hubberds Tale.* The reaction to this choleric overshooting of his malcontented self was the suppression of the *Complaints* volume. In spite of this, no doubt by the Queen's favor, the promised reward was finally given. If Cecil's anger was quenched, as Nashe suggests, he may nevertheless have been responsible for the disappointment which the poet records in the *Prothalamion.* For whatever reason, Spenser's resentment against him found its boldest expression in 1596 in the opening stanzas of the second installment of *The Faerie Queene.* At the conclusion of the last book the poet predicts that these verses, too, will be slandered by "wicked tongues" and brought into "a mighty Peres displeasure,"

> Therefore do you my rimes keep better measure,
> And seeke to please, that now is counted wisemens threasure.

Which, for a poet dedicated to ends other than merely pleasing, is tantamount to a resolve to write no more poetry.

Of Spenser's loyalty to Cecil's rival for political power, the Earl of Leicester, and to his family the Dudleys there can be no question. There is nothing remarkable in the fact that he wrote a *Stemmata Dudleiana* (presumably a eulogy of that noble house) or praised the "worthy whom shee loveth best" in 1579 even though Leicester, whose marriage to Lettice Knollys had just been revealed to the Queen, was certainly not in her good graces at the time. But the lament for the dead Earl uttered by the spirit of the ancient city of Verulam in *The Ruines of Time* shows a warmth of personal feeling beyond what might be expected as the due of a patron. And eight years after Leicester's death, in the *Prothalamion,* Spenser still remembers "that great Lord" who had aided him in his youth.

Although Leicester extended his patronage to many writers, his help went chiefly to those who composed or translated solid works of exposition on such subjects as religion, history, medicine, and philology; there are few examples of belles-lettres among the books dedicated to him.[16] One of those few is Spenser's translation of the pseudo-Vergilian *Culex,* first printed in the *Complaints* volume but "long since dedicated to the most noble and excellent Lord, the Earle of Leicester." The prologue speaks obscurely of an injury received:

> Wrong'd, yet not daring to express my paine,
> To you (great Lord) the causer of my care,
> In clowdie teares my case I thus complaine
> Unto your selfe, that onely privie are:
> But if that any Oedipus unware
> Shall chaunce, through power of some divining spright,
> To reade the secrete of this riddle rare,
> And know the purporte of my evill plight,
> Let him rest pleased with his owne insight,
> Ne further seeke to glose upon the text

The riddle remains to be solved, though not because of respect for the poet's plea. If the poem is to be read autobiographically, Spenser must be identified with the gnat who wakens a shepherd to the danger of a venomous snake and is slapped dead for his pains. It has been suggested that the danger was the proposal of marriage to the Queen by the Duc d'Alençon, but there is nothing in *Virgils Gnat* to warrant the interpretation. Whatever the wrong Spenser suffered, he remained grateful to Leicester for the rest of his life.

Spenser did not lack for other patrons. Ralegh he thanks particularly for "singular favours and sundrie good turnes shewed to me at my late being in England," that is, I suppose, when he presented *The Faerie Queene* to Elizabeth.[17] To Lord Grey he acknowledges the

> large bountie poured on me rife,
> In the first season of my feeble age [18]

Mary, Countess of Pembroke, did him "manie singular favours and great graces." [19] He is grateful for benefits given by three daughters of the Spencer family who had made noble marriages. A sonnet addressed to the Earl of Essex promises that when "the last praises of this Faery Queene" are written

> Then shall it make more famous memory
> Of thine Heroicke parts [20]

Whether or not Essex did take Leicester's place as the poet's patron, as he took his place in the palace on the Thames, we do not know. It will be remembered that he paid the costs of the poet's funeral.

Spenser's relationship with Sir Philip Sidney, Leicester's nephew, was not simply that of poet and patron. That Sidney assisted Spenser materially the dedication to him of *The Shepheardes Calender* suggests. The address to the Countess of Pembroke in *The Ruines of Time,* in which the "Immortal spirit of Philisides" is celebrated, speaks of him as "the Patron of my young Muses" and acknowledges "straight bandes of duetie." But Sidney the patron was himself a poet. In 1580, he and his friend Dyer had Spenser "in some use of familiarity" and talked with him about English versification. Spenser's report of these conversations does not suggest that familiarity became friendship. That "happy, blessed trinity," Sidney and his companions Dyer and Fulke Greville, played poetic games with each other, answering each other's sonnets, varying the same themes, toying with the same conceits. Spenser did not make a fourth. Nevertheless, these gentleman poets influenced Spenser as the academic Harvey could not. Years before, scholarly humanists like John Cheke and Roger Ascham had argued that if English poets were to achieve the eminence of their classical models they would have to abandon the barbarous "Gothic" practices of rhyme and accentual rhythm and adopt in their place the quantitative measures of Greece and Rome. Harvey had urged Spenser to follow their instruction, but it was Sidney who convinced him. Spenser writes:

I am, of late, more in love wyth my Englishe Versifying, than with Ryming: whyche I should have done long since, if I would then have followed your councell. Sed te solum iam tum suspicabar cum Aschamo sapere: nunc Aulam video egregios alere Poetas Anglicos.[21]

Apparently the example of the bright intellects of Elizabeth's court weighed more heavily with the young Spenser than the precept of the schools.

Spenser's interest in versifying in the classical manner waned early; there is no sign of it after the publication of the Harvey correspondence. Whether or not Sidney influenced him in more important and enduring ways is a difficult question. According to the author of one of the poems of commendation published with *The Faerie Queene* Spenser undertook its composition at Sidney's instance. This may well be true in the sense that Sidney encouraged him to attempt a major poem, but Sidney would not, I think, have urged him to write the poem that he did write. Although both poets subscribed to the thesis that the proper function of literature was to teach, they were in fact of very different tastes and tempers and if either did inspire the other it was rather to rivalry than to imitation. Despite the fact that Sidney disliked the "old rustick language" of *The Shepheardes Calender* Spenser continued to use a poetic vocabulary flavored with the antique in his later poems. Both wrote sonnets, but while Sidney adopted a form approximating that used on the continent Spenser devised one which deviated markedly from it. Sidney's pastorals are set in Arcadia; Spenser's

in England and Ireland. One wrote his great work in prose, the
other in verse. If Sidney had a "school" Spenser was not of it.
Nevertheless, as Spenser's association with the courtly coterie led
him to dress himself like an "Italianate signor and French monsieur,"
it may also have reinforced his interest in the fashionable literature
of the continent, in Ariosto, Tasso, Du Bellay, and Du Bartas, for
example. Harvey writes to Spenser that his *"Elvish Queene"* would
not stand comparison with the *Orlando Furioso* which "you wil
needes seeme to emulate, and hope to overgo, as you flatly professed
your self in one of your last Letters." [22] In 1579 and 1580, when
Spenser moved in court circles, he may have aspired to write a
poem like the *Orlando*. He did not finally adopt that design.

Other contemporary Englishmen who had the opportunity of mold-
ing Spenser's literary talent were Richard Mulcaster, master of the
Merchant Taylors School, and Gabriel Harvey. Of Mulcaster Spenser
says nothing, unless he is to be identified with the "good olde shep-
hearde, Wrenock" whom Colin acknowledges as his teacher in the
art of singing in the December eclogue of *The Shepheardes Calender*. The identification seems doubtful, however, since Mulcaster
was not forty years old when Spenser left the school for Cambridge,
and nobody has offered a plausible explanation of the odd pastoral
name.[23] Although Mulcaster was a highly articulate teacher who
published a considerable body of his opinions about the manner and
matter of grammar school instruction, little of what he says in print
is relevant to Spenser's development as a poet except for his contention that English is a language capable of high literary excellence—
an attitude less uncommon among Tudor schoolmasters than is
sometimes supposed.[24]

The stanza in the December eclogue which follows the tribute to
Wrenock declares that Hobbinol (Harvey in pastoral guise) thought
well of Colin's song. Spenser continued to regard Harvey as critic

and friend rather than as teacher. Harvey could have been only a few years older than the poet, though when they were both at Cambridge he was at the peak of his academic career, University Praelector in rhetoric and lecturer in Greek. A Cambridge student play of which he is the principal butt describes him as a posturing and pompous pedant, and this description is seconded not only by some vivaciously scurrilous pamphlets of Thomas Nashe but also by his own incautious habit of annotating the books in his library with intimate observations revealing his hopes and plans for advancement. But student plays are no testimony, and it is hard to say how seriously one should take a man's notes to himself. His quarrel with Nashe was certainly a mistake, as Sir John Harington remarks in an epigram:

> The proverbe sayes, who fights with durty foes,
> Must needs be soyld, admit they winne or lose,
> Then think it doth a Doctors credit dash,
> To make himselfe Antagonist to *Nash*.[25]

He seems to have got into a number of squabbles, both in and out of the university, which blocked his hopes for preferment in government service and led to his retirement from academic life. But he was "a very learned man, one of the most learned of his age" as a recent student of his works concludes.[26] And he at least tried to wear that learning lightly. The Latin orations which he delivered as professor of rhetoric are lively and witty, temperate in tone, and not unduly pretentious, at least by the standards of the age. His interests ranged well beyond the scholarly: his own doggerel proclaims his love of

> All kynde of bookes, good, and badd,
> Sayntish and Divelish, that ar to be hadd.
> Owlde, and yunge,
> For matter and tunge,

Wheresoever they dwell,
In Heaven, or in Hell;
Machiavell, Aretine, and whome you will,
That ar any renownid for extraordinary skill.[27]

In late December, 1578, Spenser thought it appropriate to give his
learned friend three jestbooks and a copy of the rogue tale *Lazarillo
de Tormes* on condition that he read them by the New Year or for-
feit his *Lucian*.[28]

We are concerned with Spenser's Harvey, and the portrait that
emerges from the poet's references to him is a consistent one. In *The
Shepheardes Calender* Hobbinol tries to assuage Colin's anguish and
urges him to return to quiet happiness in the pleasant dale; he mod-
erates Diggon's fierce anger. In *Colin Clouts Come Home Againe,*
more than a decade later, Hobbinol again tempers Colin's passionate
excess. And the same calm and independent critic appears as the
subject of the sonnet Spenser wrote in 1586 "To the right worship-
full, my singular good friend, M. Gabriell Harvey, Doctor of the
Lawes":

Harvey, the happy above happiest men
I read: that sitting like a Looker-on
Of this worldes Stage, doest note with critique pen
The sharpe dislikes of each condition

Yet much as Spenser loved and respected Harvey, there is no
reason to suppose that Harvey's criticism greatly influenced him. As
the poet himself says, the example of Sidney and his circle, rather
than Harvey's advice, drew him to his short-lived interest in experi-
menting with classical meters. His friend's taste for the "delicate
and fine conceited Grecians and Italians," Lucian, Petrarch, Aretino,
and "Pasquil," weighed little with the poet. The lack of enthusiasm
with which Harvey commented on the parcel of *The Faerie Queene*
sent to him in 1580 did not discourage Spenser from working on the
great poem. Even in minor technical matters Spenser ignores Har-

vey's advice. Harvey emphatically declares that words like "heaven" should be scanned as one syllable; Spenser continues to scan them as two when it suits him.[29]

If Spenser was no obedient follower of his friends, his associates, and his social superiors in literary matters, it is wise to proceed at least cautiously in assuming that he shared their religious and political opinions. Such caution is not always observed, however. Since Cambridge and the Earl of Leicester inclined rather to the left than to the right in the religious controversy, it has been supposed that Spenser must have tended thither also. The supposition then leads to an interpretation of *The Shepheardes Calender* designed to confirm it. Similar circles are described in the process of linking Spenser to Leicester's position opposing the marriage of the Queen to the Duc d'Alençon and consequently reading a warning against that marriage into the text of *Mother Hubberds Tale*. Arguments of this kind have only the virtue of self-consistency.

Spenser was not one of those who wrote polemical essays on the subject of the religious disputes of his day. Whatever conclusions can be drawn about his position in these matters must be derived from tangential references in the body of his writings and these are often open to several interpretations. It becomes clear, nevertheless, that he was a moderate Protestant of the kind of Richard Hooker, the great apologist of the religious compromise.[30]

Spenser's fervid opposition to the government of the Christian church by Rome is obvious if only from his portrait of Duessa as the falsehood of the Tiber in Book 1 of *The Faerie Queene*. Yet his hatred of Rome was not so violent as to make him urge the extirpation of Roman Catholicism as the first step in his program for Ireland. Political reformation should come before religious, he argued. In fact, he was more troubled by ignorance of Christian doctrine among the Irish than by their adherence to the wrong form of it, and he admired the devotion, energy, and personal courage of the "popish priests" in that country enough to wish that Protestant ministers were like them.[31] With Protestants generally he thought that the reformed religion was a return to old, true doctrine purified from the latter-day distortions of Roman Catholicism. His attack upon tithe-sharers and upon authorities who granted benefices to the unlettered echoes countless such complaints both before and after Luther's time. He shared with Chaucer and Langland a hatred for proud, self-seeking, power-hungry prelates and a love for the simple, unselfishly dedicated pastor whose life was the care of his flock. In this respect, his voice is like that of the radical Protestants heard so loudly in the earlier Elizabethan parliaments. Yet he seems to have realized, too, that a priest is a man as others are and that a life of complete dedication is humanly impossible. The "Formal Priest" of *Mother Hubberds Tale* is a bad man not because he likes to lie with his bright bride and to garb himself in beautiful vestments but because he is a hypocrite, unconcerned with the welfare of his congregation.

In matters of doctrinal controversy only the broad outlines of the poet's position are visible. If I read the Legend of Holinesse correctly, he was deeply committed to the belief that man is incapable of avoiding sin and that his salvation comes by God's grace alone. Spenser does not differ here from the established doctrine of the English church. But in the heated dispute between the radical Protestants and the English hierarchy he rather avoids than joins battle. His clearest reference to the vexed question of the meaning of the communion appears in the *Hymne of Heavenly Love*:

> the food of life, which now we have,
> Even himselfe in his deare sacrament,
> To feede our hungry soules unto us lent.   (ll. 194–96)

This is a precise statement of what Hooker declares to be the common ground of all Christian factions: "They are grown for aught I can see on all sides at the length to a general agreement concerning that which alone is material, namely the real participation of Christ and of life in his body and blood by means of this sacrament. . . . Yea, even in this point no side denieth but that the soul of man is the receptacle of Christ's presence." But Spenser takes no stand on the only issue which Hooker declares still moot: "whether when the sacrament is administered Christ be whole within man only, or else his body and blood be also externally seated in the very consecrated elements themselves."[32] While the radical Puritans of the day condemned episcopal government as without biblical warrant and railed at the bishops, calling them petty popes, Spenser gave his highest praise, not to Cartwright, intellectual leader of the radical party, but to Grindal, Archbishop of Canterbury. Grindal, it is true, earned the displeasure of the Queen because of his refusal to suppress certain dissenting proto-Presbyterian groups, but he was himself rather a moderate than an extremist of any kind.

Such political opinions as are expressed in the poems suggest that Spenser was a loyal partisan of his patrons. He reflects the interest of the "progressive party" of Leicester and Ralegh in British colonization of the new world in his reference to "fruitfullest Virginia" and in his exhortation to Englishmen to adventure boldly into the lands of the Orinoco and the Amazon:

> And shame on you, O men, which boast your strong
> And valiant hearts, in thoughts lesse hard and bold,
> Yet quaile in conquest of that land of gold.
> But this to you, O Britons, most pertaines,
> To whom the right hereof it selfe hath sold;
> The which for sparing litle cost or paines,
> Loose so immortall glory, and so endlesse gaines.   (iv.xi.22)

He describes England's unhappy intervention in the Low Countries, in which Leicester played a most important role, as though it were a heroic and successful achievement, and he portrays Lord Grey as a wise and merciful governor who would have brought

peace to Ireland had malicious slander not forced his recall. He is so
partisan, in fact, as to defend Grey's slaughter of a group of Spanish
prisoners on the ground that they bore no commission from their
king and so could not be considered soldiers.

The defense of this action of Grey's occurs in Spenser's *Vewe
of the Present State of Irelande* [33] and in this tract the most detailed
statement of his political views is to be found. Here he displays
himself as an advocate of strong, even ruthless measures for the
suppression of rebellion and the pacification 'of the country. To
achieve these ends he proposes military measures designed to starve
out the rebels and forcible alteration of laws and customs to make
the land amenable to control. Although he respects the courage
and endurance of Irish warriors and admires the technical virtuosity
(though not the morality) of Irish bards, it is evident that he thinks
of the inhabitants of the country as a brutish, uncivilized, and lawless nation that must be kept under firm rein.

If Spenser had written that second great poem of the Faerie
Queene which, according to his letter to Ralegh, was to deal with
the political aspect of the theme of the gentleman or noble person,
we should, no doubt, have a clearer picture of his philosophy of the
state. From what we have of his writing emerges principally a profoundly patriotic conviction that a harmonious England guided by
so virtuous a ruler as Elizabeth could aspire to achievement even
more glorious than that of ancient Rome. But Spenser's patriotism
is of the kind that does not ignore or gloss over shortcomings; on
the contrary, it emphasizes them by contrasting what is with what
might be. How one might become the other is a question that, except
in the tract on Ireland, he considers in moral rather than in political
terms. And since human morality is, for Spenser, a very imperfect
thing, he holds out no immediate hope that the gap between the
real and the ideal can be closed.

The poet Spenser served as clerk of the council of Munster and sheriff of Cork; the poet Chaucer served as Controller of Customs and Subsidy of Wools, Skins, and Hides, and Clerk of the King's Works. In all probability, both owed their advancement in government service in part to their poetry, or at least to their literacy. But the cases are only superficially similar. Between Chaucer's time and that of Spenser there occurred a significant change in the poet's conception of his role in the world. For Chaucer, the books one labored over at the customs office and the books one read in the chamber at home belonged to two different realms. For Spenser, the work of a civil servant was a natural extension of the vocation of a poet, that is, of a man trained in the humane discipline, learned in eloquence.

By "humane discipline" I do not mean that narrow tradition of slavish classicism and contempt for medieval thought that Mr. C. S. Lewis damns so unmercifully in a brilliant essay entitled "New Learning and New Ignorance."[34] That some humanists and some aspects of humanism were guilty as charged is unquestionably true. But humanists were far from a coherent group and their conception of the discipline they professed varied widely in breadth and emphasis.

Spenser's kind of humanism rests on the high claim for the art of expression made by Cicero in a passage of the *De oratore* which is echoed and paraphrased everywhere in the Renaissance:

To come, however, at length to the highest achievements of eloquence, what other power could have been strong enough either to gather scattered humanity into one place, or to lead it out of its brutish existence in the wilderness up to our present condition of civilization as men and citizens, or after the establishment of social communities, to give shape to laws, tribunals, and civic rights?[35]

Horace ascribes the same power to persuasive discourse in the even more famous lines of the *Ars poetica* (391 ff.) which make Orpheus civilizer of savage mankind and Amphion founder and lawgiver

of orderly society. It is in the spirit of these *loci classici* that Samuel
Daniel, eloquent defender of the intellectual accomplishment of the
Middle Ages and apologist for that "barbarous" ornament of poetry,
rhyme, is nevertheless a humanist:

> Powre above powres, O heavenly *Eloquence,*
>   That with the stronge reine of commanding words,
>   Dost manage, guide, and master th'eminence
>   Of mens affections, more then all their swords:
>   Shall we not offer to thy excellence
>   The richest treasure that our wit affoords?
>   Thou that canst do much more with one poor pen
>   Then all the powres of princes can effect:
>   And draw, divert, dispose, and fashion men
>   Better then force or rigour can direct:
>   Should we this ornament of glorie then
>   As th'unmateriall fruits of shades, neglect? [36]

And in this spirit Spenser takes upon himself the role of mentor to
mankind, beginning his literary career with a pastoral designed "To
teach the ruder shepheard how to feede his sheepe" and bringing
it to its climax with an epic poem the "general intention" of which
is "to fashion a gentleman or noble person in vertuous and gentle
discipline."

It was natural, therefore, that those who prided themselves upon
their eloquence should look to service for the commonwealth as their
proper sphere of activity. On the continent, humanist scholars found
employment as secretaries, diplomats, tutors to princes, historians,
and panegyrists. In England, too, grammarians and rhetoricians
became civil servants of various degrees of importance. Thomas
Wolsey, who had once been grammar master at the Magdalen
School, ruled the land under the king; Thomas More followed him
as chancellor; Cheke, Ascham, and Wilson taught royalty and nobility and served in the nation's diplomatic affairs. In Spenser's time
two products of the school of Cheke were members of the Privy

Council, Gabriel Harvey's kinsman Sir Thomas Smith and the great Cecil himself—Spenser seems to resent particularly the fact that one "that first was raisde for vertuous parts/ . . . Lets none shoot up, that nigh him planted bee." [37] Harvey's aspirations for a government post have been thought absurd by some, but such employment would then have been a normal expectation of a professor of rhetoric. And Spenser's intended expedition to France in the interest of Leicester, his service to Lord Grey and to Sir John Norris, his composition of the *Vewe of the Present State of Irelande* constitute not distractions from his mission as a poet but expressions of it.

The "Prince of Poets" was never more than a minor functionary in the service of the government. Yet the title of prince is not inappropriate. Spenser's sonnet in praise of Harvey compares him with

> a great Lord of peerelesse liberty:
> Lifting the Good up to high Honours seat,
> And the Evill damning evermore to dy

The description sits oddly with our impression of Harvey, but it is fitting for Spenser himself, or rather for Spenser's conception of himself. There is indeed much of the "great Lord of peerelesse liberty" about the poet. He calls Chaucer his master, but he dares to take the central plot of his great poem from the burlesque *Tale of Sir Thopas*. He models himself on Vergil, but he parodies the speech of Aeneas recognizing his mother Venus by putting it into the mouth of the ridiculous Trompart. He draws freely from the literary traditions available to him, and always with a superb disregard for the intention of the writers from whom he borrows. He is the master of his world of letters, confident that his "doomefull writing" will damn Cecil to obscurity and lift Leicester to eternal fame. The Queen herself wielded no such power.

Colin Clout

SPENSER CHOSE to present himself to the literary public of England under the pen name "Immerito," the Worthless One:

> I never lyst presume to Parnasse hyll,
> But pyping lowe in shade of lowly grove,
> I play to please my selfe, all be it ill.   (*June,* 70–72)

His election of the pastoral form, traditionally the most humble of the literary "kinds," bears out the pose of the hesitant beginner, uncertain of his abilities. And the concluding Envoy

> Goe lyttle Calender, thou hast a free passeporte,
> Goe but a lowly gate emongste the meaner sorte

echoes the well-worn formula of self-depreciation which introduces or concludes Chaucer's *Troilus,* Lydgate's *Troy Book* and *Fall of Princes,* Hawes's *Pastime of Pleasure,* and other considerable works. The poet of this tradition claims no status, he is not a competitor of the great authors, he lacks skill and training. He has written his book at command, or to eschew that idleness which might lead him to worse sins, and he hopes only that his reader will forgive his errors and correct what is amiss. Perhaps, too, his labor will turn some man to good. These disclaimers may be as conventionally rhetorical and as meaningless as "your humble servant" but their general acceptance in the late Middle Ages together with the conception of the poet's role that goes with them contrasts sharply with the humanist exaltation of the poet as civilizer of mankind.

The pastoral is a humble genre; paradoxically, Spenser's choice of it to introduce himself as the "new poet" betrays his soaring ambition. He had decided to make of his career an *imitatio Vergilis.* Cuddie sets forth the model in the October eclogue:

> Indeede the Romish Tityrus, I heare,
> Through his Mecœnas left his Oaten reede,
> Whereon he earst had taught his flocks to feede,
> And laboured lands to yield the timely eare,
> And eft did sing of warres and deadly drede,
> So as the Heavens did quake his verse to here.   (ll. 55–60)

As Vergil's pastorals prepared the way first for the *Georgics* and then for his great heroic poem, so Spenser, "following the example of the best and most auncient Poetes," begins with the pastoral, "as young birdes, that be newly crept out of the nest, by little first to prove theyr tender wyngs, before they make a greater flyght." Within a few months of the publication of the *Calender* Spenser had already finished a part of *The Faerie Queene* substantial enough to be sent to Harvey for criticism.

Although under his pastoral name of Colin, Spenser usually maintains the modest posture of a shepherd "boy," his rustic companions are lavish in his praise. The dramatic form of the eclogues may make us forget momentarily that it is the poet who makes Hobbinol say:

> I sawe Calliope wyth Muses moe,
> Soone as thy oaten pype began to sound,
> Theyr yvory Luyts and Tamburins forgoe:
> And from the fountaine, where they sat around,
> Renne after hastely thy silver sound.
> But when they came, where thou thy skill didst showe,
> They drewe abacke, as halfe with shame confound,
> Shepheard to see, them in theyr art outgoe.   (*June*, 57–64)

And Perigot:

O Colin, Colin, the shepheards joye,
    How I admire ech turning of thy verse   (*August,* 190–91)

And Cuddie:

For Colin fittes such famous flight to scanne:
He, were he not with love so ill bedight,
Would mount as high, and sing as soote as Swanne.

                                                     (*October,* 88–90)

In *December,* even Colin admits the excellence of his verse:

And if that Hobbinol right judgement bare,
To Pan his owne selfe pype I neede not yield.
    For if the flocking Nymphes did folow Pan,
    The wiser Muses after Colin ranne.   (ll. 45–48)

It is not the mere charm of his song that distinguishes Colin; the
"wiser Muses" are led by other allurements. Pan and Cuddie may
be content to "feede youthes fancie, and the flocking fry" but Colin's
aim is higher. The same Envoy which humbly urges "Goe lyttle
Calender" begins in a nobler vein:

Loe I have made a Calender for every yeare,
That steele in strength, and time in durance shall outweare:
And if I marked well the starres revolution,
It shall continewe till the worlds dissolution.
To teach the ruder shepheard how to feede his sheepe,
And from the falsers fraud his folded flocke to keepe.

The echo of the "Romish Tityrus" who "taught his flocks to feede"
dares the comparison of Spenser with Vergil and makes it clear that
the didactic intention of the *Calender* is not merely that of turning
some man to good but the betterment of the commonwealth.[1]

Appropriately, therefore, the form of the first publication of *The
Shepheardes Calender* was intended to impress the reader with a
sense of the importance of the work. This collection of English
poems by an unknown author was equipped with apparatus proper
to an edition of a Latin classic: an introduction pointing out the

singular merits of the poem, a disquisition on the nature and history of its genre, a glossary and notes. No English poet had ever been announced so pretentiously. There were four more printings in quarto, the last in 1597, after which the *Calender* was incorporated into the many editions of Spenser's collected works.

The identity of E. K., who is responsible for the editorial apparatus, is not known. There was an Edward Kirke at Pembroke Hall during Spenser's residence, and in October, 1579, a Mistresse Kerke collected and forwarded Spenser's mail. But little more is recorded of the former and nothing of the latter, so that even if they could be linked with the editor of the *Calender* the student of Spenser's poem would not be enlightened.[2] However, we do know something about E. K., both from the book itself and from references to him in Spenser's correspondence with Harvey. He claims friendship with the poet and some knowledge of his personal affairs, and he exhibits respectful admiration for Harvey to whom he addresses his dedicatory epistle. In the year following the publication of the *Calender* he was engaged in preparing an edition of another of Spenser's poems. Spenser writes to Harvey:

I take best my *Dreames* shoulde come forth alone, being growen by meanes of the Glosse, (running continually in maner of a Paraphrase) full as great as my *Calendar*. Therin be some things excellently, and many things wittily discoursed of E. K. and the Pictures so singularly set forth, and purtrayed, as if Michael Angelo were there, he could (I think) nor amende the best, nor reprehende the worst.[3]

Unfortunately, the *Dreames* never did come forth, alone or otherwise. But if E. K. was the authorized editor of that work it seems not unlikely that he was of the *Calender* also, and that Spenser knew and approved óf his introduction and notes before its publication.

Nevertheless, E. K. is not a reliable guide to the meaning of the *Calender*. Sometimes he obfuscates intentionally: in *May,* for instance, "Algrind" (transparently Archbishop Grindal) is glossed pointlessly—or as a sly joke—"the name of a shepheard." Sometimes he errs in interpreting Spenser's archaic words and in citing his sources. In larger matters, however, what W. L. Renwick justly calls the "stiffness" of E. K.'s mind makes his comment of doubtful value.[4] Pompously proud of his learning, he is more concerned with pointing out "a pretty epanorthosis" or arguing that "eclogue" should be written "aeglogue" than with explaining to the reader "the generall dryfte and purpose" of the work he is editing. Indeed, he may not have understood that drift. His Argument for the October eclogue describes Cuddie as "the perfecte paterne of a Poete, which finding no maintenaunce of his state and studies, complayneth of the contempte of Poetrie, and the causes thereof." This is, in fact, Cuddie's complaint and the complaint of pastoral poems on the same subject since the time of Theocritus, but it is not what this poem says, nor is Cuddie, obviously a foil for Colin, in any sense "the perfecte paterne of a Poete." Perhaps misreadings of this kind explain why Spenser thinks E. K.'s remarks are more often witty than excellent.

But E. K.'s criticism is sometimes excellent indeed. In defining the quality which makes the newness of the new poet, he writes: "For what in most English wryters useth to be loose, and as it were ungyrt, in this Authour is well grounded, finely framed, and strongly trussed up together." It is precisely the fine framing and strong trussing up together that distinguishes Spenser, not only from the "rakehelly rout" of his contemporaries, but also from most poets before him and after. The search for a unity, in particular a unity of the most various and even discordant elements, a unity both of form and substance, is one of the dominant characteristics of Spenser's poetry. And when the elements are considered in terms of time and change, the sought-for One becomes changeless eternity, not in opposition to the mutable but comprising it and arising from it. Hobbinol tells us in *April* that Colin tuned his lay unto the water's fall. A waterfall, single though composed of diverse and conflicting currents, stable though never the same, is no poor figure for the kind of poetry Spenser wanted to write and the conception of the world that he wanted to express.

Spenser was at least twenty-five years old when the *Calender* appeared, so that it can scarcely be described as a product of his immaturity. But in comparison with the work of his later years its contrivance is obvious enough to betray the direction of his poetic bent. He was familiar with the body of pastoral poetry, classical and Renaissance in origin. The form as he knew it had little to do with the beauty of growing things or the charm of the countryside. Particularly in its Renaissance development the pastoral standpoint required the poet to weigh the world of everyday, the world of court and city, by reducing its complexity and confusion to a conventional simplicity: simple loves, songs, and tasks, simple jealousies, ambitions, and responsibilities. So Spenser uses the form. But he elected to deviate from typical pastoral practice in several ways, most radically in the plan of his poem. Vergil's *Bucolics* consists of ten eclogues (from *eclogae,* selections); the number has no significance. Spenser's pastorals are twelve in number, firmly trussed up with the round of the year. Since the twelve eclogues, as the title page announces, are "proportionable to the twelve monethes," Spenser entitled them *The Shepheardes Calender,* "applying an olde name to a new worke." The old name is that of the *Kalendar & Compost of Shepherds,* a curious compilation which is an ancestor of innumerable "farmers' almanacs." Translated from a fifteenth-century French original in 1503 and again in 1506 and 1508, it proved hugely popular, edition succeeding edition until as late as 1656. Like its successors, the *Kalendar* contained in addition to an almanac proper a treasury of moral instruction and useful information: analyses of the vices and virtues; expositions of the paternoster, the creed, and the commandments; compendious dissertations on astronomy, physiology, and anatomy. Spenser took from it not only his title but the idea of illustrating each of his eclogues with a woodcut labeled with the astrological sign appropriate to the month.[5] He may also have noticed the chapter (No. 33) entitled "Of the commodity of the twelve months of the year with the twelve ages of man," though the notion of a correspondence between the succession of seasons and the course of human life is no doubt as old as man himself.

"We are entitled to assume," writes an editor of *The Shepheardes Calender,* "that Spenser invented the Calendar-scheme because he had written some eclogues, rather than that he invented the scheme in the air and then proceeded to write eclogues."[6] The title to this assumption rests, first, on the fact that some of the eclogues make no mention of the season, and second, on evidence tending to show that Spenser did not compose them in the order in which they appear. E. K. provides no note or gloss for that part of *August* following line 138, so that it seems likely that Colin's sestina (ll. 151–89) was interpolated after the editorial work had been completed. Again, in the November eclogue, Colin tells us that Phoebus has "taken up his ynne in Fishes haske"[a] yet the maker of the woodcuts knew that in November the sun is in the astrological sign Sagittarius, not Pisces, and so too did Spenser himself when he came to write the Cantos of Mutabilitie. Probably, Spenser decided for some reason to make a February eclogue do for November and carelessly failed to change the text accordingly. For these reasons, a number of scholars have undertaken to reconstruct the order in which Spenser composed the parts of the *Calender,* the result being an equal number of different hypothetical sequences.

But it must be the rare poet who begins with the first line of his poem and finishes with the last. In the absence of Spenser's own testimony it is impossible to decide whether he thought of a *Cal-*

[a] haske: basket, creel.

ender because he had written some eclogues or whether he invented the scheme "in the air." In fact, he would so have invented it if he remembered the famous instruction of Geoffrey of Vinsauf which his "master" Chaucer quotes in *Troilus and Criseyde* (Book I, ll. 1065–69):

> For everi wight that hath an hous to founde
> Ne renneth naught the werk for to bygynne
> With rakel [b] hond, but he wol bide a stounde,
> And sende his hertes line out fro withinne
> Aldirfirst his purpos for to wynne.

The question to be answered, at least for the purpose of understanding Spenser's meaning, is whether the book is one poem or twelve, whether the title is merely the consequence of a process of "practical bookmaking" or concerns the substance of the work. The history of the composition of a poem, however interesting biographically, is one thing; the structure of a poem is another. It is the structure to which I shall attend.

Geoffrey of Vinsauf's house has a plan, but it does not have a beginning or an end. There is a strong tendency among critics to insist upon progression or development of some kind as essential to all literary constructions. Plots must be resolved, characters "grow," ideas reveal themselves. Under the influence of this tendency, some students of the *Calender* have tried to find a "story" in it: a tale of the love of Colin for Rosalind, a poet's autobiography. There is no such story. Spenser's *Calender* does not bring us from the beginning of the year to its end; it is a circle rather than a straight line.

Although Spenser is not as rigid an architect as some of his critics, the theme of time and man pervades his poem and constitutes its principal subject.[7] The dimension of time is here employed, not primarily to expose the idea of mutability, but to examine human

[b] rakel: hasty.

states in terms of their past and their future. *January* and *December*, unlike the other eclogues, are soliloquies. In *January* Colin complains of the futile waste of his life:

> Thou barrein ground, whome winters wrath hath wasted,
> Art made a myrrhour, to behold my plight:
> Whilome thy fresh spring flowrd, and after hasted
> Thy sommer prowde with Daffadillies dight.
> And now is come thy wynters stormy state,
> Thy mantle mard,[c] wherein thou maskedst late.
>
> Such rage as winters, reigneth in my heart,
> My life bloud friesing with unkindly cold:
> Such stormy stoures do breede my balefull smart,
> As if my yeare were wast, and woxen old.
> And yet alas, but now my spring begonne,
> And yet alas, yt is already donne.   (ll. 19–30)

As *January* recalls the spring and foreshadows *December*, so *December* recapitulates:

> Whilome in youth, when flowrd my joyfull spring

Throughout the *Calender*, the matter of growth, maturity, and decay repeatedly asserts itself. *February* is a debate between youth and age; *March* presents the innocent youth as yet unacquainted with the pangs of love; *May* contrasts Palinode, who wishes he could help the ladies bear the Maybush, with Piers:

> For Younkers [d] Palinode such follies fitte,
> But we tway bene men of elder witt.   (ll. 17–18)

In *June* Colin rejects beauty and delight:

> And I, whylst youth and course of carelesse yeeres
> Did let me walke withouten lincks of love,
> In such delights did joy amongst my peeres:
> But ryper age such pleasures doth reprove,

[c] mard: marred.   [d] Younkers: youngsters.

My fancye eke from former follies move
To stayed steps (ll. 33-38)

September shows us the fortune-seeking Diggon Davie returned from his travels ragged, despondent, and bitter. In *October* Cuddie compares his youthful song-making with the improvidence of the grasshopper of the fable. In *November* Colin sings of the death of Dido: spring is the time of merriment, autumn of the mournful muse.

As the examples I have given suggest, the poles which form the *Calender* are not simply youth and age. With youth Spenser associates susceptibility to love, freedom from care, delight in song, ambitious striving. With maturity and age come pain and disillusionment in love, a profound sense of responsibility, rejection of pleasure, disappointment in life's harvest. From eclogue to eclogue, these subsidiary contraries receive greater or less emphasis, yet each recurs often enough to give unity to the whole. As the thematic stress changes, so does the pastoral conception itself. Sometimes the shepherd is primarily a lover, sometimes a poet, sometimes a priest, yet he is always all of these.

The confrontation of youth and age is most direct in the February eclogue. The introductory dialogue between the shepherd boy Cuddie and the ninety-year-old Thenot recalls the soliloquy of the young-old loving-unloved Colin of *January*. Cuddie's green love has not yet reached the point of pain:

> Phyllis is myne for many dayes:
> I wonne her with a gyrdle of gelt,[e]
> Embost with buegle [f] about the belt.
> Such an one shepeheards woulde make full faine:
> Such an one would make thee younge againe.

But Thenot answers:

[e] gelt: gilt(?).   [f] buegle: glass bead.

Thou art a fon,[g] of thy love to boste,
All that is lent to love, wyll be lost.   (ll. 64–70)

Cuddie and his flock are miserable in the bitter winter. But Thenot
has learned the lesson of the Stoics: he makes no complaint of cold
or heat, he is no foeman to Fortune,

> ever my flocke was my chiefe care,
> Winter or Sommer they mought well fare.   (ll. 23–24)

Cuddie may be careless, his youthful pride to be paid for with "weeping, and wayling, and misery," but he is alive, budding, about to
flower. So too is his "brag" bullock:

> His hornes bene as broade, as Rainebowe bent,
> His dewelap as lythe, as lasse of Kent.
> See howe he venteth into the wynd.
> Weenest of love is not his mynd?   (ll. 73–76)

Thenot, like his sheep, is dried up, crooked, fruitless:

> Thy Ewes, that wont to have blowen bags,
> Like wailefull widdowes hangen their crags: [h]
> The rather [i] Lambes bene starved with cold,
> All for their Maister is lustlesse and old.   (ll. 81–84)

Thenot concludes the eclogue with his tale of the Oak and the Briar.
Of all the stories told by the Kentish shepherd Tityrus (Chaucer, of
course, though the tale is none of his) there is "none fitter then this
to applie."

The application is obvious enough. An ancient Oak, once a goodly
tree but now barren and decaying, is challenged by a Briar, proudly
thrusting upward, gay with blossoms, the delight of shepherds'
daughters and of nightingales. When the Briar complains to the
Husbandman that the great old tree tyrannizes over him, cutting
off his light and blighting his flowers, the Oak is cut down. But the
Briar's glee is short-lived: winter comes, and the unprotected Briar,
burdened by snow, falls to the ground,

---

[g] fon: fool.   [h] crags: necks.   [i] rather: younger.

>   is trodde in the durt
> Of cattell, and brouzed, and sorely hurt.
> Such was thend of this Ambitious brere,
> For scorning Eld   (ll. 235–38)

Curiously, in *The Ruines of Time* Spenser uses the figure of an aged tree that will not suffer new growth near it to condemn the overshadowing Burghley (see above, p. 14). Here, since Thenot tells the story, the reader's sympathy goes to the Oak. The reverence—perhaps superstitiously—due to age cannot save it from decay and destruction. But youth, though it wants to live free of control, though it envies the prestige and authority which maturity brings, nevertheless depends upon maturity for its existence. The moral is not unlike that of Menenius' fable of the belly and the members: as plebeians cannot live without the nobility, so youth cannot live without age. Cuddie, naturally, thinks it a lewd tale of little worth.

In *December* the mature Colin faces his own youth. The contrasts of *February* reappear: the young man "Like Swallow swift" wanders carelessly, thinking his spring will last forever; with time comes pain, an application to things of "ryper reason," a profound sense of responsibility. And again, youth destroys age. As Shakespeare has it in Sonnet LXXIII,

> In me thou seest the glowing of such fire,
> That on the ashes of his youth doth lye,
> As the death bed, wheron it must expire,
> Consum'd with that which it was nurrisht by.

The rage of love, kindled in the young man's breast by the god of shepherds ("But better mought they have behote[j] him Hate"), blasts the promised harvest. On this dark note the *Calender* ends.

Much of the December eclogue is imitated from Clement Marot's *Eglogue au Roy*. The theme of love the destroyer, however, is Spenser's addition. It is one of the most important of the threads which

---

[j] behote: called.

bind the *Calender*. Although Cuddie thinks love is mere delight, Thenot knows it to be folly. In *August* Perigot complains,

> So learnd I love on a hollye eve
>
>   . . .
>
> That ever since my hart did greve.   (ll. 121–23)

Willy, in the March eclogue, is childish enough to suggest that

> we little Love awake,
> That nowe sleepeth in Lethe lake,
> And pray him leaden our daunce.   (ll. 22–24)

His companion, Thomalin, is wiser through experience. Cupid, in seeming play, once hit him with his shaft:

> then I little smart did feele:
> But soone it sore encreased.
> And now itranckleth more and more,
> And inwardly it festreth sore,
> Ne wote I, how to cease it.   (ll. 98–102)

The change of love from honey to gall reflects a change in the god of love himself. When Willy is told of the poison in Cupid's arrows, he remembers,

> once I heard my father say,
> How he him caught upon a day,
>   (Whereof he wilbe wroken ᵏ)
> Entangled in a fowling net,
> Which he for carrion Crowes had set,
>   That in our Peeretree haunted.
> Tho sayd, he was a winged lad,
> But bowe and shafts as then none had:
>   Els had he sore be daunted.   (ll. 106–14)

Perhaps the fowling net is intended to make the reader think of the gin in which Vulcan trapped Venus and Mars, the pear tree to re-

---

ᵏ wroken: revenged.

mind him of the tree of Eden or the one into which May climbed in Chaucer's tale. But the point of the episode is that Love, who once upon a time went about without weapons, in all innocence, now is armed with a venomous sting. Leo Spitzer reads the moral of the tale, "Rejoice not in spring, be not young!—for this is hybris, and nemesis must follow!" [8]

Colin's love for Rosalind is of this day, and the armed Cupid has taken his revenge. In youth, the heat of heedless lust engendered the flame:

> Tho would I seeke for Queene apples unrype,
> To give my Rosalind   (*June,* 43–44)

The happiness of such a love is fragile. It is destroyed by the discovery that Rosalind is disdainful ("dangerous," the medieval lover would say) and worse, fickle. The remainder is pain and waste: the harvest burnt, friendship for Hobbinol sacrificed, the shepherd's pipe broken. And the sheep in Colin's care suffer too:

> Thou feeble flocke, whose fleece is rough and rent,
> Whose knees are weake through fast and evill fare:
> Mayst witnesse well by thy ill governement,
> Thy maysters mind is overcome with care.
> Thou weake, I wanne: thou leane, I quite forlorne:
> With mourning pyne I, you with pyning mourne.
>
> (*January,* 43–48)

The case is general. As Willy says in *August:*

> Never knewe I lovers sheepe in good plight.

As the amorous shepherd cares little for his sheep, so the preoccupied pastor neglects his flock. Neither Theocritus nor Vergil would have thought of associating rustic and priest, but the authority of the Bible and the weight of medieval tradition made the connection inevitable. Out of that tradition emerged an ideal portrait of the priest: simple, humble, pure, completely dedicated to the care

of his congregation. The ideal, like all ideals, served as a principal
weapon of satire, as it did for Chaucer at his most bitter:

> For if a preest be foul, on whom we truste,
> No wonder is a lewed man to ruste;
> And shame it is, if a prest take keep,
> A shiten shepherde and a clene sheep.[9]

In the formal pastoral of the Renaissance, the equation of priest and
shepherd appears as early as Petrarch, and it occurs in the eclogues
of Spenser's English predecessors in the genre, Alexander Barclay
and Barnabe Googe. For the Protestant, the analogy was particularly
attractive because it supported both his demand for a return to the
religion of the apostles and his attack upon the pomp and pride of
Rome.[10]

May, July, and *September* are the eclogues principally devoted to
the shepherd-priest. *February* is usually included with these, but the
argument for its interpretation in this sense seems to me tenuous.
The best support for such a reading of the eclogue is found in the
lines which describe the old Oak as it is about to be felled:

> it had bene an auncient tree,
> Sacred with many a mysteree,
> And often crost with the priestes crewe,
> And often halowed with holy water dewe.
> But sike fancies weren foolerie,
> And broughten this Oake to this miserye.
> For nought mought they quitten him from decay   (ll. 207–13)

The crossing and the holy water suggest that by the Oak Spenser
may intend Catholicism or in some sense the old religion (though
a Protestant would insist that his was the religion of the apostles
and Catholicism a latter-day distortion). Once such an identification is accepted, a variety of allegories can be drawn out of Thenot's
fable. The most plausible of these interprets the tale as a warning
to those religious radicals who, in their zeal for reform, would

uproot all of the old and leave the new Tudor growth without the protection of established tradition. But Spenser may have meant no more than a passing shot at Roman rites as equivalent in vanity to the pagan magic of Druid oak-worshipers. Following Professor Renwick, I am inclined to accept E. K.'s description of the eclogue as "a discourse of old age" "rather morall and generall, then bent to any secrete or particular purpose." [11]

The subject of *May* is the dedication of the priest to his calling. Piers—his name suggests Langland's Piers the Plowman and his numerous successors of the fifteenth and sixteenth centuries—is of the line of Chaucer's poor Parson. For Piers, the life of a true "shepherd" must be altogether unworldly, altogether unlike the life of a layman. The apostles, the first Christians, had no concern with possessions, with pleasures, with ambitions. Like them, the modern shepherd must give himself up wholly to the watch of his flock, to the protection of the faith. The slightest relaxation leads to disaster, for the Enemy is wily beyond measure. To this effect Piers tells the fable of the foolish Kid whom a false Fox deceives and devours. Palinode, as his name declares (but what an odd name for a shepherd!), takes the contrary position. A shepherd is a man as other men are. The goods of the world are God-given and given to be enjoyed. The carping precisian, constantly scolding other shepherds, does more harm than good, bringing shame upon the whole calling. To these arguments Piers answers uncompromisingly:

> what concord han [1] light and darke sam? [m]
> Or what peace has the Lion with the Lambe? (ll. 168–69)

There are suggestions in Piers's fable that the Fox is to be identified with Catholicism: he carries a bag of bells, baubles, and glass trifles and he swears by "sweete Saint Charitee." E. K.'s account of the eclogue, in fact, asserts that Piers and Palinode represent "two formes of pastoures or Ministers, or the protestant and the Catholique." But

---

[1] han: have.   [m] sam: together.

the intention is surely wider than the latter alternative. Rome may be a manifestation of Satan, but the ways of error are countless. Nor is the debate as one-sided as the identification of the speakers with Protestantism and Catholicism would demand. It is true that Piers's contention is the weightier and the more emotionally charged. But Palinode's part is not specious. In *September,* Hobbinol, of whom Spenser obviously approves, is made to speak very much in Palinode's vein:

> Ah Diggon, thilke same rule were too straight,
> All the cold season to wach and waite.
> We bene of fleshe, men as other bee,
> Why should we be bound to such miseree?
> What ever thing lacketh chaungeable rest,
> Mought needes decay, when it is at best.   (ll. 236–41)

As Spenser uses it, the dialogue of a pastoral poem is not a Socratic demonstration but a valid disagreement in which the speakers explore what may best be said on either part.

The debate of *July* is between pride (or aspiration) and humility (or laziness). The symbol of the former is the hill upon which the goatherd Morrel sits; that of the latter the shepherd Thomalin's lowly plain. In the eighth eclogue of Baptista Mantuanus (Baptista Spagnuoli), the principal source of *July,* it is the peasant on the hill who persuades. Spenser gives the stronger argument to his opponent. Morrel may claim that the great god Pan dwelt upon Mount Olivet, but Thomalin knows that the "saints" of yore "lived in lowlye leas." Such was Abel

> That whilome was the first shepheard,
>   and lived with little gayne:
> As meeke he was, as meeke mought be,
>   simple, as simple sheepe   (ll. 127–30)

And such, too, were Moses and Aaron and the twelve brothers who founded the tribes of Israel. The ideal is that of Piers:

> But shepheard mought be meeke and mylde,
>> well eyed, as Argus was,
> With fleshly follyes undefyled,
>> and stoute as steede of brasse. (ll. 153–56)

The butt of Thomalin's satire is also that of Piers's, the self-seeking prelate whose great possessions and concern with power leave him no interest in the welfare of his flock. Catholic priests are of this kind, as Palinode, who has been to Rome, testifies. But the eclogue as a whole is not merely a diatribe against Catholicism. Thomalin's exemplary tale is of Algrind, the good shepherd, who once sat on a hill and suffered therefor:

> For sitting so with bared scalpe,
>> an Eagle sored hye,
> That weening hys whyte head was chalke,
>> a shell fish downe let flye:
> She weend the shell fishe to have broake,
>> but therewith bruzd his brayne,
> So now astonied with the stroke,
>> he lyes in lingring payne. (ll. 221–28)

Aeschylus' mishap is here applied to Archbishop Grindal in one of the indubitable topical references of the *Calender*. Grindal, Archbishop of Canterbury, was suspended by Queen Elizabeth in 1577, two years before the publication of Spenser's poem, for his refusal to carry out harsh measures against extreme Puritans. Morrel prophesies his restoration:

> his hap was ill,
> but shall be bett in time. (ll. 229–30)

Although Algrind was no Roman, he rose to high place and was struck down. The eclogue is concerned only in part with a condemnation of ambitious priests. It is also a warning against the temptation and the danger of the heights.

September is more obscure—or more confused—than the other

eclogues of this group. It begins with a variant of the ambition
theme: Diggon Davie has sought to better his state in "forrein costes"
but has found only misery and loss. His foil is the temperate philosopher Hobbinol:

> Content who lives with tryed state,
> Neede feare no chaunge of frowning fate   (ll. 70–71)

Diggon's complaint turns into a violent denunciation of the greedy,
proud, false shepherds whom he encountered in his travels. In some
passages those shepherds are clearly the "Popish prelates" to whom
E. K. refers, in others they appear to be intended more generally
as bad priests in high places. Diggon's fable, like that of Piers in
May, emphasizes the wiliness of the Enemy and the necessity for
sleepless watch. Its hero is Roffy: John Young, Bishop of Rochester
(*episcopus Roffensis*), whose secretary in 1578 was Edmund Spenser.
Because the Kid in the May story is foolish and unwary, the Fox
escapes with his prey, and because Roffy is "wise, and as Argus eyed,"
the Wolf of *September* is caught and killed.

This body of religious satire seems hard to reconcile with the loves
of Cuddie, Perigot, and Colin. But Spenser forges the link. The
unfortunate Kid of the May eclogue is as heedlessly lustful as Cuddie:

> His Vellet [n] head began to shoote out,
> And his wreathed hornes gan newly sprout:
> The blossomes of lust to bud did beginne,
> And spring forth ranckly under his chinne.   (ll. 185–88)

The good shepherd Abel is contrasted with Helen's Paris:

> But nothing such thilk shephearde was,
>   whom Ida hyll dyd beare,
> That left hys flocke, to fetch a lasse,
>   whose love he bought to deare:
> For he was proude, that ill was payd,

[n] Vellet: velvet, the soft skin covering the growing horns.

> (no such mought shepheards bee)
> And with lewde lust was overlayd:
> tway things doen ill agree   (*July*, 145–52)

As there was a time when Cupid went unarmed, so there was a golden age of Christianity before priests became greedy and proud. But innocence is gone and both shepherd-lover and shepherd-priest are the worse for it.

Colin himself is the principal shepherd-poet. The woodcuts for the four eclogues in which he appears all show him with a shepherd's pipe. In *January, June,* and *December,* the pipe lies shattered at his feet; in *November* Colin plays upon it his dirge for Dido as Thenot puts a laurel crown on his head. The motif of the broken pipe is the dominant one. The January eclogue announces it: since Rosalind scorns Colin's rustic muse he will sing no more. In *June* the restless, tormented Colin is contrasted with his friend Hobbinol, content with his lot:

> O happy Hobbinol, I blesse thy state,
> That Paradise hast found, whych Adam lost.

Hobbinol urges his friend to join him in his delicious dale, to leave the hills which have bewitched him. But Colin cannot recover the Eden he has lost. Once, in his youth, when he walked "withouten lincks of love," he was able to enjoy the delights of Hobbinol's paradise, to sing sweet rhymes and roundelays. But time and pain have killed his bent for such song, and his only ambition now is to make complaint so bitter that it will pierce the heart of heartless Rosalind. In *December* Colin again recalls his early song, framed "Unto the shifting of the shepheards foote," the youthful promise of his poetry, and the blighting of that promise by Rosalind's falseness. Now his Muse is hoarse and weary, and he hangs his pipe upon a tree (though the woodcut shows it broken on the ground).

It is the October eclogue which is principally devoted to the shepherd-poet. Because of its elevation of the subject to a new and

exalted level and because of its resumption of the themes that bind
the *Calender* together, it constitutes the focus of the whole. Theocritus had written about the poet unrewarded and so had Vergil,
Baptista Mantuanus, and many others. Cuddie's part in the eclogue
is imitated from Baptista, but Piers's speeches are for the most part
Spenser's own. Cuddie, like Colin, has abandoned song, but not
because of a broken heart:

> The dapper ditties, that I wont devise,
> To feede youthes fancie, and the flocking fry,
> Delighten much: what I the bett for thy?   (ll. 13–15)

The "Delighten much" was a signal to Spenser's readers—where was
the rest of the "delight and teach" formula? When Piers offers glory
as a reward, Cuddie takes it to mean words of praise, nothing but
smoke and wind. Once, indeed, there was a time when poetic genius
might fulfill itself: through the help of Maecenas, Vergil (the "Romish Tityrus") grew from the writing of pastorals to the composition of the useful *Georgics,*

> And eft did sing of warres and deadly drede,
> So as the Heavens did quake his verse to here.   (ll. 59–60)

But the modern poet lacks both means and subject matter. Maecenas
is dead, and there is no longer a "mighty manhode" to celebrate in
these degenerate, easeful times.

Piers and Cuddie are such poles apart that they can talk only at
cross purposes. For Piers, the honor of virtuous action, not earthly
fame, is the reward for the poet who inspires men to noble deeds
and keeps them from evil ways:

> O what an honor is it, to restraine
> The lust of lawlesse youth with good advice:
> Or pricke them forth with pleasaunce of thy vaine,
> Whereto thou list their trayned ° willes entice.   (ll. 21–24)

° trayned: trapped.

As Milton puts it in *Lycidas,* the payment for the homely, slighted shepherd's trade cannot be canceled by the blind Fury slitting the thin-spun life: "Of so much fame in Heaven expect thy meed." Like Cuddie, Piers believes that as the true poet matures he reaches higher. His ascent begins on the Vergilian path: when the pastoral mode is outgrown the poet should "sing of bloody Mars, of wars, of giusts." But now Piers looks to a step beyond:

> Turne thee to those, that weld the awful crowne,
> To doubted Knights, whose woundlesse armour rusts,
> And helmes unbruzed wexen dayly browne.   (ll. 40–42)

The rusted armor, like Mercilla's rusted sword in the fifth book of *The Faerie Queene,* represents a power the potentiality of which is enough to keep the peace. For subject matter Piers offers, not the embattled warriors whose absence Cuddie regrets, but those who, like Elizabeth and the great Earl of Leicester ("That first the white beare to the stake did bring"), make England so feared that none dares attack it. Nor is this the pinnacle of poetic achievement. When Cuddie protests that poetry finds no favor among the great in these corrupt times, Piers breaks into an apostrophe to "pierlesse Poesye":

> where is then thy place?
> If nor in Princes pallace thou doe sitt:
> (And yet is Princes pallace the most fitt)
> Ne brest of baser birth doth thee embrace.
> Then make thee winges of thine aspyring wit,
> And, whence thou camst, flye backe to heaven apace.   (ll. 79–84)

As poetry is divine in origin, so its final subject is the divine. And now the eclogue takes a new turn.

Though Cuddie's vision is limited, he is able to sense both the height of Piers's conception and his own inadequacy to it:

> For Colin fittes such famous flight to scanne:
> He, were he not with love so ill bedight,
> Would mount as high, and sing as soote as Swanne.   (ll. 88–90)

The bitter experience of the shepherd-lover makes it impossible for him to attain the poetic summit, the song of heaven. The result, as Cuddie sees it, is the barren waste of *January* and *December*. But for Piers, love is not a blight. "Ah fon," he says (I take it that the "fool" is Colin):

> for love does teach him climbe so hie,
> And lyftes him up out of the loathsome myre:
> Such immortall mirrhor, as he doth admire,
> Would rayse ones mynd above the starry skie.
> And cause a caytive corage to aspire,
> For lofty love doth loath a lowly eye.   (ll. 91–96)

Love the destroyer is here faced with love the creator. The opposition is central to the poet's thinking, but I must here leave it adumbrated, as the poet does.

In some sense, Colin is of course Master Edmund Spenser, the gifted young poet deeply concerned with the calling he had elected and its relation to the world about him. But Spenser's harvest was not burnt up, his career a failure and at an end in 1579; in fact, it is clear from his correspondence with Harvey that the publication of the *Calender* had spurred his poetic activity and that he was full of hopes for advancement. Hobbinol is as surely Gabriel Harvey. Spenser's portrait of him as the wise, contented philosopher does not, in truth, fit with what Nashe has to say about Harvey nor with our own impression drawn from Harvey's writings, but Nashe and we may be wrong, or Spenser may. However, we may be secure in doubting that Dr. Harvey ever sent Edmund Spenser "His kiddes, his cracknelles, and his early fruit." Hobbinol's pastoral love for Colin gives us no reason to suppose (or not to suppose) that Harvey was homosexually inclined. The search for Rosalind's identity has wasted infinite scholarly effort. Of all the speculations on the subject, the most remarkable is that which identifies her with Queen Elizabeth, partly on the ground that "Elisa R" taken together with the first syllable of "England" (with the "g" changed to "d" for euphony) is an anagram for *Rasilende,* "a name close in sound and spelling to *Rosalind*." [12] Both E. K. and Harvey's letters suggest that there was indeed a living Rosalind, but who she was and what relationship she bore to the Rosalind of the *Calender* no one knows. Cuddie, too, appears to have some connection with an Elizabethan person but our knowledge ends with that statement. In any case, it has proved impossible to read a biography of Spenser from *The Shepheardes Calender.*

In the tradition, as old as Vergil, which made the pastoral eclogue an appropriate vehicle for political comment, some of the shepherds of the *Calender* allude to public figures of the time. Roffy and Algrin, or Algrind, as has been said, refer to Bishop Young and Archbishop Grindal. Perhaps Morrel (of *July*) is Aylmer or Elmer, Bishop of London, whom Martin Marprelate ragged so unmercifully a decade later. Diggon Davie (*September*) may allude to Richard Davies, Bishop of St. David's, and Thomalin (*March* and *July*) to Thomas Cooper, Bishop of Lincoln.[13] If Spenser intended the identification of Morrel, Diggon Davie, and Thomalin with these bishops he was bold enough to criticize the morality of very powerful men indeed, a risky matter for a young poet to meddle with but something of which he was quite capable, as we know from his later attacks on Cecil. Even the undoubted reference to Grindal's suspension is evidence of that rashness of spirit of which his friend Harvey accused him.

Under other names of the poem Spenser eulogizes the great of the realm. Even E. K. admits that Elisa represents the Queen— rude shepherds, he points out, would be incapable of knowing her right name. (Drayton achieves originality of a kind by having his shepherds call her "Beta.") Lobbin, who appears in *Colin Clouts Come Home Againe* as the Earl of Leicester, may also have the same meaning in the November eclogue where he mourns the loss of Dido, though diligent research has failed to discover an appropriate Dido. Pan presents a problem of a different kind. He is always identifiable from context, but the identity in one place is that of Henry VIII (with Syrinx as Anne Boleyn?), in another a poet less meritorious than Colin, and in yet another God Himself.

The names Spenser chooses for the people of the *Calender* are not usual ones. Most Renaissance pastoralists, including Spenser's English predecessors Alexander Barclay and Barnabe Googe, were content to use the names made familiar by Theocritus and Vergil: Codrus, Daphnis, Phyllis, Menalcas, Tityrus. Clement Marot is an exception. He calls himself Colin, which Spenser imitates by adopting "Colin Clout," the pseudonym of the English satirist John Skelton. "Thenot" also comes from Marot. Spenser's Willy and Piers are plain English, harmonious with the rustic setting. But what can be made of Hobbinol, Wrenock, Palinode, and Roffy? Evidently Spenser wished to avoid on the one hand the classicism of the traditional names and on the other the commonness of the everyday. Names like these sound rude and are therefore fitting but they are not banal. Drayton follows Spenser's example, calling his shepherds Batte, Gorbo, Olcon, and Motto.

The point has some relevance to the larger question of Spenser's choice of a literary vocabulary. As he would not name his characters Daphnis and Phyllis, so he rejected the Latinate words that the English humanist tradition condemned as "inkhorn" and "smelling of the lamp." But he rejected, also, the kind of English that the humanist tradition advocated, a "standard" language which admitted only the oldest of the new and the newest of the old. For the purposes of poetry, such a language is dull and prosy, as Aristotle and Coleridge and many others have recognized. The principle of decorum, too, forbade the speech of Spenser's London to his rustics. They might have spoken a dialect, but the effect, for Spenser's audience, would have been merely ridicule. The only instance of sixteenth-century literary use of dialect for other than humorous or grotesque effect that I can think of is Shakespeare's *Henry V*, and in this case the exception really proves the rule: one of the principal points of the play is that under a true king true Englishmen who speak oddly or eat leeks are nevertheless Englishmen and those who think otherwise will find language and vegetable rammed down their throats. Spenser's solution is to mix with a basically normal vocabulary words already archaic or becoming so, words made to sound archaic by such means as the addition of the perfective prefix "y" ("yglaunst," "yshrilled"), and dialectal words which he and his London readers may have thought archaic. The result is a flavor of the antique and the rude in which sometimes the one predominates and sometimes the other. In poems written after *The Shepheardes Calender* the flavor remains, though it becomes rather less rude and much less sharp. E. K. is at pains to defend Spenser's practice on the principle of decorum and on a variety of other grounds: it reflects the poet's inheritance of the national tradition of Chaucer and other English "ancients"; the antiquity of the words "maketh the style seeme grave, and as it were reverend"; because of their harshness the words serve as discords in music to make the contrasting harmony sweeter; and their return to English usage recovers for the language "good and naturall English words, as have ben long time out of use and almost cleane disherited." Sir Philip Sidney, to whom the poem was dedicated, was not impressed with these arguments: "That same framing of his stile to an old rustick language I dare not alowe, sith neyther Theocritus in Greeke, Virgill in Latine, nor Sanazar in Italian did affect it." [14] On precisely the same ground of authoritative precedent Dryden and Pope praise Spenser for his imitation of Theocritus' use of a Doric dialect. Ben Jonson says that Spenser "writ no language" and Samuel Johnson thinks that if the shepherds of the *Calender* found it necessary to discourse on theology they might at least have taken the time to learn English. Others have come to the conclusion that Spenser is the father of English as a language of poetry. [15] That his adventure in vocabulary was a success may be doubted; that it was bold cannot.

In his verse forms, too, Spenser departs from the tradition. Following Vergil's example, the neo-Latin pastoralists of the Renaissance accepted the hexameter as their proper meter. Alexander Barclay's English eclogues are all in pentameter couplets except for a stanzaic elegy. Barnabe Googe holds faithfully to the fourteener. In contrast, there are thirteen different verse forms in the *Calender*. According to Renwick, "Of these three or four were common in his time; two at least were entirely new inventions, three were new rhyme-arrangements, two new importations, one an imitation of Chaucerian couplet peculiar to this book; and only three of the thirteen were ever used by Spenser again." [16] This variety is unique in collections of formal eclogues, apart, that is, from imitations of Spenser. But it does have a precedent in Sannazaro's Arcadian romance, a mingling of prose and verse in which there are examples of the canzone, the sestina, terza rima, and other forms. [17] The precedent is an important one since it suggested to Sidney the use of a great number of verse forms for the poems in his own *Arcadia*. At about the same time—it is impossible to tell which is earlier—both Sidney and Spenser were exploring the range of metrical possibilities for pastoral poetry. The explorations had very different results.

In Sidney's *Arcadia,* the first poem of the "Eclogues" which conclude Book I is itself a medley of meters and complex rhyme schemes. It is followed by three poems in unrhymed quantitative verse: elegiacs, sapphics, and hexameters. The last of the eclogues of Book I is a long poem in stanzas rhyming *ababababcc*. Elsewhere in the *Arcadia* are sestinas, unrhymed, double, and rhymed; dizains with a "crown" (the last line of each stanza is the first of the next); an echo poem; and more classical experiments: anacreontics, asclepiads, phaleucians.

With the exception of the sestina, to which Spenser gives a twist of his own, none of these ingenuities appears in the *Calender*. There is no quantitative verse at all, though Spenser was strongly attracted to the idea and discussed it with Harvey and with Sidney himself in 1580. Perhaps he thought so learned a kind of composition would be inappropriate in a pastoral. There are only three poems in complex verse forms in the *Calender*, and all are attributed to Colin, the nightingale of shepherds: the lay of Elisa, the sestina of *August*, and the elegy on Dido. The rest of the *Calender* is written in couplets or in simple stanzaic patterns.

It is not so much the number of the metrical forms in the *Calender* that is remarkable; it is rather their range. The sestina in which Colin gravely laments the pain of his love is set against the breathless rustic roundelay of Perigot and Willy. At one end of Spenser's scale are the long, flowing stanzas in praise of Elisa and in memory of Dido, mixing long and short verses, the rhyme schemes formally binding the units together, the complex but lucid syntax providing integrity of substance for the whole. These forms, no doubt inspired by French or Italian models, Spenser later elaborated to create the magnificent structures of his *Epithalamion* and *Prothalamion*. At the other end of his scale are the rude, lurching couplets of *February, May,* and *September*.

The lines of these eclogues are deliberately rough:

Hobbinol: Diggon Davie, I bid her [p] god day:
          Or Diggon her is, or I missaye.
Diggon: Her was her, while it was daye light,
          But now her is a most wretched wight.
          For day, that was, is wightly [q] past,
          And now at earst [r] the dirke night doth hast.

                                        (*September*, 1–6)

The irregular stress and the alliteration suggest that Spenser was imitating such revivals or survivals of Anglo-Saxon versification as *Piers Plowman* and Dunbar's *Tretis of the Tua Mariit Wemen and*

[p] her: him.   [q] wightly: swiftly.   [r] at earst: at once.

the Wedo. Some scholars have thought that Spenser's model was Chaucer as he would have been read in the sixteenth century, with final *e*'s silent. But such a reading, while it would have been more irregular than Chaucer intended, would not have resulted in the harshness of the *February* verse nor would it account for the insistent running of the letter. Whatever its derivation, the experiment was a most daring one. The generation of poets before Spenser had aspired to a perfectly regular alternation of strong and weak stresses. Sidney's line is usually free from the monotonous regularity of his predecessors, but he takes no such liberties as Spenser does. Even his attempts at quantitative verse merely substitute one kind of rule for another, while the verse of *February, May,* and *September* follows no usual rule at all. The justification for Spenser's practice must lie in the traditional Englishness of his line and in the principle of decorum as the Renaissance understood it. Since the matter of these eclogues is harsh and unpleasant, the manner should grate. The association of roughness of versification with satiric content was reinforced by the example of Juvenal. John Skelton, who claims Juvenal as his inspiration, defends his own peculiar cacophonies:

> For though my rime be ragged,
> Tattered and jagged,
> Rudely rayne beaten,
> Rusty and moughte eaten,
> If ye take well therwith,
> It hath in it some pyth.[18]

And at the end of the century the satirist Hall makes the point explicitly:

It is not for every one to rellish a true and naturall Satyre, being of it selfe besides the native and in-bred bitternes and tartnes of particulers, both hard of conceipt, and harsh of stile.[19]

It is among the "moral" eclogues, as E. K. classifies them, "which for the most part be mixed with some Satyricall bitternesse" that *February, May,* and *September* belong.

Twelve years after the publication of *The Shepheardes Calender* Spenser took up the pastoral form once more. *Colin Clouts Come Home Againe,* a title evidently intended to recall the earlier poem, repeats few of its radical experiments. The vocabulary avoids grotesque harshness, the rustic-antique appearing only in an occasional "ne" for "no," "leasing" for "lie," "yshrilled" and the like. Some of the old names of the *Calender*—Cuddy, Hobbinol, Lobbin—are retained, perhaps because of their association with real people; the others are euphonious: Marin, Alexis, Melissa. There are no violent contrasts in verse form, no jagged lines, and no display pieces. Yet the poet has not reversed direction. His aims, both poetic and didactic, are similar to those he attempted in the *Calender,* but his means have become more subtle.

The unity of *Colin Clouts Come Home Againe* is ingeniously supported by the structure of its verse. The effect of calm, unbroken flow is created by quatrains usually though not always coinciding with the syntax but organized principally as sweeping verse paragraphs. The casual reader may not even be aware of the quatrains, for Spenser disguises the pattern by beginning with seven lines linked terza rima fashion and ending with five lines rhyming *ababa*. A pervasive pastoral atmosphere arises from the simple innocence of the speakers: Colin's fearful wonder at sea and ship, Cuddy's ignorance of the existence of any land besides his own, Corylas' belief that love is to be found only among shepherds, the amazement of the whole company at the description of Cynthia's court. A single narrative device frames the whole: Colin, like Diggon Davie in the September eclogue, tells the story of his travels to a far land.

These unifying characteristics bind together a tremendous variety of mood and subject. The tone ranges from the rhapsodic to the bitter, the extremes emphasized by the comments of Colin's auditors:

Colin (said Cuddy then) thou hast forgot
Thyself, me seemes, too much, to mount so hie:

> Such loftie flight, base shepheard seemeth not,
> From flocks and fields, to Angels and to skie.   (ll. 616–19)

> Ah Colin (then said Hobbinol) the blame
> Which thou imputest, is too generall,
> As if not any gentle wit of name,
> Nor honest mynd might there be found at all.   (ll. 731–34)

Colin repeats his story of the love of the rivers Bregog and Mulla as he sang it in friendly competition with the Shepherd of the Ocean; he tells of his voyage over the sea, of incomparable England, of the poets and ladies of the court, of the great and bountiful Queen Cynthia, of the false courtier, of love counterfeit and true, of the proud Rosalind. The effect would be merely chaotic were it not for the easy run of the verse, the skillfully handled transitions, and the repeated reference to the pastoral setting of Colin's discourse.

The portrait of the poet Colin is done with delicate strokes. In the art of singing he is the peer of the Shepherd of the Ocean:

> He pip'd, I sung; and when he sung, I piped,
> By chaunge of turnes, each making other mery,
> Neither envying other, nor envied,
> So piped we, untill we both were weary.   (ll. 76–79)

His rustic companions "stand astonisht at his curious skill." But they do not proclaim him superior to Pan and the Muses. They wonder, rather, that so great a shepherdess as Cynthia should trouble to listen to him, "a simple silly Elfe." If his songs of Cynthia will not be forgotten it is because "her great excellence,/ Lifts me above the measure of my might." When he is brought to consider the poets of her court he confidently assumes the role of judge and adviser. But because he is an outsider he avoids direct competition with them, and he is even able to praise Palin "Albe he envie at my rustick quill." The pastoral pose, while it permits Colin the appearance of humility, sets him apart from the others and in an important sense above them, since he alone is a free man, unimpeded by ambition and the necessity for timeserving.

As in the *Calender,* shepherd-poet is also shepherd-lover. Since the philosophy of love which Colin expounds with such ecstasy foreshadows its fuller statement in the *Fowre Hymnes* it will be considered later. The triangle involving Rosalind and Hobbinol, however, relates directly to that of the *Calender.* The situation remains superficially the same: Colin still despairs, Rosalind scorns, Hobbinol vainly reasons. But Rosalind is no longer faithless, and her pride is not merely destructive since it is just and praiseworthy:

> Not then to her that scorned thing so base,
> But to my selfe the blame that lookt so hie:
> So hie her thoughts as she her selfe have place,
> And loath each lowly thing with loftie eie. (ll. 935–38)

Piers says in *October* that "lofty love doth loath a lowly eye" and reasons that it should therefore raise the poet's mind "above the starry skie." Colin of the *Calender* has not learned this lesson and as the poem ends he abandons his shepherd's pipe. The new Colin will continue to sing:

> Yet so much grace let her vouchsafe to grant
> To simple swaine, sith her I may not love:
> Yet that I may her honour paravant,[*]
> And praise her worth, though far my wit above. (ll. 939–42)

And this grace will bring some ease to his cureless pain.

The matter of religion, so important a subject in the *Calender,* scarcely appears at all. In its place is the court as seen by a shepherd, also part of the stock of Renaissance pastoral. With precise tact, Colin manages to explain his rejection of that court while at the same time glorifying Cynthia's bounty ("Her deeds were like great clusters of ripe grapes") and praising the noble wits and gracious ladies who surround her. For "all the rest" are proud, lewd

---

[*] paravant: preeminently.

double-dealers, and the simple swain, not daring to adventure himself among them, prefers to return to his sheep:

> it is no sort of life
> For shepheard fit to lead in that same place   (ll. 688–89)

Like Colin, Spenser went back to what he considered the rudely
barbarous isolation of Ireland from the sophisticated barbarities
of the court. Whether he did so at his own choice, like Colin, or
because the displeasure of Cecil made his position untenable is not
a matter that this poem can decide. The sensitive and intelligent
man of the Renaissance must always have been ambivalent about
the pursuit of a career at court. On the one hand, the "disordered
thrust" (as Daniel puts it) of ambitious striving was incompatible
with contemplative study; on the other, the principal justification
of contemplative study was the service it could render to the state.
This was the dilemma of Thomas More: in the first book of *Utopia*
Hythlodaye rejects the suggestion that he become adviser to a king;
within a year of the publication of that work More entered royal
service. It was the dilemma of Thomas Wyatt who wrote a satire
on court life addressed to his friend Sir John Poins during a brief
interval in his lifelong service as diplomat:

> But here I ame in Kent and Christendome
>   Emong the muses where I rede and ryme;
>   Where if thou list, my Poynz, for to come,
> Thou shalt be judge how I do spend my tyme.

The answer is Wyatt's, too:

> Yet woll I serve my prynce, my lord and thyn,
>   And let theim lyve to fede the panche [t] that list [20]

As *The Shepheardes Calender* sets that which is against that
which was, so *Colin Clouts Come Home Againe* subjects the most
civilized of institutions to the scrutiny of the rustic. In both, the

[t] panche: paunch.

grand movement is circular: the *Calender* begins and ends in
winter, Colin Clout leaves his home in the country and returns to it.
In both, corruption is a principal theme, of pristine innocence in
the one and of simple truth in the other. But the past and the pasture
are offered not as solutions but as touchstones by which this time
and this world may be tested. The *Calender* proclaims that the old
right religion "may again retorne" (which Milton thought prophetic)
and that true love should raise the poet's spirit above the dust.
Colin Clouts Come Home Againe says of Elizabeth's England:

> all good, all grace there freely growes,
> Had people grace it gratefully to use:
> For God his gifts there plenteously bestowes,
> But gracelesse men them greatly do abuse. (ll. 324–27)

The poet's task is to grapple with error, not escape from it.

The World's Vanity

WITH THE NOTABLE EXCEPTIONS of *Muiopotmos* and *Mother Hubberds Tale* Spenser's "complaints and meditations of the worlds vanitie, verie grave and profitable," are not the most attractive of his works. Most of the poems included in the volume entitled *Complaints,* as well as the elegies *Daphnaida* and *Astrophel,* are characterized by a rhetorical lushness and an exaggeratedly emotional utterance that the modern reader is likely to find distasteful, however fashionable these traits were in Elizabethan times. Nevertheless, they repay study if only because they display the range of Spenser's virtuosity in literary construction and because they reflect, in one way or another, the conceptions which underlie his greater works.

A complaint of the world's vanity arises from a sense of the inevitable decay of sublunary things. Although such meditation is to be found in the poetry of every age, there are differences in attitude which mirror differences in intellectual and spiritual temper. Like the Middle Ages, the Renaissance relied in its search for the enduring upon its hope for heaven, and rather more than the Middle Ages upon its faith in the permanence of poetry. While the late medieval concern was primarily with the end to which mankind comes, that dance of death which joins in one charnel house king and bishop, tinker and peasant, the Renaissance was awed by the spectacle of power, fame, and beauty doomed to destruction, death becoming a comment on greatness rather than greatness a comment on death. The literary consequence was a fascination with the strength which is frail, the fame which is fleeting, the beauty which is dust.

Spenser's first exercise in this kind derives from the canzone "Standomi un giorno solo a la fenestra," in which the sorrowing Petrarch tells of six marvelous apparitions: a beautiful creature of the forest, a vessel laden with precious merchandise, a paradisal laurel tree, a sparkling fountain, a phoenix purple and gold, and finally, a graceful, pensive lady. In a moment each of these is destroyed, the lady bitten in the heel by an adder. Indeed, she is not destroyed, for she is sure of heaven:

> Lieta si dipartio, non che secura

But on earth only tears endure.

Inspired by Petrarch's song of the symbols of Laura, Joachim du Bellay added fifteen symbolic visions of Rome under the title "Songe" to *Les Antiquités de Rome,* a sonnet sequence celebrating the glory and lamenting the ruin of the great city. Petrarch's canzone and Du Bellay's "Songe" made their appearance in English in a translation done by the young Spenser for a volume entitled *A Theatre Wherein Be Represented as Wel the Miseries and Calamities That Follow the Voluptuous Worldlings, as Also the Joyes and Pleasures Which the Faithfull Do Enjoy* (1569) compiled by John van der Noot, a wealthy Dutch Calvinist who had found refuge in England. The visions of Petrarch and Du Bellay, illustrated by appropriate woodcuts, here become symbols of the impermanence not of a beautiful woman or of an imperial city but of the world itself. Spenser's translations are in unrhymed verse, doubtless in deference to the humanist contempt for rhyme as a barbaric ornament. In the *Complaints* volume, many years later, Spenser included translations of the rest of *Les Antiquités* and revised versions of the "Songe" and Petrarch's canzone, the principal change consisting in the addition of rhyme. He also wrote a dozen "visions of the worlds vanitie" of his own, giving the form a new turn. In these poems, the weakness of might is manifested by the insignificance of that which overthrows or preserves it: the ant disgraces the elephant, the goose saves Rome. This is also the theme of another poem in the *Complaints,* Spenser's translation of the pseudo-Vergilian *Culex* under the title *Virgils Gnat.*

The logic of Petrarch's canzone moves from mundane transience to the particular case of Laura. *The Ruines of Time,* the first poem of the *Complaints* volume, also treats of the decay of earthly glory both generally and specifically, as the poet declares in his dedicatory letter to the Countess of Pembroke: "I have conceived this small Poeme, intituled by a generall name of the *worlds Ruines:* yet speciallie intended to the renowming of that noble race, from which both you and he [her brother, Sir Philip Sidney] sprong, and to the eternizing of some of the chiefe of them late deceased." [1] The poem is a lament uttered by the spirit of the ancient city of Verulam, or so it begins, for as the complaint proceeds Verulam's spirit seems to be replaced by the poet speaking in his own person. As Rome was empress of the whole world, Verulam declares, "So I of this small Northerne world was Princesse." As in Du Bellay's *Les Antiquités,* the emphasis falls upon the city's vanished greatness:

> High towers, faire temples, goodly theaters,
> Strong walls, rich porches, princelie pallaces,
> Large streetes, brave houses, sacred sepulchers,
> Sure gates, sweete gardens, stately galleries,
> Wrought with faire pillours, and fine imageries,
> All those (O pitie) now are turned to dust,
> And overgrowen with blacke oblivions rust.   (ll. 92–98)

Verulam is gone, but its memory lives thanks to the labors of the historian Camden, "the nourice of antiquitie." Indeed, whether be-

cause of Camden's writings or this poem of Spenser's, the ancient
city, site of the modern St. Albans, became for Elizabethans a prime
figure of the once glorious. Perhaps it was in Shakespeare's mind
when he wrote:

> When I have seene by times fell hand defaced
> The rich proud cost of outworne buried age
> When sometime loftie towers I see downe rased,
> And brasse eternall slave to mortall rage

From Verulam, figure of a vanished glory which only literature
can preserve, the subject narrows to the departed members of the
great Dudley family, especially the Earl of Leicester:

> He now is dead, and all his glorie gone,
> And all his greatnes vapoured to nought   (ll. 218–19)

and Sir Philip Sidney who has achieved immortality of two kinds:

> So there thou livest, singing evermore,
> And here thou livest, being ever song
> Of us   (ll. 337–39)

The thought of Sidney's victory over death leads to the conclusion
that he who wishes to conquer time

> on Pegasus must ride,
> And with sweete Poets verse be glorifide   (ll. 426–27)

But those who scorn the Muses—the poet's finger points at Cecil—
can expect only oblivion. Indeed, all who pride themselves on their
worldly glory should note the fate of Verulam.

The poem concludes with two sets of visions of the kind of Du
Bellay's "Songe." They are designed to teach "by demonstration"
the lesson of the spirit of the dead city. The first set presents images
of strength, beauty, and gentility: a stately tower which falls to the
ground, a beautiful garden wasted, two white bears, fair and mild,
crushed in their cave. The distraught dreamer then hears a mysterious voice:

> Behold (said it) and by ensample see,
> That all is vanitie and griefe of minde,
> Ne other comfort in this world can be,
> But hope of heaven, and heart to God inclinde   (ll. 582–85)

And he dreams again, this time of a singing swan, a harp of gold
and ivory floating down a river, a virgin in a stately bridal bed, a
knight at arms. The harp, borrowed from Ovid's account of the
death of Orpheus, is explicitly that of Sir Philip, "Immortal spirite
of Philisides." These precious creations, like those of the first set
of visions, reach their earthly end, but they leave to live forever,
the swan and the harp as signs in the firmament, the bride in the
arms of her Bridegroom, the knight in heaven.

It has been suggested that *The Ruines of Time* may be a patch-
work of pieces written at various times and for different purposes,
an *ubi sunt* for Verulam ending with a tribute to Camden; fragments of the *Dreames* and *Pageaunts* mentioned by E. K. and in
the Harvey correspondence; and an elegy on Sidney.[2] Whether or
not it evolved in this way it stands as an entirely coherent structure.
As Petrarch's images are to Laura, so Rome is to Verulam and
Verulam in turn to the dead Dudleys. As Verulam endures, despite
its destruction, in Camden's imperishable record, so the noble members of that family will live in fame "Above the reach of ruinous
decay," glorified by "sweete Poets verse." Spenser describes his poem
as a "monument" to the fame of Sir Philip, an enduring one in
contrast to the monumental Verulam. But this solution of the
problem of oblivion is valid only in a temporal frame of reference,
as the concluding visions demonstrate, for heaven alone is beyond
worldly vanity. The poem therefore ends with the injunction to
Sidney's sister:

> So unto heaven let your high minde aspire,
> And loath the drosse of sinfull worlds desire.

As if to insist upon the unity of *The Ruines of Time,* Spenser binds
the whole together by a numerical device. The main part of the

poem consists of seventy stanzas of seven lines each; the two sets of visions are comprised in twenty-eight stanzas, in each set six visions followed by an envoy rejecting the vain world and looking to heaven. Six are the days of this mutable world; on the seventh God rests and change ceases.

Daphnaida, another poem in sevens, is a pastoral elegy on the wife of Sir Arthur Gorges, a gentleman poet whom Spenser celebrates under the name of Alcyon in *Colin Clouts Come Home Againe* (ll. 384–91).[3] It is made up of twenty-eight seven-line stanzas and seven "complaints," each seven stanzas long. The narrative closely imitates Chaucer's *Book of the Duchess.* A Man in Black tells of a lost lioness (instead of a queen in chess); the dull inquirer fails to understand the riddle; the revelation, as in Chaucer, is abrupt:

> Daphne thou knewest (quoth he)
> She now is dead

In Chaucer's elegy the interview concludes with

> Is that youre los? Be God, hyt ys routhe!

and the poem itself ends at once. But Spenser's Alcyon falls to the ground in great extremity only to cry out a sevenfold passion of luxuriant rhetoric. It is a strange lamentation, quite contrary to the usual elegiac pattern which begins with weeping and ends with consolation. The death of Daphne is first recognized as a blessed release: "I goe with gladnesse to my wished rest." But the mourner grows more and more inconsolable, hating the world and everything in it, and departs finally

> As if that death he in the face had seene,
> Or hellish hags had met upon the way

Evidently, Spenser strove hard to vary the traditional form. It is not the happiest of his experiments.

If *Daphnaida* is guilty of an excess of passionate declamation, *Astrophel,* the poem Spenser composed to serve as an introduction to a group of elegies on Sidney by his sister Mary, Lodowick Bryskett, and others, is often described as lacking in emotional warmth. The shepherd hero is comely, charming, skilled in song and in pastoral sports, solely devoted to his beloved Stella. While slaughtering wild beasts he is wounded by one of them in the thigh. He dies, wept over by Stella, and she dies too in sympathy. The pitying gods transform the pair into a flower, and then the shepherds gather to make their moan. The first to sing is the hero's sister Clorinda.

Spenser, I think, deliberately avoided the personal note in this poem in order to set it apart from the lamentations which it introduces. Astrophel is not Sidney; he is rather a figure for Sidney's character, graceful in person, constant in love, bold in combat. If the shepherd's hurt thigh recalls the wound made by Spanish shot at the battle of Zutphen it also brings to mind the story of Adonis and the wild boar. Stella cannot be Penelope Rich, the Stella of Sidney's sonnets, for the poem is dedicated to Sidney's widow, nor can she be the widow, for instead of dying in sorrow the lady married the Earl of Essex. (In his contribution to the volume, Lodowick Bryskett, too, introduces a weeping Stella.) The Stella of this poem is not a real person at all but a symbol for Sidney's truth in love and the devotion that he inspired in others. *Astrophel* touches its occasion only here and there, enough to make it a fitting frame for the elegies but not enough to compete with them.

The brave beauty of the shepherd Astrophel is destroyed by a cruel, cowardly beast of accursed brood. Ugly Barbarism and brutish Ignorance have silenced the silver music of Helicon and replaced it with *The Teares of the Muses*. In the poem so entitled each of the heavenly sisters recalls her once honored role in the affairs of men, describes the low estate to which she has fallen in the degenerate present, and weeps vociferously. An introduction of nine stanzas leads into the nine complaints, the whole consisting of an even hundred stanzas. The burden of the lamentation is that in the corrupt present men in high places care nothing for virtuous learning but vulgarly seek their private ends. Perhaps this protracted outburst reflects the poet's anger at Lord Burghley as one who should but does not patronize the learned, though there is no pointed allusion to him like the passage condemning the niggardly noble in *The Ruines of Time*. No doubt our failure to sympathize with the plight of the Muses results from our loss of a feeling of urgency in the matter, the issue of the battle between learning and ignorance being no longer in doubt. But the weakness of the poem is manifest as soon as it is set beside Samuel Daniel's thoughtful, restrained, yet noble treatment of the same subject in *Musophilus*.

With these outpourings on the theme of decay and loss *Muiopotmos or the Fate of the Butterflie* seems at first to have little to do. It remains the lightest and most delicious of Spenser's poems even though generations of scholars have attempted to weigh it down with allegorical significance. Yet it is neither a trifle nor a merely pretty thing. Although the poem is obviously in the mock-heroic vein, the reader does not laugh at its hero as he does at Chaucer's Chanticleer and Pope's Belinda, for the butterfly Clarion is too beautiful to be absurd and though he is little he is not contemptible. Rather, the tragedy of his end is tempered only by his distance from us.

The opening stanzas echo the beginning of the *Iliad;* the death of Clarion at the end imitates the death of Vergil's Turnus. The promise of Spenser's introduction, however, is at odds with the fulfillment of his tale. The poet declares that he will sing of a deadly battle between two armed heroes whose mutual hatred led from "small jarre" to open war. But Clarion and his enemy, the spider Aragnoll, do not meet until the one falls into the other's web, the hatred is one-sided only, and there is no encounter between the antagonists that can properly be called either a "small jarre" or full-scale warfare. As a foreshadowing of the story this introduction

is imprecise and misleading. And to make matters worse, it closes
with the climactic utterance:

> And is there then
> Such rancour in the hearts of mightie men?

There are no "men" in the tale at all.

At the same time, that exclamation tells the reader exactly what
he must know. He is expected to remember that Vergil wrote of
Juno's hatred of the Trojans, "tantaene animis caelestibus irae?"
(Can such resentment dwell in heavenly breasts?) In *The Rape
of the Lock* Pope alludes to Vergil in almost the same way:

> In tasks so bold, can little men engage,
> And in soft bosoms dwells such mighty rage?

But his meaning is very different from Spenser's. Pope's antitheses
make the heroic tasks trivial, the divine rage absurd, very much
as the shrieking of Chanticleer's wives becomes laughable when it
is compared with the outcry of the Trojan women. The effect sought
by Pope and Chaucer depends upon the juxtaposition of two realms,
the heroic and the petty. But when Spenser substitutes human breasts
for heavenly ones in Vergil's line he sets against each other not two
realms but two proportions, that between gods and men and that
between men and insects. His equation is exactly the one made by
Gloucester in *King Lear:* "As flies to wanton boys, are we to
th'gods." [4] The poet directs his reader to sit in a godlike seat, to
look upon the little world of butterflies and spiders so that he may
understand how Olympus sees mankind. The stanzas introducing
Muiopotmos provide, not a prospectus of the tale itself, but a definition of the viewpoint upon which a comprehension of the tale
depends.

In fact, *Muiopotmos* is not one tale but three. The murder of
Clarion by Aragnoll constitutes the principal plot, but the accounts
of the metamorphoses of Clarion's mother, Astery, and of Aragnoll's
mother, Arachne, are not merely decorative digressions. In ac-

cordance with Spenser's usual practice, each part of the poem is designed to illuminate its theme. In this case, it is the idea that in this corrupt world felicitous excellence breeds that which destroys it.

No creature could be happier than Clarion. He is the darling son of a great monarch, young, swift, brave, securely armed, gorgeously beautiful, free to taste all of the world's goods:

> What more felicitie can fall to creature,
> Than to enjoy delight with libertie,
> And to be Lord of all the workes of Nature,
> To raine in th'aire from earth to highest skie,
> To feed on flowres, and weeds [a] of glorious feature,
> To take what ever thing doth please the eie?   (ll. 209–14)

Happy too is his mother Astery, one of Venus' nymphs,

> excelling all the crewe
> In curteous usage, and unstained hewe   (ll. 119–20)

Being nimbler-jointed and more industrious than the others she wins the goddess's praise for gathering the greatest quantity of flowers. Arachne's excellence at weaving is world-renowned; she is "The most fine-fingred workwoman on ground," and Pallas comes down from heaven to grant her the due reward.

But no earthly happiness is secure,

> For thousand perills lie in close awaite
> About us daylie, to worke our decay   (ll. 221–22)

Astery's downfall is swift and simply told. Her sister nymphs, envying her success in gathering "the children of the spring," tell Venus that Cupid has been helping her; the enraged goddess transforms her to a butterfly. Arachne's fate is of another kind. Her skill with the loom is so great that even

> Envie pale,
> That al good things with venemous tooth devowres,
> Could not accuse.   (ll. 301–3)

---

[a] weeds: small plants generally.

But that skill leads Arachne to the presumption of challenging Pallas herself, and she dares to disgrace the gods by portraying Jove's rape of Europa. Pallas' answer to this challenge depicts her own competition with Neptune for the worship of Athens in which her gift of a fruitful olive tree wins the prize over Neptune's war horse. It is Arachne's envy of this good and beautiful thing, the "poysonous rancor" within her, that turns her into a venomous spider. As Iago says of Cassio, "He has a daily beauty in his life,/ That makes me ugly."

Clarion falls because like Astery he arouses envy and like Arachne he presumes upon his excellence. His race derives from the beauty of flowers and from jealousy. So beautiful are his wings that ladies at court, "Beholding them, him secretly envide." Secure in the pride of his princely freedom he wanders everywhere without suspicion of friend or fear of foe. Little wonder that fate, or fortune, or an errant gust of wind blows him into the web of Aragnoll, heir to the poisonous malice of his mother.

Long before Clarion fell into the spider's snare his fate was woven by Jove's own hand and the image of a butterfly was woven by Pallas into the web of her tapestry. Mundane felicity inevitably, fatefully, arouses those dark destructive forces, the "shame of Nature,"

> That none, except a God, or God him guide,
> May them avoyde, or remedie provide.   (ll. 223–24)

Muiopotmos is a delightful teaching of the tragic lesson that on earth happiness is its own destruction, that only in heaven or by heavenly intervention is the fruitful olive victorious over chaos and death.

In contrast with *Muiopotmos* and the other "complaints" the emphasis of *Mother Hubberds Tale* is not on the inevitability of decay but on the nature of the disease which brings it about. The world which it portrays is a sick one. The astronomical beginning sets the mood: August is the month in which the sun enters the sign of Virgo, otherwise known as Astraea, the righteous goddess who fled the earth because of its sinfulness. It is also the month of the dog star, bringer of pestilence and corruption, and the poet himself is ill.

A disease is known by the state of health which it denies. Much medieval and Renaissance social comment proceeds from the assumption of a healthy or "natural" condition of the world, not that which exists or ever has existed save in Eden but that which might exist were good victorious over evil. In such a world, every plowman would, like Chaucer's paragon, thresh and ditch and delve "Withouten hire, if it lay in his myght," and every knight would fight for his lord and for Christ, not for reward or vainglory. Spenser's contemporary, George Gascoigne, sees such a world in his mirror:

> Againe I see, within my glasse of Steele,
> But foure estates, to serve eche country Soyle,
> The King, the Knight, the Pesant, and the Priest.
> The King should care for al the subjectes still,
> The Knight should fight, for to defende the same,
> The Peasant he, should labor for their ease,
> And Priests should pray, for them and for themselves.[5]

As with Chaucer, the imagined ideal leads Gascoigne to satiric comparison with the way of the world as it is. This he sees in his steel glass which reflects the truth without flattery.

Spenser's *Mother Hubberds Tale* is a general satire in this tradition. Mother Hubberd tells the sick poet a tale of "the Foxe and th'Ape by him misguided." The pair constitutes a kind of unit, a counterfeit man, the Ape mocking man in body, the Fox in mind. As the Fox explains to the Ape when they are arguing about which should be king:

And where ye claime your selfe for outward shape
Most like a man, Man is not like an Ape
In his chiefe parts, that is, in wit and spirite;
But I therein most like to him doo merite
For my slie wyles and subtill craftinesse,
The title of the Kingdome to possesse.   (ll. 1041–46)

In successive episodes, the pair passes itself off as the various kinds
of man, peasant, priest, courtier, and king—just Gascoigne's division.
In each case the consequence is the same: betrayal of responsibility,
damage to the commonwealth, and eventually exposure and expulsion of the culprits. But in a manner typically Spenserian, each
episode is handled differently.

Ape and Fox are introduced as malcontents, unwilling to lose
their "freedom" by tying themselves to productive labor. The division of mankind into classes they reject as unjust:

as we bee sonnes of the world so wide,
Let us our fathers heritage divide,
And chalenge to our selves our portions dew
Of all the patrimonie, which a few
Now hold in hugger mugger in their hand,
And all the rest doo rob of good and land.   (ll. 135–40)

Like the egalitarian giant of the Legend of Justice of *The Faerie
Queene* they echo the old cry of the Peasants' Revolt:

When Adam delved and Eve span
Who was then the gentleman?

With the protection of a forged passport the Ape pretends to be
an old soldier and the Fox his dog. An unwary Husbandman is
fooled into giving them the ward of his sheep, a kindness they
repay by eating their charges. But the day of reckoning comes and
they must fly.

This brief adventure announces the pattern of the rest. Again
Ape and Fox disguise themselves, now with gown and cassock, and

again they provide themselves with a forged license testifying that they are "Clerkes booke-redd." They encounter a "formall Priest" through whose advice the Fox secures a benefice while the Ape becomes his parish clerk. Abuse of their responsibility inevitably leads to the day of judgment and hasty flight. But the actions of the Ape and Fox do not bear the weight of the satire in this episode; their tenure in office is dismissed almost casually. The principal butt is the priest in form only, as much a counterfeit as they are. He is a false Protestant, a hypocrite Piers. The simple man cannot read the license, in fact he cannot read at all, because

> Of such deep learning little had he neede,
> Ne yet of Latine, ne of Greeke, that breede
> Doubts mongst Divines, and difference of texts,
> From whence arise diversitie of sects,
> And hateful heresies, of God abhor'd:
> But this good Sir did follow the plaine word,
> Ne medled with their controversies vaine.   (ll. 385–91)

He scolds the Fox and the Ape for their vagabondage, urging them to try for advancement in the church,

> In the meane time to live in good estate,
> Loving that love, and hating those that hate;
> Being some honest Curate, or some Vicker
> Content with little in condition sicker.[b]   (ll. 427–30)

When the Ape, rather out of character, fearfully remembers the terrible responsibility of those who are charged with the feeding of men's souls the Priest speciously answers with a text teaching that divine grace alone can justify:

> We are but charg'd to lay the meate before:
> Eate they that list, we need to doo no more.
> But God it is that feedes them with his grace,
> The bread of life powr'd down from heavenly place.   (ll. 435–38)

[b] sicker: secure.

Indeed, he has no use for the old Roman Catholic ways, services morning and evening, fasts, haircloth, clerical celibacy. Now there is but one "small devotion" on the Sabbath, and besides,

> we may have lying by our sides
> Our lovely Lasses, or bright shining Brides.   (ll. 475–76)

It is easy to attain this pleasant life, he explains. All that is necessary is to pretend gravity and saintliness, lie, face, forge, crouch, fee a courtier, or split the income of the living with the lord of the manor.

The adventure at court preserves the scheme and varies it again. The Ape disguises himself as a gentleman

> And his man Reynold with fine counterfesaunce
> Supports his credite and his countenaunce.   (ll. 667–68)

Because he is dressed like a gentleman the court accepts him, he cheats, at length is discovered and banished "by such as sate in justice seate." The substance of the satire appears in Mother Hubberd's contrasting descriptions of the true courtier and the false. A great body of Renaissance literature provides the matter for this contrast. These writings are commonly though inadequately represented by Castiglione's *Il Cortegiano,* a treatise which despite its popularity and its literary excellence is rather more urbane than most of its kind and perhaps lacks their moral dedication and seriousness of purpose.[6] Spenser's true courtier resembles Castiglione's only superficially. He will not abase himself, flatter, or traduce a man behind his back. He rides, hunts, wrestles, recreates himself with "Ladies gentle sports" and with the Muses, not frivolously but with "wise discourse." He spends his days in his prince's service, not to win wealth or place but to win honor "To which he levels all his purpose." He therefore trains himself both for arms and for counsel

> To learne the enterdeale of Princes strange,
> To marke th'intent of Counsells, and the change

> Of states, and eke of private men somewhile,
> Supplanted by fine falshood and faire guile;
> Of all the which he gathereth, what is fit
> T'enrich the storehouse of his powerfull wit   (ll. 785–90)

He is Thomas Elyot's Governor rather than Castiglione's Courtier. The foil for this ideal is the Ape. His sports are dicing and cards; he plays the poet but only to make divine poetry a servant to base affection; he tries to

> allure
> Chast Ladies eares to fantasies impure.   (ll. 819–20)

He and his man the Fox cheat simple folk who repose confidence in those who give the impression of being "on the inside." His only purpose is his own advancement.

The final usurpation is that of the robes and royalty of the Lion, king of beasts. While the Lion carelessly sleeps, the Ape with the Fox as his chief counselor acts the role of the tyrant, the anti-king. In this action, the final judgment cannot be made by a mortal agent. News of the suffering realm at last reaches

> high Jove, in whose almightie hand
> The care of Kings, and power of Empires stand   (ll. 1225–26)

Mercury, having confirmed the chaotic injustice of the kingdom, wakes the Lion who "uncases" the Fox, cuts off the Ape's long tail and pares his ears, and resumes his rightful rule. There is no description here of a true king, as there is of a true courtier in the preceding episode. But the portrait of the tyrant implies the portrait of the king, and both are the products of a tradition reaching back to the beginnings of European civilization. Sometimes these portraits are imagined in literature, or historical fiction, as in Xenophon's *Cyropaedia,* Thomas Elyot's *Image of Governaunce,* and Shakespeare's *Henry V* and *Richard III;* sometimes they are drawn in didactic treatises like Erasmus' *Education of a Christian Prince.*

The characteristics of Spenser's tyrant are by no means exceptional; almost all of them, in fact, can be found in Erasmus' brief description of an evil ruler. In the Ape's first royal act,

> to his Gate he pointed a strong gard,
> That none might enter but with issue hard:
> Then for the safegard of his personage,
> He did appoint a warlike equipage
> Of forreine beasts, not in the forest bred   (ll. 1115–19)

Says Erasmus: "The tyrant guarantees safety for himself by means of foreign attendants and hired brigands." [7] The Ape makes all the beasts the "vassals of his pleasures"; Erasmus' tyrant keeps his subjects "like slaves." [8] The Ape "enlarg'd his private treasure" with the spoils of his subjects; Erasmus contrasts the tyrant with the king who considers "that his purse is represented by the wealth of his subjects." [9] The Ape rules by fear; Erasmus says, "the tyrant strives to be feared, the king to be loved." [10] The Fox, as chief minister, shares the royal vices and adds some of his own. He keeps low the nobility of the kingdom, the men of arms and letters, just as Erasmus' tyrant uses "every means to reduce the wealth and prestige of any of his subjects, and especially the good men." [11] Here the Fox is an extension of the conventional tyrant; he also plays a separate role as the equally conventional evil minister who gathers all power into his own hands, allows nobody to appeal to the king, and even cheats the king to enrich himself.

Spenser's Fox, in fact, is identical in almost every respect with the butt of John Skelton's *Speak, Parrot; Colin Clout;* and *Why Come Ye Not to Court?* Skelton too rails at a chief minister who acts as though he were sole ruler, handles all business himself and for himself, denies access to the king, builds royal mansions while the commonwealth suffers. In Skelton's satire, the chief minister is Thomas Cardinal Wolsey. Is Spenser's tale of Mother Hubberd a direct attack upon William Cecil, Lord Burghley? The comparison

does not lead to easy conclusions. Skelton, like Spenser, draws upon
the traditional descriptions of tyrant and tyrannical administrator
for his portrait of Wolsey. In fact, he poses as a satirist of vice, not
of a vicious individual:

> For no man have I named:
> Wherfore sholde I be blamed? [12]

Nevertheless, he constantly nudges his reader to think of one who
rides

> upon a mule
> With golde all betrapped,
> In purple and paule belapped,[13]

of a "braggyng bocher" (Wolsey's father was said to have been a
butcher), and unequivocally of the builder of Hampton Court.
Puns and topical innuendoes insist upon the identification. This is
not the atmosphere of *Mother Hubberds Tale*. Much of the attack
upon the Ape and the Fox echoes contemporary attacks upon Cecil,
but it also echoes Aristotle, Erasmus, and Skelton. To be sure, the
Latin for "ape" is "simia," and Simier was a French ambassador
who tried to arrange a marriage between Queen Elizabeth and the
Duc d'Alençon. To be sure, Burghley was a "foxy" chief minister
who opposed Leicester in favoring the marriage (the Queen, however, called him her "Camel"). But the text of the poem simply will
not bear a consistent identification of Ape with Simier and Fox
with Burghley.

There are two passages in *Mother Hubberds Tale* which do demand a topical interpretation. One of these is the bitter complaint
of the suitor who is disappointed of his promised reward. I have
already suggested that these lines were interpolated shortly before
the publication of the poem, and that they reflect Spenser's resentment at Burghley's interference with or delay of the reward promised by Elizabeth for *The Faerie Queene*. For the other, which also
appears to be a late addition, no satisfactory explanation has been

offered and I can present none. To the Ape's inquiry as to which courtiers bear the greatest sway at court the Mule answers:

> Marie (said he) the highest now in grace,
> Be the wilde beasts, that swiftest are in chase;
> For in their speedie course and nimble flight
> The Lyon now doth take the most delight:
> But chieflie, joyes on foote them to beholde,
> Enchaste with chaine and circulet of golde:
> So wilde a beast so tame ytaught to bee,
> And buxome to his bands is joy to see.
> So well his golden Circlet him beseemeth:
> But his late chayne his Liege unmeete esteemeth;
> For so brave beasts she loveth best to see,
> In the wilde forrest raunging fresh and free. (ll. 619–30)

At first the Lion seems to be ruler, as he is in the final episode of the poem. Then the plural "beasts" whom he enjoys seeing turn into a singular "beast," and finally a feminine "liege"—surely Queen Elizabeth—expresses disapproval of the Lion himself or of one of the other beasts. Spenser is here extraordinarily recondite or extraordinarily careless, perhaps both. But apart from these two apparently patched-in passages, *Mother Hubberds Tale* needs no explanation in terms of personal or political reference.

However, no writer of power comments on the state of the world without looking at the world before him. Nor does his audience read such a comment without reflecting upon contemporary affairs. The applications of writer and reader do not necessarily coincide: there may be general agreement about what a tyrant is but little about who is a tyrant. Evidence outside of the text of the *Tale* suggests that at the time of its publication Spenser thought Burghley a bad man, and we may therefore suppose that whatever he intended when he wrote the poem in the "raw conceipt" of his youth Burghley came to his mind as he reconsidered the lines in which he had described an evil minister. He may have hoped that his readers would think of Burghley too but, except in his reference to the peer whose grace he lacks, he does not ask them to do so.[14]

Considered as a story, *Mother Hubberds Tale* suffers from a defect so obvious that it is hard to understand how a skilled writer could have overlooked it. The world of the first two episodes is clearly a world of men into which the shiftless villains can intrude only by disguising themselves. The setting becomes vague in the third episode, for although the Ape dresses as a gentleman and the Fox as his groom, a Mule tells them the tidings of court, a Lion appears to be its king, and wild beasts his servants. The final episode takes place wholly in a world of animals except that the Ape justifies his taking of the Lion's place by explaining that he looks like a man.

The poet's failure to arrive at a clear conception of the circumstances of his story can be explained in either of two ways. It has been suggested that the inconsistencies of *Mother Hubberds Tale* are the result of a hasty and radical revision made after the poem had been laid aside for many years.[15] This is similar to the explanations that have been devised to account for the difference between promise and performance in *Muiopotmos,* the fading away of the spirit of Verulam in *The Ruines of Time,* and the many slips in storytelling that have been detected in *The Faerie Queene.* But the very necessity of explaining so much carelessness demands an understanding of the poet's attitude toward his own fictions. He pays little attention to their consistency and verisimilitude because they are not ends in themselves but servants of idea, of moral intention. In the "complaints" and satires considered in this chapter, as everywhere in Spenser's poetry, the object is to portray the nature of the world in which we live by contrasting it with a state of excellence from which we have declined and to which we may aspire. The decay of the one and the hope for the other therefore constitute a principal theme of his works.

Love Creating

THE BROKEN PIPE OF *The Shepheardes Calender* asserts that love is a barren and destructive power. Piers's outburst in the October eclogue and Colin's rhapsody in *Colin Clouts Come Home Againe* state the contrary proposition, that love justifies its inherent pain by stimulating and ennobling the lover, by generating virtuous and heroic deeds, and by maintaining the coherence and the life of this world. It is this justification which is the principal subject of the *Amoretti*, the *Epithalamion*, and the *Fowre Hymnes*. The history of such a fruitful love is narrated in the sonnets and in the marriage song; its nature and its relationship to the divine constitute the matter of the *Hymnes*.

The manuscripts of the *Amoretti* and the *Epithalamion* came to England in the same ship, and Ponsonby published them together, taking pains to make the volume appear a unit. Each sonnet and each stanza of the marriage song is given a page to itself, and the pages are tied together by an ornamental band running across the top and bottom throughout. The two works are linked in substance by their common autobiographical reference to Spenser's courtship and marriage. They are linked in form, too. Petrarch had varied his collection of sonnets by the inclusion of canzoni, a practice imitated by Sidney in his *Astrophel*. The *Epithalamion* is a kind of canzone which Spenser sets outside his sequence to bring to a fitting conclusion the love story of the *Amoretti.*

To the casual modern reader, one Renaissance sonnet sequence seems much like another. There is an inevitable sameness about these posies of love poems, inevitable because the long-established convention included not only a specified verse form but also a specified set of themes and subjects, like the pieces in chess, with which the sonneteer might play. The lover's unhappiness and unwavering devotion; the lady's heartlessness and beauty; the paradoxes of inflamed lover and icy beloved, of painful joy and joyous pain; meditations on the moment of hope and the moment of despair, on time, eyes, hair, jealousy, the perdurability of poetry—all these are to be found in the *Amoretti* as in other sonnet collections of the time. The ingenious poet, indeed, attempted rare and remarkable combinations, and the poet of power transcended the convention, but their election of the form showed that they willingly imposed upon themselves those limitations that they wished to challenge. The Renaissance reader was no doubt expert enough to detect and enjoy subtle differences of technique, approach, mood, and idea among the innumerable sonnets of his time, differences which are now blurred. But some of the special qualities of Spenser's *Amoretti* are not difficult to discover.

As *The Shepheardes Calender* differs in form from Spenser's models, so too does the *Amoretti,* both in the structure of the sonnets which compose it and in the organization of the group as a whole. The nature of Spenser's innovation in the structure of the individual sonnet is best understood against the history of the development of the English form. Almost from its first appearance, the English sonnet had taken a turn away from its continental model. The traditional pattern of eight and six—two nearly equal divisions of the whole—began to disintegrate when the fourteen lines ended, as often in Wyatt, with a couplet rhyming independently of the rest. There are a few examples of couplet endings in continental sonnets, but typically, in these exceptional cases, the final rhyme repeats the end-sound of another line in the sestet so that the integrity of the sestet is maintained. Surrey's usual practice further obscured the crucial division between eight and six, the first twelve lines becoming three cross-rhymed quatrains and the concluding couplet a thing apart. The organization of the poem as three fours and two, or twelve and two, accommodated the English sonnet to the definition of the verse epigram, most popular of the short forms practiced by the neo-Latin writers of the Renaissance: "a short poem ending in a witty or ingenious thought or sententious comment to which the rest of the composition is intended to lead up." [1] The relationship between the two forms was not unknown to continental criticism, Sebillet, for example, writing: "Le Sonnet suit l'épigramme de bien près, et de matiére, et de mesure: Et quant tout est dit, Sonnet n'est autre chose que le parfait épigramme de l'Italien, comme le dizain du François." [2] The English verse pattern rendered the connection even stronger, so that Sir John Harington could distinguish between sonnet and epigram only on the ground that one was sweet and the other salt. [3] At the same time, the continued English imitation of French and Italian sonnets gave persistent life to the traditional division of thought between octave and sestet. Several types of Elizabethan sonnet pattern appear, therefore: at one extreme a poem identical in structure with the epigram in which the final couplet comments on, summarizes, or overturns the sense of the preceding twelve lines; at the other a sonnet in the continental tradition in which the thought is divided eight and six without reference to the formal independence of the couplet; and a compromise between the two in which the sense breaks after the octave while the couplet remains epigrammatic.

Both Sidney and Spenser deviate from the English type of sonnet, but in opposite directions. Sidney returns to the continental verse

form, or to Wyatt's version of it. Though there is often a witty
or ingenious turn at the end of his sonnets (as in Petrarch's and
Ronsard's), he regularly rhymes the octave as a unit, distinguishing
it from the sestet, and he rarely makes a syntactic division between
the last two lines and the rest of the poem. In contrast, Spenser
links Surrey's three quatrains together with common rhymes (*abab
bcbc cdcd*), so creating an entity sharply distinguished from the
independently rhymed conclusion. Sometimes, it is true, the sense
of the sonnet ignores this formal pattern and obeys the continental
structure (*Amoretti* x, xvi, xliii). But normally the first twelve
lines present a single idea whether as a seamless unit or subdivided
into octave and quatrain or into three parallel quatrains. The couplet
therefore stands by itself, a *clausula* as it would be called in an
epigram:

> What then remains but I to ashes burne,
>   and she to stones at length all frosen turne?   (xxxii)

> That ship, that tree, and that same beast am I,
>   whom ye doe wreck, doe ruine, and destroy.   (lvi)

> Fondnesse it were for any being free,
>   to covet fetters, though they golden bee.   (xxxvii)

Of course, similar sonnet patterns may be identified in the poems
of Shakespeare and the other sonneteers of the period. Spenser's
variation on the traditional English rhyme scheme did not make a
new thing of the sonnet; it did recognize and emphasize tendencies
that were already present.

It is often said that the individual sonnets of the *Amoretti,*
though lucid, graceful, and finely wrought, lack the poetic fire which
makes so many of Sidney's and Shakespeare's memorable, and
this failure is attributed to Spenser's inability to work at his best
in so restrictive a medium. The counter to this judgment asserts
that the *Amoretti* must not be thought of as a collection of indi-

vidual lyrics: "Taking the sonnets as a whole, the critic must find
in them the truest sequence of this decade. There is a progression
in the story and in the poet's moods, from the beginning to the end,
and each sonnet has its inevitable place. The series is really but
one poem in which each sonnet is a stanza, and each stanza, as in
the *Epithalamion,* a lyric unit."[4] While this is surely an overstate-
ment of the case, it remains true that the *Amoretti* is a better unified
work than the typical "sequence" of the tradition.[5] The opening
sonnet presents the whole collection, "Leaves, lines, and rymes,"
to "my soules long lacked foode, my heavens blis," and looks to
the separation of the lovers at the end:

> Dark is my day, whyles her fayre light I mis,
>   and dead my life that wants such lively blis.

The impression of unity is reinforced by recurrent references to
the time of the year: it is New Year's Day in Sonnet IV, Spring in
XIX, Lent in XXII, a year since the beginning of the poet's love in
LX, Christmas in LXVIII, and Spring again in LXX. (The *Epithalamion*
celebrates the wedding on Midsummer Day.) A sense of the passage
of time is provided by the "story," too. After his long anguish, the
lover at last achieves his victory (Sonnet LXIII) and there follows a
period of ecstatic happiness marred only by a few intermissions of
absence until a "venomous tongue" intervenes and the sequence
concludes on a note of separation and sorrow but not despair.

More important to the structure of this work is its pattern of
thematic oppositions, traditional in amatory sonnets but here most
strongly emphasized: appearance and essence, earth and heaven,
pain and ecstasy, despair and hope, separation and union, lust and
love, smile and frown. Such contraries appear in a single line:

> Sweet is the Rose, but growes upon a brere   (XXVI)

in a quatrain:

> For with mild pleasance, which doth pride displace,
>   she to her love doth lookers eyes allure:

> and with sterne countenance back again doth chace
> their looser lookes that stir up luste impure (xxi)

in successive sonnets:

> Mark when she smiles with amiable cheare (xl)

> Is it her nature or is it her will
> to be so cruell to an humbled foe (xli)

and in the sharp changes of mood from one group of sonnets to the next.

Among the most prominent of the matters so treated is the lady's "pride." The conclusion of *Colin Clouts Come Home Againe*, it will be remembered, presents the opposing views of Hobbinol and Colin on the subject. The sonnets of the *Amoretti* that deal with it are almost equally divided between those that praise pride or self-assurance as nobility of spirit and those that blame it as haughtiness, vanity, cruelty. The debate is given added emphasis by a pair of sonnets (lviii and lix), the first of which attacks "her that is most assured to her selfe":

> Weake is th'assurance that weake flesh reposeth
> In her owne powre, and scorneth others ayde:
> that soonest fals when as she most supposeth
> her selfe assurd, and is of nought affrayd.
> All flesh is frayle

. . .

> Why then doe ye proud fayre, misdeeme so farre,
> that to your selfe ye most assured arre?

The second is a palinode:

> Thrise happie she, that is so well assured
> Unto her selfe and setled so in hart:
> that nether will for better be allured,
> ne feard with worse to any chaunce to start,
> But like a steddy ship doth strongly part
> the raging waves and keepes her course aright;

. . .

> Most happy she that most assured doth rest,
>   but he most happy who such one loves best.

From one point of view the lady is a tyrant, a tiger, hard as stone. The pain she causes moves the lover even to praying the god of love for vengeance

> That I may laugh at her in equall sort,
>   as she doth laugh at me and makes my pain her sport.   (x)

Like Rosalind of the *Calender,* the proud lady of the *Amoretti* silences the poet. He explains his failure to complete *The Faerie Queene* almost in the words of Cuddie accounting for Colin's abandoned pipe:

> How then should I without another wit,
>   thinck ever to endure so taedious toyle?
> sins that this one is tost with troublous fit,
>   of a proud love, that doth my spirite spoyle.   (xxxiii)

But if pride is in one sense associated with love the destroyer, in another it is associated with love the creator.

For the lady is proud, not of her flesh, but of the divinity of her spirit. She is "full of the living fire,/ Kindled above unto the maker neere" (viii); she is "divinely wrought,/ and of the brood of Angels hevenly borne":

> what reason is it then but she should scorne
> base things that to her love too bold aspire?
> Such heavenly formes ought rather worshipt be,
>   then dare be lov'd by men of meane degree.   (lxi)

The very difficulty of attaining her love makes the eventual victory more precious. And the sovereign beauty of spirit which is the source of her pride lights a "heavenly fire" in the lover and raises him from baseness. Instead of putting an end to poetry it provides divine inspiration:

> Deepe in the closet of my parts entyre,
>   her worth is written with a golden quill:

> that me with heavenly fury doth inspire,
> and my glad mouth with her sweet prayses fill.
> Which when as fame in her shrill trump shal thunder,
> let the world chose to envy or to wonder. (LXXXV)

And if the poet has made little progress on *The Faerie Queene* it is only because he has been gathering his forces. His love is a spur, not a rein:

> the contemplation of whose heavenly hew,
> my spirit to an higher pitch will rayse. (LXXX)

"Ah, fon," cried Piers, "for love does teach him climbe so hie."

As the lady's beauty arouses sexual passion so her pride of spirit keeps it under control. Not Cupid but angels shoot arrows through her eyes; the effect is not "base affections wound" but the leading of "fraile mindes to rest/ in chast desires on heavenly beauty bound" (VIII). The chastity of those desires may seem suspect to the reader:

> on the sweet spoyle of beautie they did pray.
> And twixt her paps like early fruit in May,
> whose harvest seemd to hasten now apace:
> they loosely did theyr wanton winges display,
> and there to rest themselves did boldly place. (LXXVI)

And in the sonnet following, too, the lover's thoughts go to his lady's breasts, two golden apples in a silver dish. When he says that he wishes to feed on those apples is he confessing unregenerate lust? The sense of the poem denies it. These sonnets occur in that part of the sequence which is concerned with the ecstatic victory, a part in which there is no darkness, no bitterness, no ugliness. The breasts themselves are "Exceeding sweet, yet voyd of sinfull vice/ . . . sweet fruit of pleasure brought from paradice." This pleasure —and it is carnal pleasure, certainly—is not only void of sin but is of heavenly derivation. Yet even in victory, the purity of the lady's spirit requires the tight reining in of the passion she arouses:

> Let not one sparke of filthy lustfull fyre
> breake out, that may her sacred peace molest:

    ne one light glance of sensuall desyre
    Attempt to work her gentle mindes unrest.
But pure affections bred in spotlesse brest,
    and modest thoughts breathd from wel tempred sprites,
    goe visit her in her chast bowre of rest,
    accompanyde with angelick delightes.   (LXXXIV)

How difficult is the resolution of passion and purity is shown by the tragic suffering of Amoret and Scudamour in the third book of *The Faerie Queene.*

The lady of the *Amoretti* is proud, but there is a point at which her pride turns to gentleness. In what seems to me (and to others) the most beautiful sonnet of the sequence the poet compares himself to a weary hunter resting after his long, futile chase of the deer. But the deer returns to quench her thirst at the stream nearby, and, unlike Petrarch's "candida cerva,"

        beholding me with mylder looke,
    sought not to fly, but fearelesse still did bide:
    till I in hand her yet halfe trembling tooke,
    and with her owne goodwill hir fyrmely tyde.
    Strange thing me seemd to see a beast so wyld,
    so goodly wonne with her owne will beguyld.   (LXVII)

The poet does not speak of a promise of marriage—there are few marriages in Renaissance sonnet sequences. But the meaning is clear.

The autobiographical reference of this collection of sonnets is, in fact, one of its distinctive features. I do not mean that the lyrics record the history of Edmund Spenser's courtship of Elizabeth Boyle any more literally than the poem *Astrophel* recounts the events of the skirmish at Zutphen. But the person who speaks in the sonnets is not any passionate and sensitive lover with a gift for imaginative utterance; he is a man of forty years of age, his mother's name is Elizabeth, he is friend to Lodowick Bryskett, he has completed six books of a great poem entitled *The Faerie Queene,* and he is in love, not with an intangible Petrarchan lady, but with a young woman of wit and will and good humor.[6] By inflecting and manipulating the devices of the sonnet tradition Spenser both assimilates his private love to the public convention and at the same time declares its particular nature.

Between the *Amoretti* and the *Epithalamion,* Spenser or Ponsonby interpolated some curious verses about Venus and Cupid which derive ultimately from Theocritean or Anacreontic traditions. If the arrangement of the book reflects Spenser's intention, these verses serve primarily to mark the interval between the separation which concludes the *Amoretti* and the union of the marriage song.[7]

In that song, the *Epithalamion,* Spenser again renders an established genre peculiarly his own. The singer in this classical tradition (the Greek means "upon the bedchamber") wishes the wedded pair happiness and good fortune; he is outside the frame of reference or one of the attendant crowd.[8] By identifying singer and bridegroom, by praying the Muses who in the past have helped him to praise others now to help him his "owne loves prayses to resound," the poet adds to the form a new emotional dimension. Yet even though he says that "I unto my selfe alone will sing" the reader does not become an embarrassed eavesdropper, for the conventional and ritual elements are too strong. The *Epithalamion* is at once intensely private and a public ceremony.

Here again Spenser uses time as a structural principle. He begins by calling upon the Muses to rise

> Early before the worlds light giving lampe,
> His golden beame upon the hils doth spred   (ll. 19–20)

and wake his love to meet the bridal day. The sun rises high, the marriage ceremony is performed, darkness is wished for and comes at last, and the poet sings of the joys and hopes of the night. The poem ends, a full day after its beginning, as the wedded pair falls to rest not long before dawn. The temporal movement is emphasized in a variety of ways: the poet pleads, "But let this day let this one day be myne"; he calls upon the Hours to be the first to attend the bride; her coming to church is likened to

> Phoebe from her chamber of the East,
> Arysing forth to run her mighty race   (ll. 149–50)

As night falls the refrain changes to "The woods no more shall answer." The poet hopes for "the timely fruit of this same night," and at the close ceases "our tymely joyes to sing." But though the great day is St. Barnaby's, the longest day of the year, it does not encompass the poem. The frame breaks at the end as the poet prays to the "high heavens"

> That we may raise a large posterity,
> Which from the earth, which they may long possesse,
> With lasting happinesse,
> Up to your haughty pallaces may mount,
> And for the guerdon of theyr glorious merit
> May heavenly tabernacles there inherit,
> Of blessed Saints for to increase the count.   (ll. 417–23)

The mundane day becomes eternity.

It has been suggested recently that the time motif of the *Epithalamion* is echoed and reinforced by previously unrecognized characteristics of its verse structure.[9] The poem consists of twenty-three stanzas and an envoy—twenty-four units in all. The "day" refrain, varying "The woods shall to me answer," ends the first sixteen stanzas; the "night" refrain, "The woods no more shall answer," concludes the remainder, a division corresponding to the number of hours of daylight and dark at the summer solstice in the latitude of England and southern Ireland. An even more remarkable observation depends upon the fact that the poem is made up of clearly distinguishable long lines (five feet or longer) and short ones. There are 365 of the former. All this may be merely coincidence, but it fits with Spenser's use of number as a structural element elsewhere: the twelve eclogues of the *Calender,* the hundred stanzas of *The Teares of the Muses,* the patterns of sevens in *The Ruines of Time* and *Daphnaida.* Numerical composition of this kind was practiced occasionally in classical times and became common in the Middle Ages. Sometimes, the number appears to have been chosen without reference to the content of the poem, or as a substitute for a logical system of organization. In the most famous example, however, the hundred cantos of the *Divine Comedy* (made up of the introductory canto and three books of thirty-three cantos each, thirty-three recalling, of course, the number of years of Christ's life), the numerical system is indissolubly bound up with the meaning of the work. This appears to be the case with the *Epithalamion.*

However, the very fact that the numerical scheme of the *Epithalamion* has remained unnoticed for so long is evidence that it is not its basic structural element. Rather, the symmetry of the whole gives the poem that sense of gracious unity which has been apparent to generations of readers who have never troubled to count the stanzas or the long lines. The opening invocation of the Muses, the Nymphs, the Hours, and the Graces is matched by concluding prayers to Cynthia, Juno, Genius, Hebe, and the "high heavens." The bride is roused from sleep at the beginning and is sung to sleep at the end. The rising sun has its balance in the evening star, the moon, and the "thousand torches flaming bright." In the morning the Hours are asked to adorn and array the bride; when the sun sets the attendant damsels disarray her and "Lay her in lillies and in violets." As she comes to church the minstrels shrill aloud and the boys run shouting; as she leaves the maidens sing their carols and the young men ring the bells. And precisely at the midpoint of the poem the temple gates open for the solemn ceremony of marriage.[10]

Within this pyramidal structure are incorporated many moods:

ecstatic expectation of the approaching fulfillment, humble reverence, bacchic frenzy, impatience, grotesque humor, sensual delight, inspired prophecy. The stanzaic units which present this constantly shifting emotional scene are themselves subtly changing patterns. Each is a long, lucid statement, superbly adapted to reading aloud; each is composed of long lines and short, the short ones regularly completing couplets; each combines alternating and consecutive rhyme groups; each ends with an echoing refrain. But the refrain changes constantly: "The woods shall to me answer," "That all the woods may answer," "The woods shall to you answer." A study of the metrics discloses the fact that some of the stanzas are eighteen lines long, some nineteen, and one seventeen, and that the rhyme schemes are not uniform. But the reader will sense, rather than know, these irregularities.

The *Epithalamion* brings to its natural end the history of courtship narrated in the *Amoretti*. As the gentleness of the self-tamed deer prophesies, there is no haughtiness in the bride of the marriage song. She is more beautiful than ever, and the beauty of her body is exceeded by the beauty of her spirit over which Virtue reigns as queen with the "base affections" subservient—but not absent. When she walks to church, her modest eyes fixed to the ground, she blushes to hear her praises sung,

> So farre from being proud.   (l. 164)

She lies in her bride bed, covered with silk and arras:

> Behold how goodly my faire love does ly
> In proud humility.   (ll. 305–6)

It is only in oxymoron that her pride remains.

The sonneteer's dream of his lady's body is at last realized. Carnal joy is accepted as eagerly and thankfully as it is, for example, by the neo-Latin poet Joannes Secundus whose *Basia* was much admired by the lighter spirits of the Renaissance. But Spenser insists, as

Joannes does not, that such pleasure is without sin. He calls upon the classical god of procreation:

> And thou glad Genius, in whose gentle hand,
> The bridale bowre and geniall bed remaine,
> Without blemish or staine,
> And the sweet pleasures of theyr loves delight
> With secret ayde doest succour and supply,
> Till they bring forth the fruitfull progeny,
> Send us the timely fruit of this same night. (ll. 398–404)

The end of these sweet pleasures is generation; the end of generation, Spenser goes on to say, is the preservation of the species and the increase of heaven.

In the *Fowre Hymnes* Spenser undertakes to expound his philosophy of love. There is a kind of preliminary sketch of this philosophy in Colin's rhapsody in *Colin Clouts Come Home Againe,* and the theme of generation, in particular, is the principal subject of the Garden of Adonis episode in the third book of *The Faerie Queene.* As a work devoted wholly to the philosophy of love the *Fowre Hymnes* stands alone, I think, in English literature of its time, though it belongs to a numerous company of such essays written in Renaissance Italy and France. The genre derives principally from the *Vita Nuova* and from Ficino's translations of Plato and Plotinus and his commentaries on them, especially his exposition *De amore* of Plato's *Symposium.* Some of the literary treatments of this kind are in prose, like Bembo's *Gli Asolani,* the speech which Castiglione attributes to Bembo in *Il Cortegiano,* the *Dialoghi d'Amore* of Leone Ebreo, and *Le Sympose de Platon de l'Amour et de Beauté . . . avec trois livres de Commentaires* of Louis Le Roy; others are in verse, like Benivieni's *Canzona dello Amore celeste et divino* which was published with a commentary by Pico della Mirandola.[11] Each of these works undertakes by Platonic or neo-Platonic means to discover the relationship between earthly and heavenly love.

Two of the sonnets of the *Amoretti* bear directly on this problem, one of them in Christian terms, the other in Platonic. In the first of these (LXVIII) the poet draws an earthly lesson from a contemplation of the surpassing love of Christ for mankind:

> So let us love, deare love, lyke as we ought,
>   love is the lesson which the Lord us taught.

The second (LXXII) must be quoted in full:

> Oft when my spirit doth spred her bolder winges,
>   In mind to mount up to the purest sky:
>   it down is weighd with thoght of earthly things
>   and clogd with burden of mortality,
> Where when that soverayne beauty it doth spy,
>   resembling heavens glory in her light:
>   drawne with sweet pleasures bayt, it back doth fly,
>   and unto heaven forgets her former flight.
> There my fraile fancy fed with full delight,
>   doth bath in blisse and mantleth ª most at ease:
>   ne thinks of other heaven, but how it might
>   her harts desire with most contentment please.
> Hart need not wish none other happinesse,
>   but here on earth to have such hevens blisse.

The object of both poems is to justify the earthly as an illustration or reflection of the heavenly. When Sidney treats this theme he writes wittily rather than seriously, and not only his manner but his meaning contrasts with Spenser's. Astrophel's love for Stella directly opposes reason and philosophy:

> Plato I have read for nought, but if he tame
> Such coltish yeeres
>
> With what strange checkes I in my selfe am shent,
> When into Reasons Audit I doe goe:
> And by such counts my selfe a Banckerowt know
>
> Reason, in faith thou art well serv'd, that still
> Would'st brabling be, with sence and love in me [12]

ª mantleth: spreads its wings while on its perch, as a hawk does.

And the lesson of Christ teaches Sidney not to love his dear love but
to turn away from that which reaches but to dust to "Eternall
Love." [13] For Italian Platonists like Benivieni and Castiglione human
love is not indeed antithetic to reason; it is rather a first step to be
left behind as the true lover rises to a truer love, "grade by grade
to the uncreated sphere/ . . . whence fashioned were/ All beauties
in the loved one manifest." [14] But Spenser neither declares the earthly
incompatible with the heavenly, as Sidney does, nor does he envision
an unbroken ascent which spurns earth in its aspiration for heaven.
He would have both loves, the one infinitely good, the other good
too because, though finite, it imitates the infinite.

These are the two goods of the earthly and the heavenly hymns.
In his dedication Spenser explains that the former hymns were written "in the greener times" of his youth, and since they "too much
pleased those of like age and disposition," feeding their strong passions, he was moved to add the hymns of "celestiall" love and beauty
"by way of retractation." Some scholars have argued that this account
is a fiction designed to preserve decorum by associating sexual love
with youth and contemplative love with maturity. They may indeed
be right, for I find it hard to believe that even in his greenest times
Spenser would have thought his paean of love complete without
reference to a realm transcending the mundane.

As the poet says, the hymns of heavenly love and heavenly beauty
constitute a palinode for the earthly pair:

> But all those follies now I do reprove,
> And turned have the tenor of my string,
> The heavenly prayses of true love to sing.   (*HHL*, 12–14)

A palinode makes little sense unless one knows what it is opposed
to, and it is evident that the two later hymns are designed to gain
strength and meaning from the two former. The method is a complex system of parallels and contrasts. Each hymn begins with an
invocation and ends with a paradisal vision. The two hymns of love
are linked by their common concern with motive; the hymns of

beauty by their common concern with the goal toward which that
motive drives. But between earth and heaven there lies a great gulf.

Both hymns of love invoke the god, but the home of earthly love
is Venus' lap while that of heavenly love is "heavens hight." Earthly
love is the son of Venus and at the same time "Begot of Plentie and
of Penurie"—the Plenty of Beauty and the Penury which is the hunger for Beauty. In *Colin Clouts Come Home Againe* Love's gene-
alogy is explained differently: he is the child of the hermaphrodite
Venus, born pure and spotless of a beautiful conjunction of opposites.
Heavenly love is Christ, derived not from a desire for something
lacking nor from a mixture of contraries but from single Plenty
alone, for the "high eternall powre"

> lov'd it selfe, because it selfe was faire;
> (For faire is lov'd;) and of it selfe begot
> Like to it selfe his eldest sonne and heire   (*HHL*, 29–31)

The creation of the mutable world is a history of the works of earthly
love: Love reconciled the warring elements of chaos, binding together contraries "with adamantine chains," setting bounds to the
things so created, dividing the heavens and the earth, the land and
the sea. The Almighty, too, is described as the generative force,

> that loves to get
> Things like himselfe, and to enlarge his race   (*HHL*, 51–52)

and it is He who created the angels and their dwelling place, "the
heavens illimitable hight,/ Not this round heaven." And after the
fall of Lucifer He made man "of clay, base, vile, and next to nought,"

> and breathd a living spright
> Into his face most beautifull and fayre,
> Endewd with wisdomes riches, heavenly, rare.   (*HHL*, 110–12)

But apart from man, nothing is said of His creation of "this round
heaven" and the living world within it, so that there is no direct
contradiction of the earlier hymn by the later.

As Cupid generates the world so he inspires in its creatures the desire for generation. Beasts seek their mates blindly, unaware of the nature of the force that urges them and ignorant, too, of its procreative purpose. But man, who occupies a special and exalted place within the animate world, retains within his spirit some trace of "that heavenly fire" which is defined in *Colin Clouts Come Home Againe* as "the sparke of reasons might." He therefore knowingly seeks Beauty "borne of heavenly race," and

> Not for lusts sake, but for eternitie,
> Seekes to enlarge his lasting progenie.   (*HL,* 104–5)

His search is terribly difficult, for Love "enmarbles" the lady's proud heart and makes her pitiless so that the lover suffers anguish. This suffering tests the validity of the lover's passion. "Baseborne mynds" which feel only "loose desyre" will not endure it. The high distance of the lady cleanses the lover's soul of "dunghill thoughts" and spurs him to great deeds in the hope of winning her favor. Even when the victory is in sight, however, the purgation continues, for the lover can be satisfied only by the knowledge that he alone is loved in return. Until that time he suffers from countless fears, surmises, envies, rumors, delays, and worst of all, from jealousy. But after purgatory comes paradise—an earthly paradise, for it rewards an earthly love, a paradise of nectar and ivory beds arrayed with roses and lilies:

> There with thy daughter Pleasure they doe play
> Their hurtlesse sports, without rebuke or blame,
> And in her snowy bosome boldly lay
> Their quiet heads, devoyd of guilty shame,
> After full joyance of their gentle game   (*HL,* 287–91)

Point for point, the nature of this earthly love is compared with that of the realm of heaven. There, "pride and love may ill agree"; Lucifer falls through pride but in Christ "no jot/ Of loves dislike, or pride was to be found." The parallel to the lover's anguish is that of Jesus, caused by the

> huge and most unspeakeable impression
> Of loves deepe wound, that pierst the piteous hart   (*HHL,* 155–56)

If earthly love lifts himself "out of the lowly dust,/ On golden plumes up to the purest skie," heavenly love descends "Out of the bosome of eternall blisse"

> like a most demisse
> And abject thrall, in fleshes fraile attyre   (*HHL,* 136–37)

For the "brave exploits" of the one there is the "humble carriage" of the other. The earthly lover demands to be loved alone; Christ asks us to love Him and also "our brethren to his image wrought." Yet the jealous exclusiveness of human love has its counterpart in heaven:

> With all thy hart, with all thy soule and mind,
> Thou must him love, and his beheasts embrace:
> All other loves, with which the world doth blind
> Weake fancies, and stirre up affections base,
> Thou must renounce   (*HHL,* 260–64)

And with renunciation and purification the lover of Christ attains a vision, not of ivory beds, but of "Th'Idee of his pure glorie."

The search for true Beauty discloses similar contrasts. The movement of the earthly hymn is down, beginning with the aboriginal "wondrous Paterne" according to which "the worlds great workmaister" fashioned all things "as comely as he could," and descending with the soul to be embodied past the sphere of the sun to the living lady, fair in spirit and therefore in body. The movement of the heavenly hymn is up,

> Beginning then below, with th'easie vew
> Of this base world, subject to fleshly eye   (*HHB,* 22–23)

and rising through the elements and the spheres of the mutable world to the "Unmoving, uncorrupt" heaven beyond, organized like this one in nine degrees of increasing beauty.[15] The discovery of mundane beauty demands the distinction between essence and appearance. It must be identified not with features, colors, proportions that fade and die but with the source of which these appearances are the reflection, the inward beauty of the soul which is divinely derived and therefore immortal. Similarly, even the intelligible aspects of the universe offer only a hint of the celestial beauty from which they arise:

> Cease then, my tongue, and lend unto my mynd
> Leave to bethinke how great that beautie is,
> Whose utmost parts so beautifull I fynd,
> How much more those essentiall parts of his,
> His truth, his love, his wisedome, and his blis,
> His grace, his doome, his mercy, and his might,
> By which he lends us of himselfe a sight. (*HHB*, 106–12)

In the realm of the earthly hymn, beauty manifests itself to those who love. Spenser does not say with Marlowe (and Shakespeare), "Who ever lov'd that lov'd not at first sight?" Beauty of appearance may stir the beholder—so fancy is bred—but

> all that like the beautie which they see,
> Streight do not love: for love is not so light,
> As streight to burne at first beholders sight. (*HB*, 208–10)

In *Colin Clouts Come Home Againe* the shepherds are taught that when Beauty darts her beams into the mind of man he seeks cure for his pain from her that wounded him. In the hymn, the poet makes it clear that only when the lover-to-be apprehends essential rather than apparent beauty does he truly fall in love. The first step is liberation of the sensible image from "fleshes frayle infection." Next, this purer form is "conformed" to the sun-derived light of his own spirit, the result being a heavenly beauty which is the "mirrour of his owne thought." This is "fairer, then it is indeede" when "indeede" refers to the lady's appearance, "And yet indeede her faire-nesse doth exceede" when "indeede" refers to that more profound beauty which even the sharp-sighted lover cannot fully see. With this achievement, the lover perceives beauty at its earthly summit:

Sometimes upon her forhead they behold
A thousand Graces masking in delight,
Sometimes within her eye-lids they unfold
Ten thousand sweet belgards,[b] which to their sight
Doe seeme like twinckling starres in frostie night:
But on her lips like rosy buds in May,
So many millions of chaste pleasures play.   (*HB*, 253–59)

These are the attributes of Beauty, the "handmaides" of Venus.

The way to a vision of Heavenly Beauty begins, like the path to
Venus, with beautiful appearance in this world, but Spenser distinguishes the two journeys by beginning the one with a fair countenance and the other with the fair world of sense. The rise to the
celestial is accomplished through heavenly contemplation of the
"high flying mynd." At the pinnacle of heaven is the Highest, bathed
in light so brilliant that the sun, source of beauty for the lower
universe, seems dark. Neither men nor angels can look directly at
those bright beams, but some happy mortals "whom God so much
doth grace" may, like the angels themselves, see God's "owne Beloved" Sapience who sits in His bosom, dimming the beauty of
Venus.

As the earthly hymns, then, distinguish love from lust and essential from superficial beauty, so the heavenly hymns oppose Christ
to Cupid and Sapience to Venus. At the same time, these oppositions
declare the relationship, however distant, between the blind generative passion of beasts and the love of Christ, between the beauty
of mundane creation and the unimaginable splendor of God.

This fabric of love is a weaving of Spenser's own. The strands
which compose it are diverse, indeed incompatible by philosophic
standards. They derive from the *fin amor* of Provence, from the
ancient conception of Nature as a generative force, from Christian
doctrine and Christian mysticism, and from what must loosely be
called Platonism. In full accord with the spirit of most Renaissance

[b] belgards: loving looks.

thinking Spenser's effort in the *Fowre Hymnes,* as in his other poems, is to discover common direction in the traditions which he inherited, even at the cost of blurring distinctions logically necessary. The very diversity of the traditions which enter into it is therefore essential to the conception of the work.

The language and thought of the hymns insistently echoes that of the amorists of the Middle Ages. Like Spenser, they make much of the distinction between true love and beastly lust, of the play of the eyes, the haughtiness of the lady, the monomania and suffering of the lover, the sickness of jealousy, the stimulation to noble deeds and poetic utterance, and the purification of the lover's spirit. The goal of the lover is sexual union, whether in the form of a token smile or kiss or in physical consummation, and it is conceived of as a "joy" or ecstasy beyond the experience of ordinary mortals. By Chaucer's time, at least, even marriage can be accommodated to the convention, for if Troilus has no thought of wedding, the prize of the *Knight's Tale* is not merely Emily's heart but her hand as well, and it is essential to the *Franklin's Tale* that the true union of Dorigen and Arveragus is the consequence of a most courtly courtship. While this love of the troubadours and their followers is at base sensual, it is not without its links to heaven. If Andrew the Chaplain retracts his art of courtly love in a concluding book of divine love he by the same token associates the two. The love language of the Provençal poets becomes the language in which nuns are taught to express their adoration of Christ. With Dante, the lady herself becomes an angel and the final ecstasy of love the divine vision.

Despite these resemblances, Spenser's understanding of the nature of love differs significantly from that of the courtly amorists. When the writer of the medieval tradition distinguishes between love and lust he does so on the basis of the involvement of the heart rather than the body, his touchstone being the gentility of the enamored spirits. Spenser says this too, but his distinction depends primarily upon man's "more immortal mind," his "sparke of reasons might." For the troubadour and his heirs, reason characterizes a heavenly love, not an earthly. Indeed, it is the enemy of earthly love, however "gentle." Dante, it is true, asserts that Beatrice's image was of such virtue "that no time did it suffer Love to rule over me without the faithful counsel of reason, in those things where such counsel were useful to hear," [16] but even this is to make reason love's handmaid, not love's guide.

Although Dante and the courtly amorists speak of love as a creative force they do not concern themselves with the kind of creation represented by the bearing of children and the peopling of the earth. For this aspect of his philosophy Spenser drew upon the ancient conception of Nature as a beneficent and fecund power. Ovid's account of the making of the world [17] closely resembles that of Spenser in the *Hymne of Love;* both tell of an original Chaos of antagonistic and unlimited elements drawn into harmony and set in bounds by the creator. Ovid is not sure whether this power is Nature or some other god; Claudian identifies her with Nature, governor of marriage and generation. The twelfth-century philosophical poets Bernard Silvestris and Alain de Lille find a place for *Natura* between God and the world, associating her both with the creation and ordering of the cosmos and with childbearing. Jean de Meun's *Romance of the Rose* assigns to Nature and her high priest Genius (the Roman god of generation) the final victory of the lover, and it is Nature who presides over the marriage contest of Chaucer's *Parlement of Foules*. Spenser's familiarity with this tradition is made evident by his description of Genius as the porter in the Garden of Adonis and by his choice of the goddess as the arbiter of Mutabilitie's claim to dominion over the world.

Natura or Physis has other names. Sometimes she is identified with Venus, and this version Spenser also knows, Lucretius' invocation to *Venus genetrix* serving as the model for his hymn to the goddess in the tenth canto of Book IV of *The Faerie Queene*. Boethius gives her role to Love, significantly linking love and marriage. Chaucer translates him:

Al this accordaunce of thynges is bounde with love, that governeth erthe and see, and hath also comandement to the hevene. And yif this love slakede the bridelis, alle thynges that now loven hem togidres wolden make batayle contynuely, and stryven to fordo the fassoun of this world, the which they now leden in accordable feith by fayre moevynges. This love halt togidres peples joyned with an holy boond, and knytteth sacrement of mariages of chaste loves; and love enditeth lawes to trewe felawes.[18]

Whatever her appellation, Spenser's homage to her is his pervasive emphasis upon the fecundity of sea and land, upon the conquest of death by the species, upon the mysteries of generation and regeneration.

Although Christian writers speak of the goddess Natura as an emanation of the Godhead, she still somehow retains a pagan autonomy, so much so that Ralegh feels it necessary to argue "That Nature is no *Principium per se*." [19] For an orthodox justification of marriage and childbearing, Spenser need have looked no further than the beginning of the office of holy matrimony in the Book of Common Prayer. Marriage "is an honorable estate instituted by God in paradise, in the time of mannes innocencie, signifying unto us the misticall union that is betwixte Christe and his Churche . . . not to bee enterprised, nor taken in hand unadvisedlye, lightelie, or wantonly, to satisfie mens carnal lustes and appetites, like brute beastes that have no understanding, but reverently, discretely, advisedly, soberly, and in the feare of God." Restricting the ideal of sexual abstinence to the status of a gift granted by God to very few, not necessarily more holy than others, Reforming preachers dwelt on the virtues of loving, productive wedlock.[20] If marriages are

made in heaven, some of them say, those destined for happy union
must have been created with a secret sympathy between them, and
as Spenser puts it,

> wrong it were that any other twaine
> Should in loves gentle band combyned bee   (*HB*, 204–5)

Human love, now become a religious duty, takes on qualities with
which it is endowed in alien traditions. It is praiseworthy for love
to be blind, for man and woman to see each other as more beautiful
and more virtuous than indeed they are. Not only the heart but the
eye also should be pleased in marriage: husbands and wives "may be
the sweetest, and most pleasing objects, upon earth; to take up each
others eyes, from all the world besides, that no other in this regard
may once be thought worth looking upon." [21] Protestant and puritan
glorification of the wedded state does not extend to a parallelism
between the joys of the marriage bed and those of heaven, but the
Prayer Book does answer the deep need of the lover for a justification beyond sense by making marriage a symbol of the "mystical
union" of God and the souls of the saved.

Christian mystics, themselves indebted to pagan contemplatives,
make a special contribution to the two "heavenly" hymns. The approach to God through contemplation of His works is closely allied
to Platonic method. More common in the Middle Ages is the approach through meditation on the life of Christ. Spenser follows
the former path in the *Hymne of Heavenly Beautie,* the latter in the
Hymne of Heavenly Love. Both ascents are marked by three stages
defined in the writings of medieval mystics, a cleansing of the seeking spirit, its illumination by the light of truth, and its achievement
of the sight of the divine and the annihilation of self. The language
of these writers constantly stresses the motive power of love, the
purity of immaterial beauty, and the rapture of the summit.

Inextricably mixed with these strains in Spenser's thinking is the
Platonic. The teaching of Plato came to the poet and his contem-

poraries along a tangle of paths: from the philosopher himself and from his followers Porphyry and Plotinus; from Greek and Latin moralists like Plutarch, Vergil, Cicero, Macrobius, and Boethius; from St. Augustine and other fathers of the Christian church; from philosophers and poets of the high Middle Ages; and from the revivified Platonism of the Italian Renaissance. *Fin amor* was itself influenced by Platonic notions and Italian Platonism was in turn indebted to *fin amor*. It is only rarely possible, therefore, to assert of an aspect of Spenser's philosophy that it derives, let us say, from Ficino and not from Plotinus, Vergil, or Chaucer. But the connections between Spenser's ideas and the Platonic grand scheme of things are clear enough.

There are two distinct tendencies in the Platonic tradition, a centripetal one seeking the immaterial, all-inclusive, self-sufficient heart of all, and a centrifugal one, accounting for the infinite universe in terms of the unselfish, creative richness of that heart.[22] The nexus of those tendencies is God, or the good, or Beauty. The Renaissance believed this pagan conception to be even older than Plato, Sir Walter Ralegh, for example, referring it to the Orphic hymn:

> The first of all is God, and the same last is he.
> God is the head and midst, yea from him all things be.
> God is the Base of Earth, and of the starred Sky.
> He is the Male and Female too, shall never die.
> The spirit of all is God, the Sun, the Moon, and what is higher.
> The King, th'original of all, of all the end.
> For close in Holy Breast he all did comprehend,
> Whence all to blessed light, his wondrous power did send.[23]

In its creative aspect, that "high eternall powre" began the begetting by loving itself "because it selfe was faire"—this passage in the *Hymne of Heavenly Love* paraphrases the *Timaeus*. Its beauty impresses itself everywhere throughout the material world although it is visible to mortal eyes only dimly through its temporal vesture.

Since man retains within himself some trace of the beauty from which he was derived, some memory of his "first countries sight," he is drawn back toward it by the hunger which is love. In its striving to see beauty plain the seeking spirit is refined and elevated, as is the courtly lover by his devotion to the unattainable lady, with the difference that the Platonic claims to follow reason while the courtly lover rejects it. And since love of the essential beauty is rational it is also virtuous and the happiness which rewards it is a good.

For many of Plato's Renaissance followers, the most important teaching of his love philosophy was the progressive ascent from the material to the immaterial described by Diotima in the *Symposium*. But Spenser's earthly and heavenly loves are sharply distinguished. His earthly lover learns to perceive the inward beauty of his lady, but climbs at last not to a perception of the essence which generated it but into bed. The lover of the heavenly hymns begins with a recognition of the admirable beauty not of a particular woman but of "the frame of this wide universe." The ascent of the lower slope may be a reflection or a symbol of the higher, perhaps even a preparation for it; it is not part of the same expedition.

In his recognition of earthly love as in itself valid and virtuous Spenser comes close to the position taken by Plotinus in the *Enneads*. Although the influence of that work seems to me evident not only in the *Fowre Hymnes* but also in the description of the Garden of Adonis and in the Mutabilitie cantos, I would not insist that Spenser knew it directly. The ideas which it contains may have filtered to him through lectures at the university or conversations with Harvey or by way of medieval or Renaissance works as yet undiscovered by students of his philosophy. Yet I do not know why it should be more probable that a well-educated Englishman of the sixteenth century depended upon popularizations or intermediaries rather than upon the original, published with Ficino's Latin translation and his commentary, surely one of the most intellectually exciting books of the Renaissance. The principle of parsimony does not lead inevitably to the conclusion that writers of the period drew all their learning from handbooks, abridgments, and translations.

For Plotinus as for Spenser, the heavenly kind of beauty and love is immeasurably superior to the earthly. But significantly, Plotinus thinks human beauty and sexual love (of the right kind) true goods. The beauty which we see reflects a beauty of spirit, from which it follows that

nothing base within can be beautiful without—at least not with an authentic beauty, for there are examples of a good exterior not sprung from a beauty dominant within; people passing as handsome but essentially base have that, a spurious and superficial beauty: if anyone tells me he has seen people really fine-looking but interiorly vile, I can only deny it; we have here simply a false notion of personal beauty; unless, indeed, the inner vileness were an accident in a nature essentially fine; in this Sphere there are many obstacles to self-realization.[24]

This beauty is not merely symmetry or a certain charm of color but rather the Principle from which these characteristics derive. Although Eros takes his name, Plotinus supposes, from *horasis,* the act of seeing, love is not aroused at first sight:

So long as the attention is upon the visible form, love has not entered: when from that outward form the lover elaborates within himself, in his own partless soul, an immaterial image, then it is that love is born, then the lover longs for the sight of the beloved to make that fading image live again.[25]

But the immaterial image does not inspire only a fleshless passion. Beauty stirs in man "a copulative love which is the will to beget in beauty." Pure love, indeed, seeks beauty alone, but

there are those that feel, also, a desire of such immortality as lies within mortal reach; and these are seeking Beauty in their demand for perpetuity, the desire of the eternal; Nature teaches them to sow the seed and to beget in beauty, to sow towards eternity, but in beauty through their own kinship with the beautiful.[26]

Plotinus is careful to distinguish this procreative desire from lawless or unnatural carnality:

All the natural loves, all that serve the ends of Nature, are good, in a lesser Soul, inferior in rank and in scope; in the greater Soul, superior; but all belong to the order of Being. Those forms of Love that do not serve the purposes of Nature are merely accidents attending on perversion.[27]

There is difference, too, between lovers who look no further than the beauty of earth and those who

venerate also the beauty of the other world while they, still, have no contempt for this in which they recognize, as it were, a last outgrowth, an attenuation of the higher. These, in sum, are innocent frequenters of beauty, not to be confused with the class to whom it becomes an occasion to fall into the ugly—for the aspiration towards a good degenerates into an evil often.[28]

This acceptance of the world and the flesh with the recognition at the same time of the existence of a far better world beyond is pervasive in the *Enneads*. To those who teach hatred and abandonment of the body Plotinus answers with a parable:

Two people inhabit the one stately house; one of them declaims against its plan and against its Architect, but none the less maintains his residence in it; the other makes no complaint, asserts the entire competency of the Architect and waits cheerfully for the day when he may leave it, having no further need of a house.[29]

Indeed, even while he lives there, content with his quarters, man may look beyond his limits. Like the earthly lover who molds himself to his beloved, trying to increase the attraction of his person, his moral qualities, and other graces, the lover of a higher beauty strives to make himself fit for the object of his desire. Plotinus compares the ecstatic self-annihilation of the soul mounted to the highest with the joy of sexual union:

She has turned away from all about her and made herself apt, beautiful to the utmost, brought into likeness with the divine—by those preparings and adornings which come unbidden to those growing ready for the vision—she has seen that presence suddenly manifesting within her, for there is nothing between: here is no longer duality but a two in one; for, so long as the presence holds, all distinction fades: it is as lover and beloved here, in a copy of that union, long to blend.[30]

And in this ultimate union all earthly values fade away:

All that she had welcomed of old,—office, power, wealth, beauty, knowledge—of all she tells her scorn as she never could had she not found their better; linked to This she can fear no disaster . . . ; let all about her fall to pieces, so she would have it that she may be wholly with This, so huge the happiness she has won to.[31]

Or as Spenser puts it, in the rapture of his vision of Sapience:

> And that faire lampe, which useth to enflame
> The hearts of men with selfe consuming fyre,
> Thenceforth seemes fowle, and full of sinfull blame;
> And all that pompe, to which proud minds aspyre
> By name of honor, and so much desyre,
> Seemes to them basenesse, and all riches drosse,
> And all mirth sadnesse, and all lucre losse.   (*HHB*, 274–80)

The significance of the comparison between Spenser's philosophy of love and that of Plotinus does not lie in the correspondence of one or another idea. Point by point, with greater or less emphasis, these notions are endemic in classical times, the Middle Ages, and the Renaissance. The value of the parallels depends rather upon their revelation of an attitude toward the mundane common to the philosopher and the poet. Neither rejects the life of this world as without purpose, or useful only as a steppingstone to the other. Its worth, to be sure, arises from its imitation, however dim and distorted, of the brilliance beyond, earthly love being a good while celestial love is an infinite, not merely a greater good. But instead of destroying the finite, the infinite justifies it. Even though the bright angels' tower of the New Jerusalem "quite dims" this world's Panthea, the Red Cross Knight was not wrong in thinking Cleopolis "for earthly frame/ The fairest peece that eye beholden can."

Spenser was of course first of all a Christian. There is nothing in Plato or Plotinus that corresponds to the descent of God into the flesh and His sacrifice for mankind. But it is idle to ask whether Spenser was a Christian Platonist or a Platonic Christian. From the time of the Fathers, Christianity had itself been Platonic, and St. Augustine's admiration for Plato and his debt to Plotinus are well known. Medieval theologians adapted to Christian uses whatever they could of classical philosophy, sometimes stretching the literal sense of the Bible in order to make it consonant with pagan teaching, sometimes reinterpreting pagan teaching to fit it to the Bible. By appropriate changes in form and function even the ancient gods were made to serve true religion. Furthermore, classical writers and philosophers were themselves turned almost Christian in the sense that their morality and striving for truth were thought to arise from some apprehension of the as yet unrevealed verity of Christ. Some Platonic tenets, such as the belief in the eternity of the world and in metempsychosis, proved difficult to accommodate to Christianity; others, like the complex series of hypostases between the One and the realm of matter, held little interest for most Christians. But both Platonists and Christians identify the highest with ultimate good and ultimate beauty, both find material existence in comparison shadowy and poor, both urge man to break from the bounds of earth toward the celestial. The Sapience who sits in God's bosom in the *Hymne of Heavenly Beautie* has been variously interpreted as the Holy Ghost, Christ, the Sapience of the Book of Wisdom, and the Platonic Heavenly Venus, and she has qualities of each of these. Since Spenser does not tell us specifically which she is, he no doubt intends what is common to all, a wealth and wisdom of which this world's riches and knowledge are only a token, an entity associated with God yet not altogether beyond the apprehension of the purified human soul. The high "Ideas . . . which Plato so admyred" are ranged in the celestial realm between the souls of the happy and the Powers and Dominations of the Bible. The Hill of Contemplation from which the Red Cross Knight sees the New Jerusalem is likened to Sinai, the Mount of Olives, and Parnassus.

Spenser's system of love, as even so cursory a study shows, reaches upward from this world but keeps foothold within it. Examined as a logical construct, it disintegrates at once into a conglomeration of inconsistencies and even absurdities. But it has a coherence of another kind. The poet was attempting to justify by the authority of literature, the wisdom of the ancients, and revealed religion his deep feelings about the relationships of man and woman and man and God. He saw a likeness between the love that draws the sexes together, producing noble deeds and perpetuating the race, and the love that draws man to God and fills the world with beauty. To testify to this likeness he summoned his cloud of witnesses.

That True Glorious Type

IN THE STRANGE and various forest of *The Faerie Queene* many lose their way and succumb at last to the monster Error or, worse still, to exasperation and boredom. Omens for the journey are particularly unpropitious if the traveler enters upon it guided by the Aristotelian dictum that plot is the "first principle, and, as it were, the soul" of an epic poem, for here it will lead him only into a morass. He is better off if he comes armed, like the Red Cross Knight, with faith, faith in the book itself and in the guiding signs within it. By faith in the book I mean a disposition to believe that whatever the history of its composition may have been, the poem as it was presented to Queen Elizabeth is neither an incoherent and improbable tale worth reading only for the charm of its quaint and delicious passages nor a farrago of bits and pieces hastily thrown together to make a volume but, like Spenser's other poems, a carefully considered composition in which theme, rather than fable, is the central structural element. And by faith in its signs, I mean the belief that Spenser's announcements of his intention, both in the text itself and in the letter addressed to Sir Walter Ralegh which was appended to the first edition, are designed to give "great light to the Reader" rather than to mislead him. It would hardly be necessary to make these affirmations were it not for the number of interpreters of *The Faerie Queene* who begin by denying them. Of course, the reader may conclude (as I do not) that the only order in *The Faerie Queene* is of the kind imposed by the stargazer upon the scattered lights of the sky, and that the poet's professions of purpose, like those of many a Renaissance author, are no more than a formal bow to the critical dogma of his time. The proof lies in the poem.

The first lines of *The Faerie Queene* are themselves a sign to the reader, though their meaning is hidden in an obscurity not of Spenser's making. Had he begun with the words "I sing of arms and the man" no reader could doubt that he wished his poem to be recognized as of the genre of the *Aeneid*. But in Spenser's edition of Vergil's poem, as in all Renaissance editions, the opening words were not "Arma virumque cano" but the following verses, probably Vergilian indeed but rejected by Vergil's first editor, Varius:

> Ille ego qui quondam gracili modulatus avena
> Carmen, et egressus silvis, vicina coegi
> Ut quamvis avido parerent arva colono
> Gratum opus agricolis: at nunc horrentia Martis
> Arma virumque cano . . .

The beginning of *The Faerie Queene* is an unmistakable allusion to these lines:

> Lo I the man, whose Muse whilome did maske,
>   As time her taught in lowly Shepheards weeds,
>   Am now enforst a far unfitter taske,
>   For trumpets sterne to chaunge mine Oaten reeds

The poet so announces that his principal model is Vergil's *Aeneid*. If Spenser's text of the poem he wished to imitate differs from our own, his understanding of its intention and method differs even more radically. Since he was a man of independence and originality it would be risky to assume that he accepted without question the standard textbook interpretations of Vergil current in his time. Nevertheless, a comparison of his letter to Ralegh with a typical Renaissance introduction to the *Aeneid* helps to make clear what he meant by beginning as he did. Among the many sixteenth-century editions of Vergil's poems a considerable number are substantial folio volumes in which the text is surrounded by a sea of commentary. Commonly, such editions include the annotations of various scholars, the work of the late classical grammarians Servius and Donatus and of Renaissance humanists. Of the later commentaries that of Jodocus Badius Ascensius, otherwise Josse Bade van Assche, famous Flemish scholar and publisher, is surely one of the most frequently reprinted.[1]

After explaining the form of the title of Vergil's poem, Badius announces its purpose as "simul et iucunda et idonea dicere vitae." This is the second line of that distich of Horace's *Ars poetica* which Ben Jonson translates:

> Poets would either profit or delight
> Or mixing sweet and fit, teach life the right.[2]

The poet, Badius declares, undertook the task of teaching "life the right" because he knew that there could be nothing more useful to a commonwealth than to be led by a prince who was clement, prudent, brave, temperate, and endowed with the other virtues. He therefore depicted such a prince in the *Aeneid,* prophesying that he would be imitated by Augustus, just as Xenophon had portrayed a Cyrus, not exactly as he was, but as he should have been ("ut Xenophon de Cyro fecisse perhibetur, non semper qualis fuit, sed qualem fuisse decuit perscribens"). By this means he suggested to Augustus both the necessity of imitating the ancestor to whom he traced his origin, a man whom he described as most pious, just, brave, temperate, etc., and the disgrace that he would incur if he degenerated from the honorable customs and virtues of his forebears. Besides this general intention which he shares with all good writers, Badius explains, Vergil had a number of particular ones ("speciales atque peculiares"). He wished to crown his poetic career with a work in the grand manner, as he had begun it in his youth with the humble pastoral and progressed in his maturity to the middle style of the *Georgics*. And since he had equaled Theocritus in his eclogues and Hesiod in his *Georgics* he desired in his great work to equal that prince of poets and fountain of ingenuity, Homer. Indeed he overwent Homer ("illi praestare demonstrat"). What the Greek poet needed the forty-eight books of his *Odyssey* and *Iliad* to express, Vergil said in twelve. For Homer had described the contemplative life in the person of Ulysses and the active life in his account of the Trojan war, while Vergil combined them both in one, treating of the former (which he signified by the word *virum* in "arma virumque cano") in his first six books and of the latter (*arma*) in the last six books. Besides considering other "special" intentions of the *Aeneid,* Badius summarizes the events of its story in chronological or historical order, pointing out as he does so that poetical narration follows a very different sequence.[3]

Some verbal correspondences between this essay and Spenser's letter are worth noting. Like Badius, Spenser distinguishes between his general intention and "particular purposes or by-accidents." His choice of a historical fiction to embody his meaning he defends as "most plausible and pleasing," and since the word *plausible* must here have its old meaning of "deserving of approval," the expression translates Horace's "iucunda et idonea." [4] And like Badius Spenser cites the precedent of Xenophon who "in the person of Cyrus and the Persians fashioned a governement such as might best be." But phrases of this kind are so much the common currency of Renaissance criticism that they demonstrate rather Spenser's familiarity with the tradition than his use of Badius as a "source."

It is in terms of matter and emphasis that Spenser's letter shows itself to be modeled after the kind of introductory essay that is found in sixteenth-century editions of the *Aeneid*. As Vergil's intention is said to be the portrayal of a virtuous prince, so Spenser begins by asserting his purpose "to fashion a gentleman or noble person in vertuous and gentle discipline." For the fabulous Aeneas Spenser offers Arthur "before he was king." Arthur cannot serve as a figure for Elizabeth, as Aeneas for Augustus, but Spenser explains that she is "shadowed" in Arthur's beloved Gloriana and in Belphoebe. If Vergil's method is justified by an appeal to the precedents of Homer and Xenophon, Spenser relies for authority upon those two writers, upon Vergil himself, and upon Ariosto and Tasso. Badius' division of the subject of the nature of the hero-prince into the branches designated by *virum* and *arma* is paralleled by Spenser's partition into *ethice* and *politice*. The list of virtues ascribed to Aeneas is like the list of virtues combined in Arthur and represented separately by the twelve subsidiary heroes; the one catalogue begins with "pius," the other with "Holinesse." And Spenser's letter ends with a summary of the events of his story told, not according to "the Methode of a Poet historical," but in the manner of a historiographer who "discourseth of affayres orderly as they were donne, accounting as well the times as the actions."

For his linking of Ariosto and Tasso with Homer, Vergil, and Xenophon as writers on the theme of the virtuous hero, Spenser had ample authority in contemporary comment on their poems. The editions in which he must have read the Italian poets were supplied with introductions resembling that of Badius to the *Aeneid*. Tasso himself provided explanatory prefaces to his *Rinaldo* and his *Gerusalemme Liberata,* and his essay on the latter, like the letter to Ralegh, repeats the accepted dogma concerning the division of the great subject:

Of the life of the Contemplative Man, the Comedy of Dantes and the Odysses, are (as it were) in every part thereof a Figure: but the civil Life is seen to be shadowed throughout the Iliads, and Aeneids also, although in this there be rather set out a mixture of Action and Contemplation.[5]

There has been much argument as to whether Tasso's moralizations of his poems reflect his original intention or a more or less grudging concession to the pressures of counter-Reformation critical theory, but the question is irrelevant to the present purpose. Like Tasso's poems, the *Orlando Furioso* came to Spenser's hands as a work in this didactic tradition. Few readers today will believe that Ariosto's purpose was to portray a prince like Aeneas or Cyrus. But there are a number of plainly moralistic episodes in the *Orlando,* fully equipped with appropriately named allegorical personages, and the problem of extracting a useful meaning from the rest of the poem was easily within the capacity of the critics of the time. Sixteenth-century editors of the *Orlando* regularly discovered in it a portrait of the heroic leader, and one of them, Orazio Toscanella, compiler of *Belleze del Furioso di M. Lodovico Ariosto* (1574), describes Ariosto's method in just the way that Spenser describes his own. Ariosto, he says,

placed several virtues in several individuals, one virtue in one character and another in another character, in order to fashion out of all the characters a well-rounded and perfect man. A well-rounded and perfect man is one adorned with all the virtues.[6]

Spenser calls this well-roundedness "magnificence . . . which vertue . . . (according to Aristotle and the rest) . . . is the perfection of all the rest, and conteineth in it them all."

By Spenser's own account, then, the intention of *The Faerie Queene* is "to fashion a gentleman or noble person," and this he confirms by announcing in the prologue to his poem that its "argument" is "that true glorious type" of Queen Elizabeth, the type of gentleness and nobility. The word "fashion" in his statement of purpose is open to misconstruction. It may be taken to mean that Spenser proposed to show how experience and training make a truly virtuous man out of one who is only potentially virtuous. But in the present case, Spenser's use of "fashion" echoes a long-established tradition which shows that he must intend by it not "educate" or "train" but "represent," "delineate." Cicero's *De oratore* introduces its subject with the statement "we have to picture to ourselves in our discourse (*fingendus est nobis oratione nostra*) an orator from whom every blemish has been taken away."[7] Castiglione makes Sir Frederic propose that one of the company "take it in hand to shape in wordes (*formare con parole*) a good Courtier," and the author declares his intention to "fashion such a Courtier as the Prince that shall be worthie to have him in his service, although his state be but small, may notwithstanding be called a mighty Lord."[8] It is in this acceptation that the *Oxford English Dictionary* understands "fashioning" as it appears on the title page of Spenser's poem: "The Faerie Queene. Disposed into twelve bookes, Fashioning XII. Morall vertues." And in the sentence immediately preceding that in which "to fashion a gentleman" occurs, Spenser explains that the purpose of his letter is "to discover unto you the general intention and meaning, which . . . I have fashioned." Furthermore, Spenser goes on to explain that in fulfillment of his design he has labored "to pourtraict in Arthure, before he was king, the image of a brave knight, perfected in the twelve private morall vertues." He does not say that he has shown Arthur in the process of achieving that perfection. Of course, since the "fashion" of a man includes that which determines his character, training and experience enter into it to the extent that one believes them to be effective agents. But Spenser announces here, not that he has written the story of an education, but that, like Badius' Vergil and Toscanella's Ariosto, he has described a man who combines in himself the chivalric and the moral disciplines, a virtuous gentleman. And when he exclaims at the beginning of the last canto of the Legend of Temperaunce,

> Now gins this goodly frame of Temperance
> Fairely to rise

he is saying that he has portrayed the virtue itself, not the growth of that virtue in its champion.

It is difficult for most modern readers to disabuse themselves of the idea that character development must be an essential feature of any extended narrative that pretends to be more than merely an entertainment. Stories in which the growth of the hero is a principal motif are of course not uncommon in medieval and Renaissance literature: *Parzifal* is a notable instance, and the progressive lightening and illumination of Dante's soul is obviously important to the structure of the *Commedia*. The humanist Christophoro Landino reads the *Aeneid* as an ascent of the hero from the fleshly concerns of Troy to the purity of the contemplative life symbolized by the conquest of Latium.[9] But although the question of the role of character in an epic poem was endlessly discussed by Renaissance critics, no writer on the subject with whose work I am familiar recommends the growth or education of the hero as a subject for the narrative poet. Indeed, the Aristotelian principle of consistency ("The fourth point [with respect to character] is consistency: for though the subject of the imitation, who suggested the type, be inconsistent, still he must be consistently inconsistent" [10]) and the Horatian emphasis on decorum were read as prescribing stability of character, so that one Italian critic says flatly, "The poet, once he has undertaken to imitate somebody, keeps him always and everywhere exactly the same as he was when first introduced." [11] Tasso's Godfrey is typical, I think, of the kind of heroic figure envisaged by Renaissance criticism. His victory is achieved, not through the perfecting of his nature, but through the overcoming of obstacles which prevent that nature from exercising its proper functions. These are the victories won by Spenser's gentle knights.

A gentleman or nobleman is distinguished from Everyman by the fact that he bears both a private and a public character. Spenser's use of the words *ethice* and *politice* to describe the study of these two aspects of the gentle nature suggests a reference to Aristotle's *Ethics* and *Politics,* linked treatises the first of which concerns the good man, the second the state in which men are made good. In describing the *Odyssey* and Tasso's *Rinaldo* as concerned with the

former, the *Iliad* and the *Gerusalemme* with the latter, and the
Aeneid and the *Orlando Furioso* with both, Spenser accepts the
conclusions of the criticism of his time. His own work is to deal with
"ethics," as portrayed in Arthur before he became king, "which if
I finde to be well accepted, I may be perhaps encoraged, to frame
the other part of polliticke vertues in his person, after that hee came
to be king." [12]

The division between the "ethical" and "political" realms needs
to be understood as precisely as possible, particularly because Spenser
is often accused of abandoning it in the later books. What he has
to say about Queen Elizabeth and the role she plays in the poem
helps to clarify the matter. After identifying Gloriana as "glory"
in his general intention but "the most excellent and glorious person
of our soveraine the Queene" in his particular, Spenser continues:
"For considering she beareth two persons, the one of a most royall
Queene or Empresse, the other of a most vertuous and beautifull
Lady, this latter part in some places I doe express in Belphoebe."
The poet's language indicates a familiarity with the famous legal
doctrine of "the king's two bodies," a doctrine which a recent
student describes as "a distinctive feature of English political thought
in the age of Elizabeth and the early Stuarts." [13] The doctrine is
carefully set forth in connection with a much-discussed case of the
fourth year of Elizabeth. The decision was agreed upon by all of the
crown lawyers and reported by the great Elizabethan jurist Edmund
Plowden (" 'The case is altered,' quoth Plowden") :

For the King has in him two Bodies, *viz.*, a Body natural, and a Body
politic. His Body natural (if it be considered in itself) is a Body mortal,
subject to all Infirmities that come by Nature or Accident, to the Imbecility of Infancy or old Age, and to the like Defects that happen to
the natural Bodies of other People. But his Body politic is a Body that
cannot be seen or handled, consisting of Policy and Government, and
constituted for the Direction of the People, and the Management of the
public weal, and this Body is utterly void of Infancy, and old Age, and

other natural Defects and Imbecilities, which the Body natural is subject to, and for this Cause, what the King does in his Body politic,
cannot be invalidated or frustrated by any Disability in his natural
Body.[14]

The bodies are joined in somewhat the same way as the membership
of a corporation and the corporation itself, or as humanity and
divinity in Christ.

Spenser's Gloriana was evidently intended to represent this union
and so the necessary connection between *The Faerie Queene* and
that second "polliticke" poem. Often it required great legal subtlety
to distinguish between the king natural and the king politic. But
Spenser's understanding of the difference appears most clearly, I
think, where it has been most often challenged. In the Legend of
Justice, Queen Mercilla sits surrounded by the emblems of her
regality as presiding officer at the trial of Duessa. But when the
court, the body of which she is the head, arrives at its verdict, she
does not pronounce it. She does not let "due vengeance" light upon
the culprit but

> rather let in stead thereof to fall
> Few perling drops from her faire lampes of light;
> The which she covering with her purple pall
> Would have the passion hid, and up arose withall. (v.ix.50)

The passion and tears, inevitable and praiseworthy in a virtuous
queen natural, are nevertheless the sign of an "imbecility" to which
the queen politic, by definition, cannot be subject.[15]

The theme of the noble man as "body natural" having been
determined, Spenser then chose the "historicall fiction" of Arthur
as the most suitable means by which to express it. So, at least, he
describes the process. It has been argued most ingeniously that in
fact he did not begin in this way at all, that the moral intention
came late and was superimposed upon what was originally a
romantic narrative.[16] In the absence of unambiguous independent

testimony—and it is absent—such an argument cannot be decisive. It may be that in 1589 Spenser himself would not have been able to say whether it was a dream of Britomart or a determination to benefit the commonwealth that led to the composition of his poem. But the question in any case is not directly pertinent to an attempt to understand the meaning of *The Faerie Queene,* a poem which we read, not as it evolved in the mind of its author, but as it was dedicated to Queen Elizabeth and published in 1590 and 1596.

The choice of Arthur as hero was dictated by a number of considerations, among them those which Spenser mentions: he was "most fitte for the excellency of his person, being made famous by many mens former workes, and also furthest from the daunger of envy, and suspition of present time." Certainly the myth so sedulously fostered by Henry VII that Arthur was of the line of British kings whom the Tudors claimed as their ancestors and a descendant of Vergil's Aeneas also played a part in his election. Spenser recalls the story by deriving the family of Elizabeth from his own fictions, Artegall and Britomart, and so eventually from Aeneas' grandson, Brutus. That the poet placed any credence in the tale of the ancient Trojan ancestry of the Tudors or in the reliability of Geoffrey of Monmouth as a historian is at least doubtful. In a passage in *A Vewe of the Present State of Irelande* [17] he laughs at the vanity of Englishmen who believe that Brutus was the founder of Britain, and Sidney similarly refuses to take the story seriously.[18] But Spenser was not striving for historical accuracy in *The Faerie Queene,* and for his poetic purpose the myth of the Tudor descent from Troy, used with deliberate vagueness, provided him with a useful parallel to Vergil's link between Aeneas and Augustus.[19]

It is Arthur "before he was king" who is to provide the historical fiction for the delineation of the "private morall vertues." Since the tradition told Spenser very little about Arthur before the beginning of his reign he was free to invent what actions he liked. How he would have adapted the more fully documented story of Arthur the king to an exposition of the politic virtues it is impossible to guess; perhaps he never formulated the plan except in the most general terms. It was this *Iliad* to complement Spenser's *Odyssey,* a poem about Arthur as defender and lawgiver of the commonwealth, that Milton intended to write, I think. The scattered references to his proposed "Arthuriad" suggest a matter of battling armies and national crises, the kind of matter that finds no place in Spenser's poem about Arthur as a private man. Milton, it is believed, gave up the idea of an "Arthuriad" because of his doubts as to the historicity of the accounts of ancient Britain. If so, he belonged to that considerable Renaissance school that held that a true poem must be true in its fable as well as in its meaning. Spenser did not.

The Faerie Queene does not pretend to be an account of events that actually took place. We are now so accustomed to the convention of serious fiction that it requires an effort to recapture the attitude that demanded of a writer that he account to the world for his telling of a story palpably false. The argument of Sidney's *Apology for Poetry* in fact turns upon such a justification: a poem is not a lie, he says, both because the reader is not invited to accept it as history and because it is tied to "the general reason of things" if not to "the particuler truth of things." [20] It is this "general reason of things" that Spenser claims to be expressing when he describes his work as "a continued allegory or darke conceit."

In recent years a number of brilliant studies have thrown much light on the use of allegory in the Middle Ages, and that use was surely a powerful influence upon later allegorists. But what may be said of the method of the *Divine Comedy,* the *Romance of the Rose,* and *Piers Plowman* does not necessarily apply to *The Faerie Queene.* Spenser claims as his models not those poems but the *Aeneid,* the *Orlando,* and the *Gerusalemme.* Whatever *allegory* may have meant in medieval usage, it had both a particular and a

general acceptation in the Renaissance, the particular defined in
terms of its nature, the general in terms of its function. The former
sense, that given in textbooks of rhetoric from classical times onward,
makes allegory a species of metaphor, "a Trope of a sentence, or
forme of speech which expresseth one thing in words and another
in sense." It is distinguished in its class by the fact that its literal
elements and the meanings they signify are multiple rather than
single: "In a Metaphore there is a translation of one word onely,
in an Allegorie of many, and for that cause an Allegorie is called
a continued Metaphore." [21] The examples of this figure of speech
given by the rhetoricians are derived indifferently from prose and
poetry, the Bible and secular letters. One writer offers as a typical
instance the following line from Vergil's eclogues:

Stop up your streames (my lads) the medes have drunk ther fill

explaining it thus:

As much to say, leave of now, yee have talked of the matter inough: for
the shepheards guise in many places is by opening certaine sluces to
water their pastures, so as when they are wet inough they shut them
againe: this application is full Allegoricke.[22]

Spenser's familiarity with this sense of "allegory" is obvious both
from his application to the word of the standard epithet "continued" and from his frequent use of such extended metaphors in
the poem. Amoret with her heart laid open and bleeding is a figure
of speech for a woman tormented in spirit; Orgoglio deflated like
an empty bladder tells us that pride is merely puffed up; Arthur's
dream of Gloriana is a metaphorical statement of the noble vision
of glorious achievement. These are "allegories" within the definition of the rhetoricians and there are many like them in *The Faerie
Queene*. In Spenser's practice they are often presented dramatically
or pictorially, a technique resembling that of medieval allegory and
of the allegorical pageants, paintings, and "emblems" of the Renais-

sance. But Spenser says that his poem is an allegory, not merely that there are allegories in it.

It is the functional significance of the word which is uppermost in Spenser's mind. Tasso's explanation of his *Gerusalemme Liberata* provides the gloss:

Heroical Poetry (as a living Creature, wherein two Natures are conjoyned) is compounded of Imitation and Allegory: with the one she allureth unto her the Minds and Ears of Men, and marvellously delighteth them; with the other, either in Vertue or Knowledge, she instructeth them. And as the Heroically written Imitation of an Other, is nothing else but the Pattern and Image of Humane Action: so the Allegory of an Heroical Poem is none other than the Glass and Figure of Humane Life. But Imitation regardeth the Actions of Man subjected to the outward Senses, and about them being principally employed, seeketh to represent them with effectual and expressive Phrases, such as lively set before our Corporal Eyes the things represented: It doth not consider the Customs, Affections, or Discourses of the Mind, as they be inward, but only as they come forth thence, and being manifested in Words, in Deeds, or Working, do accompany the Action. On the other side, Allegory respecteth the Passions, the Opinions and Customs, not only as they do appear, but principally in their being hidden and inward; and more obscurely doth express them with Notes (as a Man may say) mystical, such as only the Understanders of the Nature of things can fully comprehend.[23]

Beyond the vague statement that it is difficult to understand and is expressed by obscure "notes"—a "dark conceit" in Spenser's phrase —Tasso is not concerned with the method of allegory. What is salient for him is its purpose, instruction in virtue and knowledge and investigation of the inward as well as the outward motions of man, the presentation of "the Glass and Figure of Humane Life." Sir John Harington's "Briefe and Summarie Allegorie of Orlando Furioso" shows how such a definition is applied.[24] The "two principall heads and common places" of the *Orlando* he takes to be love and arms. Under the former he expounds the meaning of Rogero's adventures with Alcina, the temptation of pleasure, and Logestilla, or virtue. These episodes are "allegories" in method. But Harington also declares that "the whole booke is full of examples of men and women, that in this matter of love, have been notable in one kinde or other." His exposition of the theme of arms begins with "the example of two mightie Emperours, one of which directeth all his counsels by wisdom, learning, and Religion; But the other being rash, and unexperienced, ruined himselfe and his countrie." These are exemplary fictions, metaphoric only in the sense that their characters are types representative of many individuals, but they find place in the "generall Allegorie of the whole worke" because they contribute to its didactic purpose. Renaissance allegorical explanations of the *Aeneid* similarly depend indifferently upon the elucidation of "continued" metaphors and the lessons to be learned from the example of the characters of the story. Spenser himself makes no sharp division between allegory and fictional example: although at one point he describes his work as "clowdily enwrapped in Allegoricall devises," at another he declares the method of the *Cyropaedia* to be doctrine "by ensample" and adds, "So have I laboured to doe in the person of Arthure."

Spenser's method is in fact best disclosed by his practice. The episode of Malbecco, Hellenore, and Paridell, the principal subject of the ninth and tenth cantos of the Legend of Chastitie, serves as a convenient illustration, for while its intention is unmistakable, the rhetorical techniques employed in its telling are marvelously varied and complex. The tale begins as a fabliau of the hoariest type, a comedy involving the miserly, jealous husband, his pretty, wanton wife, and the polished seducer. Such situations are sometimes called "realistic," yet the names of the characters at once give the story a meaning beyond the particular: "Malbecco" is from the Italian *becco* which means both "cuckold" and "he-goat"; "Hellenore" and "Paridell" are intended to suggest the types of Helen

and Paris of Troy. Malbecco's passions for his money and his wife
are presented in parallel so that one becomes a figure for the other:
he is not properly entitled either to the gold or to the girl, he makes
no use of either, he keeps both locked up and fears constantly for
their loss. His blindness in one eye serves as a metaphor for the
watchful blindness of jealousy, for although he keeps up a sleepless,
self-tormenting vigil he is unable to see what goes on at his side,
the seduction of Hellenore by Paridell. That affair is described
realistically: Paridell "sent close messages of love to her at will";
metaphorically: "She sent at him one firie dart, whose hed/ Em-
poisned was with privy lust, and gealous dred"; and symbolically:
"[she] in her lap did shed her idle draught,/ Shewing desire her
inward flame to slake." That inward flame leads to the fire set
by Hellenore to cover her escape, a fire compared with the con-
flagration which consumed Troy, Helen and Hellenore, wantons
both, joying in wanton destruction. Now the realm of realism is
left quite behind, for Hellenore, having been abandoned by the rake
Paridell, finds refuge as the common mistress of a band of satyrs,
half-goats who herd goats, her sexual passion satisfied at last. And
when Malbecco tries to rescue her from her happy predicament,
the goats butt him with their horns—give him the "horn" for
which he was named at his christening. Finally, consumed by the
"long anguish and self-murdring thought" of his jealous nature he
is changed into a strange creature with crooked claws dwelling
in a cave overhung by a tremendous cliff

> which ever and anon
> Threates with huge ruine him to fall upon,
> That he dare never sleepe, but that one eye
> Still ope he keepes for that occasion   (III.x.58)

There he lives forever, so deformed "that he has quight/ Forgot he
was a man, and Gealosie is hight." [25]

This is not a story in the ordinary sense of the word, for the movement is inward, not onward. The transformations of Malbecco and Hellenore are not really transformations at all but revelations of their essence. The poet's purpose has been to lay bare the sterile, destructive, and dehumanizing power of the passions of greed, jealousy, and lust, and to this end he has made use of every means at his command, exemplary tale, myth, metaphor extended and simple, simile, symbol, and direct statement. As narrative, the episode is self-contained, for neither Malbecco nor Hellenore appears earlier or again, but the ideas which it expresses are presented in parallel and contrast, echoed, analyzed, developed, and refined throughout the Legend of Chastitie. To distinguish among the rhetorical tools by which this is accomplished is a task which would require the sharpest of definitions and infinite subtlety in applying them, for the poetical stream flows unbroken from one into another. Fortunately, it is not a task that need be undertaken here, for it offers little help in understanding the poem. Rather, the theme of discourse suggests itself through its repeated statement in a variety of forms, and once manifested reciprocally illuminates the "dark conceits" by which it is expressed.

The models for his method which Spenser acknowledges in the letter to Ralegh include only classical and Renaissance works. He is also indebted, though I think not as profoundly, to specifically medieval traditions. The influence of the morality drama is particularly evident in the Legend of Holinesse. Since the subject of many of these plays is human salvation, their protagonists meet obstacles similar to those which hinder the Red Cross Knight, and like that Knight they must be saved by God's mercy. The central characters of the later moralities—for their popularity persisted well into the sixteenth century—tend to be one or another kind of human rather than Mankind in general, and John Skelton's *Magnificence* presents a prince, or magnificent man, as its hero. The trials of Magnificence parallel those of St. George. The vicious influences playing upon him are disguised as virtuous ones, just as Duessa poses as Fidessa and Archimago as the Red Cross Knight. As a result of his delusion he falls into the clutches of Despair and is about to commit suicide when Good Hope snatches away his dagger and he is regenerated by Redress, Sad Circumspection, and Perseverance. The influence of the long tradition of medieval allegorical poetry on *The Faerie Queene* is also clear. Spenser owes to it such devices as the gardens of love, the pageant of the sins, the arms of the Red Cross Knight, the masque of Cupid, and the Blatant Beast. An analogue to the Beast occurs in a late example of such poetry, Stephen Hawes's *Pastime of Pleasure,*[26] a poem which is strikingly similar to *The Faerie Queene* in general conception, for Graunde Amour, like the Red Cross Knight, is clad in the armor described by St. Paul,[27] and his passion for La Belle Pucelle is as much a metaphor for the noble man's hunger for glory as Arthur's love for Gloriana. Indeed, the idea of a quest for a high goal as the central motive is common to medieval story of many kinds, from saints' lives to chivalric adventures. And since a heroic quest is central to the *Aeneid* also, Spenser found it appropriate to his Vergilian treatment of the matter of Arthur.

But the goal is not Prince Arthur's guide, as the hope of a new Troy is for Aeneas and the conquest of Jerusalem for Tasso's Godfrey. The narrative structure of *The Faerie Queene* is, in fact, almost frivolously weak. Having fallen in love with the Faerie Queene in a dream, like Sir Thopas in Chaucer's burlesque tale, Arthur thereafter wanders in and out of the poem, rescuing the unfortunate, contending with villains, and chasing the beautiful Florimell. Only a parenthetical observation that he wished his beloved were as fair as Florimell reminds the reader that his romantic attachment persists. The chivalric quests of the titular heroes of the successive books can be taken no more seriously. St. George sets out to kill the dragon besieging the castle of Una's parents and that is all we hear of his interest in the matter until the very end of his legend. In the second book, Guyon's task is to destroy Acrasia's Bower, but he is otherwise occupied for most of his career. Britomart is absent from much of her Legend of Chastitie and she learns of Amoret's imprisonment and undertakes to rescue her only in the eleventh canto. The story of Cambel and Triamond is merely an episode in the Legend of Friendship. Neither the rescue of Irena nor the hunt for the Blatant Beast dominates the action of the last two books, and there is no sign of a champion or of a quest in the fragmentary seventh. There are, to be sure, hundreds of stories in Spenser's poem, many of them brilliantly told, but *The Faerie Queene* is not, in any significant sense, a story. If plot is soul, the poem cannot escape damnation.

Nor does *The Faerie Queene* become coherent if the reader seeks for a continuing moral tale of which the literal one is a metaphor. In the first episode of the first book, the Red Cross Knight enters the Wandering Wood and conquers monstrous Error. When he leaves the Wood does he leave Error behind him and thereafter walk in the way of Truth? In fact, he, like all men, spends his mortal life in the Wood battling with the monster. Has he done with despair when he escapes from Despair? Even in his final struggle with the Old Dragon he wishes he were dead. Seduced by Will and Grief, he abandons Una, his true faith. If he is therefore faith-less he is nevertheless able to conquer Sans Foy, or faithlessness. Then he enters Lucifera's House of Pride in company with the figure of Falsehood, Duessa. In this state he fights with Sans Joy and is at the point of defeat when his "quickning faith" rescues him and turns the tide. This happens in Canto v, yet St. George is not reunited with his Faith until the end of Canto viii. By the dwarf's help he escapes from that House of Pride only to be caught in the arms of Duessa by the giant of pride, Orgoglio. Those commentators who read the Legend of Holinesse as a Christian's progress make a difference between Lucifera and the giant; I cannot find it in the text. To be sure, the carcasses behind Lucifera's palace are those guilty ones who have been destroyed by the sin of pride while the bodies on the floor of Orgoglio's castle are the innocents and martyrs who have been destroyed by the sinfulness of the proud. Lucifera, usurping queen of man's soul, is attended by the mortal sins of which she is chief and source; Orgoglio, usurping tyrant of the world, by a seven-headed monster whose tail reaches to the house of the heavenly gods. These are inward and outward aspects of the same sin, that sin of pretended glory which is false at its foundation, as the House of Pride is built on a hill of sand and the great Orgoglio is brought down by a blow at the leg. A recent student of *The Faerie Queene* analyzes the Legend of Holinesse into ten "acts," [28] but if the episodes are properly so described the whole is scarcely a neatly constructed play.

Confusion also besets the reader who follows the characters of *The Faerie Queene* in the hope of extracting from their adventures an orderly lesson in morality. In the course of Florimell's desperate flight from her various pursuers she escapes from a horrid spotted beast by leaping into the boat of a poor old fisherman. As she does so she loses her golden girdle. Since in later books we learn that this girdle will not stay bound about ladies who are unchaste we may be led to conclude that Florimell has now lost her maidenhead. One commentator [29] accepts this logic and finds confirmation for it in "the apparently innocent line that she was driven to great distress 'and taught the carefull Mariner to play' (III.viii.20)" although the grammar of the passage in question makes it quite clear that Fortune, who drove Florimell to distress, taught her to play the troubled mariner, not that Florimell taught the fisherman erotic games. Surely, the unhappy girl is here made to lose her girdle only in order that Satyrane may have it to bind the spotted beast, for when the fisherman attacks her she cries to heaven, and not in vain:

> See how the heavens, of voluntary grace
> And soveraine favour towards chastity,
> Doe succour send to her distressed cace:
> So much high God doth innocence embrace   (III.viii.29)

Even if God is deluded about Florimell's chastity, it seems unlikely that the poet is also. Yet later in the same canto he exclaims in her praise, "Most vertuous virgin!" The fallacy of reading Spenser's allegory rigidly becomes patent when it is observed that the Snowy Florimell, who is not enough of a virgin to wear the girdle in the fourth book (v.19–20), has somehow become able to bind it about her waist by the time of her trial in the fifth (iii.24).

Reading the Florimell story as a continued narrative leads to the suggestion that she is a kind of Proserpina, that her imprisonment beneath the sea by Proteus and her eventual betrothal to Marinell constitute a retelling of the vegetation myth.[30] Indeed, her flowery name, the icicles on Proteus' beard, and the effect of the warmth of her presence on the moribund Marinell seem to support such a reading. But if this is what Spenser intended by the story taken as a whole, he was perverse enough to addle his readers unmercifully by making the duration of Florimell's bondage not six months but seven.

If Spenser had thought that the greatness of his poem rested upon its fable and its characters, I presume that he would have been careful to make them coherent and consistent. Yet when he came to write the letter to Ralegh he described the beginning of Sir Guyon's quest in a manner directly contradicted by the text he was introducing. He brings Amoret to the point of reunion with her long lost Scudamour only to forget all about her and allow her to drop out of sight. In the space of twenty stanzas "lewd Claribell" unaccountably becomes "good Sir Claribell" (IV.ix.20, 40). Britomart's traveling companion is now called the Red Cross Knight and now Sir Guyon; it does not seem to matter to the author who he is. However Spenser came to make the errors in the first place they apparently did not bring themselves to his attention when he revised. Spenser was no hasty publisher of his works, and he must have read his manuscript through thoroughly before permitting it to assume the immortality of print. What escaped his notice must have been those matters to which he paid little attention.

Sometimes, in fact, Spenser sees fit to introduce a note of burlesque into his narration of even the most heroic and pathetic actions. This should not surprise us, for the combination of jest and earnest is a firm and ancient rhetorical tradition.[31] Spenser uses humor occasionally only, for in general he strives to maintain the mood of "beautifull old rime,/ In praise of Ladies dead, and lovely Knights." But its presence, though often overlooked, should warn us not to read his stories too solemnly. The beautiful and virtuous Serena has been captured by fierce cannibals. After consultation, they decide

> to let her
> Sleepe out her fill, without encomberment:
> For sleepe they sayd would make her battill [a] better. (VI.viii.38)

And when she is saved by her beloved Calepine she cannot say a word because she is in "so unwomanly a mood." The unhappy wife of Sir Bruin adopts a child rescued from the jaws of a bear, taking it as "her owne by liverey and seisin" [b] (VI.iv.37). The heroine Britomart meets an Amazon in mortal battle:

> The Trumpets sound, and they together run
>   With greedy rage, and with their faulchins smot;
> Ne either sought the others strokes to shun,
>   But through great fury both their skill forgot,
>   And practicke use in armes: ne spared not
> Their dainty parts, which nature had created
> So faire and tender, without staine or spot,
> For other uses (v.vii.29)

[a] battill: become fat and fleshy, as cattle do.
[b] by liverey and seisin: legal language for the delivery of property into the corporal possession of a person.

Britomart tilts with Scudamour, and

> entertaind him in so rude a wise
> That to the ground she smote both horse and man;
> Whence neither greatly hasted to arise,
> But on their common harmes together did devise.   (IV.vi.10)

After Artegall has laid low the immense giant Grantorto at the climax of the fifth book, "He lightly reft his head, to ease him of his paine" (xii.23). Lines of this kind are common enough to qualify the tone of the poem.

Sometimes it is difficult to tell whether Spenser is being intentionally witty or unintentionally absurd, for he does not signal his reader as Ariosto and Chaucer do. No one doubts that Chaucer is mocking a literary convention when he says, in his account of the battle between Palamon and Arcite, "Up to the ancle foghte they in hir blood." But when Spenser tells of the wound inflicted on the Old Dragon by the Knight of the Red Cross,

> Forth flowed fresh
> A gushing river of blacke goarie blood,
> That drowned all the land, whereon he stood;
> The streame thereof would drive a water mill   (I.xi.22)

he is thought to be straining so hard for effect that he falls into nonsense.

Perhaps he is guilty here, though he is so sophisticated a writer that one must suspect the judgment. But it cannot be argued that Spenser's hydraulic metaphor must be taken seriously because the inner meaning of the battle between St. George and the Dragon is deeply in earnest. Such an argument depends upon the critical assumption that in proper poetry the story and its significance must both tend to the same effect. If the assumption is valid—and I am not sure that it is—then Spenser's method is often quite improper. In terms of the narrative, Guyon's faint when he emerges from the Cave of Mammon can arouse only sympathy for his plight—he has been without food and water for three days and the fresh air is too much for him. But the meaning of this swoon is that Guyon is a wicked man, undeserving of his rescue by the freely given grace of God. A monster that vomits up a collection of books and papers is merely ridiculous; as a symbol of the kind of error into which man's blindness leads him she is no laughing matter. There is, to be sure, a point of contact between the mood of these tales and what they signify, for if human weakness is sinful it is also pathetic, and if human error is damnable it is also grotesque. The story may so serve to inflect its underlying meaning in much the same way as a shadow influences the perception of the object which produces it. But one does not confuse shadow and object.

One kind of inconsistency in Spenser's narrative which is sometimes ascribed to changes in his plans and to shifting literary influences upon him is, I think, an essential part of his grand design, although it has not previously been recognized as such. It is apparent and it has often been remarked that the style of *The Faerie Queene* is not uniform throughout: the Legend of Holinesse is the life of a saint, an *imitatio Christi;* the Legend of Chastitie is notably in Ariosto's manner; the Legend of Courtesie has the character of pastoral romance. If this is inconsistency, it is of the kind the reader should be led to expect from a consideration of Spenser's practice in his other poems. In *The Shepheardes Calender* he evidently strives for the greatest possible range of meter, mood, and manner. The four episodes of *Mother Hubberds Tale* are bound together by a common theme, yet each is handled differently. And the letter to Ralegh makes clear the poet's desire to avoid monotony in *The Faerie Queene:* "But of the xii. other virtues, I make xii. other knights the patrones, for the more variety of the history."

The varying styles of the successive books of *The Faerie Queene* serve a purpose of greater weight than the avoidance of monotony. The "patrons" of those books are indeed different from each other and engage in different kinds of action. This is so, I believe, because Spenser intended his readers to recognize in them reflections of particular literary models in just the same way as they recognized in the first half of the *Aeneid* an imitation of the *Odyssey* and in the latter half an imitation of the *Iliad*. The Legend of St. George echoes the saint's life in *The Golden Legend*. Sir Guyon is a hero of classical epic, like Aeneas and Odysseus. Britomart and Florimell inevitably recall Ariosto's Bradamante and Angelica. The titular story of Cambel and Triamond in the Legend of Friendship is based on Chaucer's unfinished *Squire's Tale,* and reminiscences of that story and the one told by the Knight recur frequently throughout the book. Artegall is compared directly with Hercules, Bacchus, and Osiris, the mythical founders of civilization. The adventures of Sir Calidore are of the type found in the Greek romances and imitated by Sidney in the *Arcadia*. The fragmentary Cantos of Mutabilitie clearly imitate Ovid's *Metamorphoses*. In the following chapters I shall suggest why Spenser may have thought these models suitable to the subjects which he wished to treat. It was surely in his character as a poet not only to seek the greatest variety possible in the general form of the epic poem as he understood it but also to display his technical virtuosity by imitating within the compass of a single work a great range of the literary models available to him and to his contemporaries.

This hunger for complexity, for binding into one the multiple and for revealing the multiple in the one, shows itself in almost every aspect of Spenser's technique. The stanza which he invented for the poem is itself such a various unit. Its closest relatives are the Italian ottava rima (*ababababcc*), rhyme royal (*ababbcc*), and the stanza used by Chaucer in the *Monk's Tale* (*ababbcbc*). In the first two forms the final couplet rhymes independently of the rest; the *Monk's Tale* stanza lacks a clear-cut conclusion. By adding an alexandrine rhyming with *c* to this last verse pattern, Spenser introduces metrical variety and at the same time supplies an ending which is linked to rather than separated from the remainder. Stanza is joined to stanza by frequent echoes in the first line of one of the sound or thought of the last line preceding it, and analogous links tie together canto with canto and book with book. To the amalgamation in his stanza of Italian and English forms Spenser adds a Vergilian touch by occasionally leaving a verse unfinished in the manner of the *Aeneid*.

The invention of the names of the characters of *The Faerie Queene* betrays a similar habit of mind. They are designedly derived from different languages: Pyrochles is Greek, Munera Latin, Alma Italian (and also both Latin and Hebrew), Sans Foy French, the first half of Ruddymane English. Many of the names are portmanteaus into which Spenser has stuffed a multiplicity of meanings. "Britomart," for example, reminded his Elizabethan readers of Ariosto's heroine Bradamante as well as of Britomartis, the chaste daughter of Carme whom ancient myth identified with Diana,[32] while at the same time the etymology "martial Briton" must have been inescapable, for Boccaccio calls Britomartis "Britona, Martis filia." [33]

The key ideas of his moral teaching are expressed by as many different symbols as the poet can imagine: the power which binds the disparate or antagonistic is represented by the figure of Concord flanked by Love and Hate; by the hermaphrodite Venus and the snake about her legs whose head and tail are joined together; by the lady Cambina, her team of angry lions, her Aesculapian rod, and her cup of nepenthe. These reciprocal processes of unification and multiplication reflect a conception of the universe which makes it all one, yet unimaginably rich.

There is a plenitude of story in *The Faerie Queene,* martial, amatory, and domestic; myth, fairy tale, chivalric adventure, and anecdote. Some of these tales Spenser invents himself; others he borrows from biblical, classical, medieval, and contemporary sources. He has no sense of impropriety in setting together the true and the fabulous, the familiar and the heroic, the Christian and the pagan. Rather, he seems to seek occasion to do so, either "for the more variety of the history" or to demonstrate the universality of the theme he is expounding. What he borrows he makes his own, without the slightest respect for the integrity or the intention of the original. His ruthless use of Vergil's story of Dido and Aeneas serves as an example. The words spoken by Aeneas when he meets his mother on the Carthaginian shore are put into the mouth of the buffoon Trompart, while the portrait of Venus is made over into a portrait of the Diana-like Belphoebe. Aeneas' account of his past experiences at dinner with Dido inspires Guyon's table conversation with Medina. Dido's alternate name, Elissa, is given to Medina's morose sister. Dido's dying speech is echoed by the suicide Amavia, and as Iris shears a lock of hair from the one so Guyon does from the other. Again, elements of the legendary story of St. George are used in several ways in Book I, but the incident of George's binding the dragon with a girdle and leading it about as a tame thing is transferred to Sir Satyrane in Book III. Chaucer's *Squire's Tale* provides the basis for the story of Cambel and Triamond; the episode in which a love-sick bird is restored to its fickle mate "By mediacion of Cambalus" suggests the reconciling of Timias and Belphoebe by mediation of a lovesick bird.

Sometimes Spenser seems almost perverse in the way he turns his borrowed matter upside down. The pathetic interchange between the heroine of Chastity, Britomart, and her nurse Glauce is taken almost verbatim from that between Ciris, or Scylla, daughter of the king of Megara, and her nurse Carme in a poem attributed to Vergil. This is the Carme whose daughter Britomartis once fled from the embraces of Minos into some fishermen's nets at the seashore, like Florimell in Spenser's tale. Ciris, maddened by love for the same Minos who is now besieging Megara, rapes from her father's head the crimson lock which protects the city, and so brings destruction upon her home, her kindred, and herself. She is as bad a girl as Spenser's Britomart is a good one, a symbol of lust as Britomart is of chastity. Arthur's miraculous shield is another instance of imitation by reversal. It was originally the property of Atlante, in the *Orlando Furioso*. Sir John Harington explains its principal significance:

In the shield, whose light amazed the lookers on, and made them fall down astonied, may be Allegorically meant the great pompes of the world, that make shining shewes in the bleared eyes of vaine people, and blind them, and make them to admire and fall downe before them . . . either else may be meant the flaring beauties of some gorgeous women that astonish the eyes of weake minded men.[34]

But in Spenser's version this trumpery shield becomes the divine power that destroys illusion:

> all that was not such, as seemd in sight,
> Before that shield did fade, and suddeine fall. (1.vii.35)

That which hides the truth Spenser turns into that which reveals it.

This reshaping and reworking of borrowed material is neither random nor perverse. Behind it lies the constant determination to make story the servant of intention. The process can be seen clearly in the different coloring given to parcels of a continuous narrative when it is used to express different ideas. The history of Britain from its beginnings in the judgment of Paris and the fall of Troy is told in three installments, in Arthur's book of *Briton moniments* in Book II and in Merlin's prophecy to Britomart and Paridell's account of his ancestry in Book III. Arthur reads his book in the House of Alma, the house which is well governed because each division of it obeys its mistress. The theme of this part of the history of Britain suits the house in which it is read, for it

> of this lands first conquest did devize,
>   And old division into Regiments,
> Till it reduced was to one mans governments.   (II.ix.59)

Merlin's contribution to the history is a glorious prophecy which interprets and justifies the pain of the lovesick Britomart:

> For so must all things excellent begin,
>   And eke enrooted deepe must be that Tree,
>   Whose big embodied braunches shall not lin,[c]
>   Till they to heavens hight forth stretched bee.
>   For from thy wombe a famous Progenie
>   Shall spring, out of the auncient Troian blood,
>   Which shall revive the sleeping memorie
>   Of those same antique Peres the heavens brood,
> Which Greeke and Asian rivers stained with their blood.
>
> (III.iii.22)

When it is revived by the false lover Paridell, however, that sleeping memory becomes an exemplum of the sterile consequence of the lust of his ancestor Paris:

> Troy, that art now nought, but an idle name,
>   And in thine ashes buried low dost lie,
>   Though whilome far much greater then thy fame,
>   Before that angry Gods, and cruell skye
>   Upon thee heapt a direfull destinie,
>   What boots it boast thy glorious descent,
>   And fetch from heaven thy great Genealogie,
>   Sith all thy worthy prayses being blent,[d]
> Their of-spring hath embaste,[e] and later glory shent.   (III.ix.33)

Urged by Britomart, Paridell remembers that the Trojan line did not altogether die out, for Aeneas, son of "Venus faire," after long suffering married the daughter of old Latinus:

> Wedlock contract in bloud, and eke in blood
>   Accomplished, that many deare complaind:

---

[c] lin: cease.   [d] blent: hidden from sight.   [e] embaste: debased.

> The rivall slaine, the victour through the flood
> Escaped hardly, hardly praisd his wedlock good.　　(III.ix.42)

Not Paridell but Britomart celebrates the glory of Rome, the second
Troy, and prophesies the rise of that third Troy, Britain,

> That in all glory and great enterprise,
> Both first and second Troy shall dare to equalise.　　(III.ix.44)

In the context of Prince Arthur, the history demonstrates the necessity of rule; in that of Britomart, the creativeness of love; in that of
Paridell, the destructiveness of lust.

Within *The Faerie Queene,* the unit is the book or legend. It is
made up of episodes and "allegories" invented to illuminate its theme.
Typically, a book begins with an encounter between new characters
and those of its predecessor, there is a climax or shift of emphasis
approximately at midpoint, and the end is marked by some great
action. Apart from these loose formal characteristics, however, the
constituent elements are not sequential in their arrangement; they
are truly episodic, obeying no law of progress or development.
Rather, they are so placed as to produce effects of variety and contrast. They are tied not to each other but to the principal subject
of discourse, and to this they contribute analytically or comprehensively, directly or by analogy, by affirmation or denial.

In Spenser's poem, intention is the soul, while the stories, characters, symbols, figures of speech, the ring of the verse itself constitute
the body:

> of the soule the bodie forme doth take:
> For soule is forme, and doth the bodie make.　　(*HB*, 132–33)

Only from the made body can the form be inferred, however, and
this is the kind of inference that Spenser expects of his readers. One
may take hold of the meaning of a book almost anywhere in it, for
it is everywhere there. I have entitled the chapter dealing with the
Legend of Holinesse "The Cup and the Serpent," the symbol which

Fidelia holds, but it might as well have been called "Mount Sinai and the Mount of Olives," "Sans Joy and the Promise," "Hope in Anguish," "The Burning Armor," "Una and the Veil," or "The Tree and the Living Well." Each of these in its own way and with its own inflection is a figure for the paradox of life and death which I take to be central to the book. What that paradox means and how it may be resolved Spenser never says directly. I think it was the nature of his mind rather than the fear of losing his audience that kept him from delivering his discipline "plainly in way of precepts." He could no more state his abstract theme apart from its expression in this world than a painter could draw the idea of a chair. The result is the richness of *The Faerie Queene*.

The Legend of Holinesse

THE CUP AND THE SERPENT

THE FIRST APPEARANCE of the Red Cross Knight in the Legend
of Holinesse announces the Christian paradox which is its principal
subject:

> on his brest a bloudie Crosse he bore,
> The deare remembrance of his dying Lord,
> For whose sweete sake that glorious badge he wore,
> And dead as living ever him ador'd (i.2)

Christ dying is the focus, dying and in torment, but about to pass
by means of death into life. The riddle "dead as living" develops
the theme. Superficially, the words mean only that the Knight loved
his Lord both before and after His death. But beneath this meaning
is the essential one, that Christ dead is Christ living. About the
reconciliation of death and life cluster related ideas: the life of the
body, inevitably sinful and therefore damnable by God's law, is as a
death, yet the sacrifice of the dying Christ is God's gift of a true life.
The "too solemne" sadness of the Red Cross Knight arises from the
death which is this life, his "soveraine hope" from the life which is
His death.

The theme recurs constantly throughout the first book of *The
Faerie Queene*. The portraits of Fidelia and Speranza, sister per-

sonifications of the House of Holinesse, state it emphatically. Fidelia holds in one hand a "sacred Booke, with bloud ywrit" from which she preaches heavenly documents:

> For she was able, with her words to kill,
> And raise againe to life the hart, that she did thrill.[a]   (x.19)

"For the letter killeth, but the Spirit giveth life," wrote Paul to the Corinthians (II Corinthians 3:6). As the gloss in the Geneva Bible explains it, by "the letter" is meant the Law of Moses, "a writting of it selfe dead, and without efficacie"; by "the Spirit" the New Testament, "the very vertue of God it selfe, in renewing, justifying, and saving of men. The Law propoundeth death, accusing all men of unrighteousnesse: The Gospell offereth and giveth righteousnesse and life."

In her other hand Fidelia holds

> a cup of gold,
> With wine and water fild up to the hight,
> In which a Serpent did himselfe enfold,
> That horrour made to all, that did behold;
> But she no whit did chaunge her constant mood   (x.13)

Spenser's readers would have recognized this golden vessel as the emblem of John the Evangelist, a token of the power of faith which, according to an apocryphal story, permitted him to drink the liquor of a poisoned cup without harm. The cup has a complex of associations. When the people of Israel wandered in the desert many were bitten by poisonous serpents and died, but Moses made a serpent of brass which cured those who looked upon it. The lifting up of this serpent, John says (3:14–15), is the lifting up of Christ. (John Donne describes the serpent in his family crest: "He is my death: but on the cross my cure.") [1] As Fidelia's cup is filled with wine and water, it is also the sacrament. It is therefore both death and life, no mere

---

[a] thrill: pierce.

opposites since they derive from each other and imply each other, as the word of God is the same in the death of the Old Testament and the life of the New.

Like Fidelia, the false Duessa carries a golden cup "replete with magick artes" (viii.14). From it she pours death and despair on Arthur's Squire. For the witch knows that Christ is dead, but she does not know, or pretends not to know, that He lives again:

> His blessed body spoild of lively breath,
> > Was afterward, I know not how, convaid
> And fro me hid: of whose most innocent death
> When tidings came to me unhappy maid,
> O how great sorrow my sad soule assaid.   (ii.24)

This is part of the truth, but not the whole of it. It is the killing word of Fidelia's book without the Spirit which revives. Fidelia's sister Speranza is sad too:

> > whether dread did dwell,
> Or anguish in her hart, is hard to tell   (x.14)

But her name means Hope, and she carries a silver anchor on her arm.

The story of St. John and the poisoned cup was told also of St. George. According to the version in *The Golden Legend,* after George had suffered terrible torments yet remained faithful to Christ the tyrant Dacian summoned an enchanter to put him to a further test:

The enchauntour . . . dyde take stronge venyme and medled it with wyne / and made invocacyon of the names of his false goddes and gave it to saynt George to drynke [.] Saynt George toke it and made the sygne of the crosse on it / and anone dranke it without grevynge hym ony thynge. Than the enchauntour made it moche stronger than it was tofore of venyme and gave it hym to drynke / and it greved hym no thynge. Whan the enchauntour sawe that he kneled downe at the fete of saynt George and prayed hym that he wolde make hym crysten.[2]

Because St. George was the patron of England and because he was at once a knight and a saint Spenser chose him to be the champion of the first book of *The Faerie Queene*. As a knight of some ancient time when chivalry meant truth, courage, and love, he is like the other heroes of the poem, and his adventures, like theirs, are often drawn from the stock of medieval romance. As a saint he stands alone.

No Renaissance humanist could have thought the legendary life of St. George a respectable literary model. By the sixteenth century accretions of impossible adventure and the buffoonery of village St. George plays must have rendered the story ridiculous; in fact, it had been denounced as apocryphal as early as the fifth. Spenser is able nevertheless to turn it to serious uses because such a legend, however incredible or even absurd it may be, asserts ideals of nobility, love, and holiness which are consonant with his purpose. Both a saint's life and a knight's tale tell of arduous and dangerous quests for high goals. The ways are full of pitfalls and temptations; knight and saint will stumble or be drawn from the path and suffer in consequence. The end is the end because the set task is performed, the lady won, the saint seated in heaven. In Spenser's version the end is not reached: the wedding takes place but the Knight must return to Cleopolis to finish his service to Gloriana; heaven is seen and promised but the Saint must first live out his term on earth.

The Red Cross Knight learns of his name and destiny only in the tenth canto, during his talk with the Hermit on the Hill of Contemplation. The alert reader, however, would have identified him at the very beginning not only because of his red cross and his dragon-killing mission but also because of his companions, the Princess and her milk-white lamb. According to *The Golden Legend,* a poisonous dragon besieging the city of Silene in Libya could be appeased only by the daily supply of two sheep. As sheep grew scarce, a human was substituted for one of them and eventually the sacrificial lot fell on the king's daughter. At this point St. George made his rescue, and illustrations of his fight with the dragon usually depict the princess in the background with a lamb at her feet or held by a gold string. In his opening stanzas, therefore, Spenser is reminding his readers of this familiar tableau.[3]

The allusions to the legendary life of St. George in the Legend of Holinesse have a purpose deeper than such a reminder, for both works are essentially concerned with the problem of human salvation. The first of the etymologies for the saint's name provided by *The Golden Legend* is the following: "George is sayd of geos / which is as moche to saye as erthe and orge / that is tilyenge [i.e., tilling] / so george is to saye as tilyenge the erthe / that is his flesshe."[4] For this reason the Hermit calls the Red Cross Knight "thou man of earth" and tells him that he was found as an infant in "an heaped furrow" and brought up in "ploughmans state." And the same agricultural trope is in Spenser's mind when he describes his hero in the letter to Ralegh as "a tall clownishe young man" who rests himself on the floor in Gloriana's palace because he is "unfitte through his rusticity for a better place." Indeed, as earth he is unfit for heaven. Yet he may attain it. After his overthrow by the terrible dragon, the Knight is revived and strengthened by a trickle of water flowing from the "well of life." Fradubio and Fraelissa, too, will be released from their wooden prisons when they are bathed in water of the "living well." This life-giving water is biblical, to be sure, but it is also part of the story in *The Golden Legend*. After George had subdued the dragon, the tale goes, "the kynge dyde do make a chirche there of our lady and of saynt George. In the which yet sourdeth [springs] a fountayne of lyvinge water / whiche heleth the seke people that drynken therof."[5]

In the conflict between sickness and health, between death and life, as in the dread or anguish at the heart of Speranza and in the serpent of Fidelia's cup, may be found the crisis of the soul about which the Legend of Holinesse is constructed. That crisis is reflected most brilliantly in the episode of St. George and the "man of hell, that cals himselfe Despaire" (Canto ix). Here Spenser sets knight's tale and saint's legend side by side as though to illustrate the analogy between them. After the Red Cross Knight has been freed from the castle of Orgoglio, he meets Sir Trevisan, his heart "bloud-frozen," who tells how he and a companion, Sir Terwin, fell into the clutches of Despair and how Terwin killed himself while Trevisan barely escaped the same fate. Terwin is described as the traditional lovesick youth enamored of a proud lady, his despair the despair of a rejected suitor. The tale is briefly told and neither Terwin nor his lady is heard of again. But the story serves to introduce the terrible encounter between St. George and that man of hell in which the hero is brought to the point of self-destruction. The Knight, like Terwin, is heartsick because of the failure of his hope. If Terwin dies because he cannot win a woman, St. George is almost damned because he fears that he cannot win heaven. His own sense of divine justice, of divine foreknowledge, of the joylessness and tribulation of earthly things makes him vulnerable to despair; his very Christianity betrays him to the most fearful of sins, abandonment of his hope for salvation. He is tempted to escape from his consciousness of guilt and his fear of hell by damning himself everlastingly.

The paradox which associates the desolation of despair with true Christian faith is a topic frequently discussed in the religious literature of Spenser's time. The preacher Thomas Becon wrote *A Dialogue between the Christian Knight and Satan, Wherein Satan Moveth unto Desperation, the Knight Comforteth Himself with the Sweet Promises of Holy Scripture*.[6] As in Spenser's version, the devil's principal weapons are Old Testament texts and the Knight's own conscience. Burton's *Anatomy of Melancholy* closes with a discourse on religious despair, a disease which afflicts "poor distressed souls, especially if their bodies be predisposed by melancholy, they religiously given, and have tender consciences." [7] In a sermon on faith in the elect Richard Hooker teaches:

Happier a great deal is that man's case, whose soul by inward desolation is humbled, than he whose heart is through abundance of spiritual delight lifted up and exalted above measure. Better it is sometimes to go down into the pit with him, who beholding darkness, and bewailing the loss of inward joy and consolation, crieth from the bottom of the lowest hell, "My God, my God, why hast thou forsaken me?" than continually to walk arm in arm with angels, to sit as it were in Abraham's bosom, and to have no thought, no cogitation, but "I thank my God it is not with me as it is with other men." No, God will have them that shall walk in light to feel now and then what it is to sit in the shadow of death.[8]

Although they may be thinking of different degrees or kinds of "inward desolation," Burton regards it as a disease, Hooker as a sign of health. For Spenser it is both.

The higher the ambition, the more terrible the sense of frustration. For the Red Cross Knight heaven is the ultimate goal, so that when he listens to the teaching of Fidelia in the House of Holinesse he is driven to a despairing wish for death:

> The faithfull knight now grew in litle space,
>   By hearing her, and by her sisters lore,
>   To such perfection of all heavenly grace,
>   That wretched world he gan for to abhore,
>   And mortall life gan loath, as thing forlore,
>   Greev'd with remembrance of his wicked wayes,
>   And prickt with anguish of his sinnes so sore,
>   That he desirde to end his wretched dayes:
> So much the dart of sinfull guilt the soule dismayes.   (x.21)

In his last battle with the Old Dragon he is once more brought to desperation:

> Faint, wearie, sore, emboyled, grieved, brent
>   With heat, toyle, wounds, armes, smart, and inward fire

> That never man such mischiefes did torment;
> Death better were, death did he oft desire,
> But death will never come, when needes require.   (xi.28)

The "inward fire" kindled by the flame issuing from the dragon's hell-mouth sears his body so

> That he could not endure so cruell cace,
> But thought his armes to leave, and helmet to unlace.   (xi.26)

It is the "whole armour of God" that burns him, and the "helmet of Salvation" that he cannot endure. Faith itself creates despair: "That erst him goodly arm'd, now most of all him harm'd."

The theme of hopelessness and the wish for death touches other characters of the book besides St. George and Sir Terwin. The "deadly cold" or "carefull cold" which is regularly its symptom creeps to the heart of Una, so that Arthur must rouse her from her acceptance of the defeat of the Knight by Orgoglio. Again, as the Knight is about to stab himself "The crudled cold ran to her well of life" (ix.52). Arthur's Squire is "with sudden dread dismayd" by the poison of Duessa's cup:

> Death and despeyre did many thereof sup,
> And secret poyson through their inner parts,
> Th'eternall bale of heavie wounded harts   (viii.14)

Even Despair himself, frustrated in his hope for the Knight's damnation, tries vainly to commit suicide (ix.54).

Despair is personified again in Sans Joy, youngest brother of Sans Foy and Sans Loy, the hellish counterparts of the heavenly sisters of the House of Holinesse, Speranza, Fidelia, and Charissa. He may be identified from the corresponding antinomies set up by Richard Hooker: "But infidelity, extreme despair, hatred of God and all godliness, obduration in sin, cannot stand where there is the least spark of faith, hope, love, or sanctity." [9] Hooker makes two of Sans Loy (hatred of God and obduration in sin) and two again of Charissa (love and sanctity); otherwise his analysis is the same as Spenser's.

Sans Joy's name is carefully chosen: the word *joy* means the reward of the successful lover and it also means paradisal bliss. When he first appears in the story the reader is told,

> He seemd in hart to harbour thoughts unkind,
> And nourish bloudy vengeaunce in his bitter mind. (iv.38)

"Goe guiltie ghost" he cries in his struggle with the Red Cross Knight, the struggle which reaches its climax as the hero is afflicted with "creeping deadly cold" (v.11–12).

When Sans Joy is overcome by St. George, Duessa takes his body to Hades to seek help of Aesculapius. He is "nigh voyd of vitall spright," which is just what his name implies, for the cold of despair is the antagonist of the life spirit. She carries him over the "bitter waves" of the river Acheron. The name of that river, according to Badius, is derived from the Greek words α' and χαρά, meaning "absque laetitia," i.e., Sans Joy.[10] Then they pass the ghosts condemned for their guilty lives to eternal torment, classical ghosts in a pagan hell but otherwise like those whom Despair later shows to the Red Cross Knight "painted in a table plaine":

> The damned ghosts, that doe in torments waile,
> And thousand feends that doe them endlesse paine
> With fire and brimstone, which for ever shall remaine. (ix.49)

Finally they reach Aesculapius, suffering endlessly for his presumption in reviving the dead. The physician protests:

> Is not enough, that thrust from heaven dew
> Here endlesse penance for one fault I pay,
> But that redoubled crime with vengeance new
> Thou biddest me to eeke?

To which Duessa:

> Not so (quoth she) but sith that heavens king
> From hope of heaven hath thee excluded quight,
> Why fearest thou, that canst not hope for thing,

>And fearest not, that more thee hurten might,
>Now in the powre of everlasting Night?   (v.42, 43)

This is paradox triumphant: since the life of hell is death, the incurably damned healer Aesculapius restores life to life's enemy.

A paradox is a question, not an answer. Why should St. George, elect for heaven, be subject to an overwhelming sense of guilt and inflict upon himself the torments of the damned? Why, indeed, does he not obey the terrible Law of Moses? The good and true is so beautiful and the evil and false so hideous that—granted freedom of choice—not even an unreasoning creature would stand doubtful between them. At the sight of Una's angelic face the ramping lion forgets his furious passion and licks her lily hands. A sermon of Hooker's provides the text: "Lions, beasts ravenous by nature and keen with hunger, being set to devour, have as it were religiously adored the very flesh of faithful man." [11] Like a lion rescuing a lamb from a wolf, as the poet puts it, a "rude misshapen monstrous rablement" of fauns and satyrs saves Una from the rape of Sans Loy, and like the lion the rude creatures of the wood smooth their frowning foreheads and lay aside their rustic horror to worship her sovereign beauty, kissing her feet (vi.10–13).[12] Evil, on the other hand, is so monstrous that man is inevitably repelled by it. Duessa, stripped of her disguise, is a "filthy foule old woman," her "neather partes misshapen, monstruous" (ii.41), no sooner seen than rejected. The creature in the cave of Error must hide in its darkness; it is woman above and hideous serpent below, a conflation of Satan tempting Eve and Hesiod's Echidna.[13]

The very idolatry of barbarous pagans, according to Calvin, is a sign of the attraction which Truth instinctively arouses in mankind.[14] But instinct alone is not enough. The lion is overcome by Sans Loy, whom Spenser identifies as "lawless lust": the passionate beast succumbs to uncontrolled passion. Despite Una's best efforts the satyrs remain incapable of Truth; they

worshipt her in vaine,
And made her th'Image of Idolatryes;
But when their bootlesse zeale she did restraine
From her own worship, they her Asse would worship fayn.

(vi.19)

The lesson that dominance of the passions and lack of reason impair the instinct to Truth is taught in reverse by the example of Satyrane, who is part man and part beast (as all men are). His only education consists in the taming of fierceness, of lion, bear, panther, and tiger. He learns to force the antelope and the wolf to draw together as a team, to make the wild creatures obey his behest as "a tyrans law." Unlike the lion, therefore, he governs passions and is able to fight the ungovernable Sans Loy on equal terms; unlike the satyrs, he is a rational creature and able to learn Una's "discipline of faith and veritie" (vi.21–31).

The Red Cross Knight does not suffer from the fatal defects of the lion and the satyrs. He sets out from Cleopolis fully equipped for his ultimate battle with the infernal fiend, clad in the armor of Christianity, upon his shield the red cross, emblem of his hope for salvation. With him goes Una, his true faith, leading the white lamb which represents her innocence and purity. Lagging far behind follows a dwarf carrying Una's "bag of needments." He is the faculty of reason, necessary to faith but faith's follower, not her guide. The Knight's fierce horse—his passionate nature—foams at the bit, but the Knight curbs the beast (as Satyrane curbs wild animals) and sits him fair. So accoutered and so accompanied, he is nevertheless unable to cleave to the good and to flee evil.

The reason for his failure is the veil which hides Una's sunlit face. She wears it in token of her sorrow for the imprisonment of her parents, the King and Queen of Eden, by the Old Dragon—that is, for the fall of man. In one form or another, the veil which obscures Truth, the corruption of human vision, becomes a principal theme of the Legend of Holinesse. Hooker writes:

For evil as evil cannot be desired: if that be desired which is evil, the cause is the goodness which is or seemeth to be joined with it. Goodness doth not move by being, but by being apparent; and therefore many things are neglected which are most precious, only because the value of them lieth hid.[15]

The shadows fall at the moment the quest begins. A storm drives the little party into a grove

> Whose loftie trees yclad with sommers pride,
> Did spred so broad, that heavens light did hide,
> Not perceable with power of any starre   (i.7)

In the darkness one cannot find one's way; False seems true and True seems false. The shadowy Wood of Error "seems" a fair harbor; the evil magician Archimago "seems" sagely sad; Duessa is a "seeming simple maid"; Lucifera's palace "seemd to be" the house of a mighty prince. Only when the victory is won at last Una

> in her selfe-resemblance well beseene,
> Did seeme such, as she was, a goodly maiden Queene.   (xii.8)

The light-obscuring forest which leads the Red Cross Knight astray is a strongly evocative symbol. It reminds one at once of that *selva oscura* in which Dante finds himself at the beginning of the *Inferno,* a forest usually interpreted as sinfulness or worldliness. Dante himself speaks in the *Convivio* of youth in his first age entering "the wandering wood of this life." [16] Tasso also writes of an allegorical forest, and in his explanation of the *Gerusalemme Liberata* asserts that "the Inchantments of Ismen in the Wood, deceiving with Illusions, signifie no other thing than the Falsity of the Reasons and Perswasions which are ingendred in the Wood; that is, in the variety and multitude of Opinions and Discourses of Men." [17]

There is another forest which an epic hero enters at the beginning of his adventures, a forest with an allegorical meaning about which Spenser and his contemporaries must have learned at school. It is the wood in which Aeneas meets his mother Venus in the garb of a huntress as he is seeking game to feed his shipwrecked companions. The fourth-century scholar Servius, first of Vergil's commentators, explicates the word *silva* in *Aeneid,* 1.314 as equivalent to the Greek ὕλη, and like ὕλη double in meaning: forest, specifically a wild, uncultivated forest; and the chaos of elements out of which everything is created.[18] Servius' note on the forest of the sixth book of the *Aeneid* in which the hero searches for the golden bough expands on this idea of the material congeries and gives it a moral meaning: "for by forests, darkness, and wilderness he [i.e., Vergil] signifies that in which beastliness and passion dominate." [19] The commentary of Servius remained standard throughout the Middle Ages. In Renaissance times his definition of *silva* enters the dictionaries, and Cooper defines the word not only as "wood" but also as "store of mattier digested together." The interpretation becomes the basis for the new commentaries of the humanists and is printed together with them in the great "variorum" editions of Vergil. The reference to "hyle," a term of technical philosophy, linked the *Aeneid* with Platonic tradition, a connection particularly attractive to such scholars as Landino and Badius. The Vergilian forest so becomes a figure variously signifying the material stuff upon which divine ideas are impressed, the activities of this world, the passions of the body, the earthly or fleshly aspect of human life. Badius is copious in his comment: "By *sylva,* therefore, is signified to us the diversity of influences in which it is difficult to find that golden bough." "From this wood, which is the business of this world, let us emerge into the light; the goal is the golden bough, that is *sapientia.*" "Because the stars draw us into various perturbations, it is difficult to hold always to the right way; or [an alternative explanation] the woods, that is, the passions of the body, obstruct virtue." [20]

The influence of this interpretation of *silva* upon Renaissance writers may be illustrated by a passage in the popular *Zodiacus Vitae*

of Marcellus Palingenius as translated by Barnabe Googe. Calliope
addresses the poet:

> Then Jove hys daughter deare
> With smiling lippes began to say thou rovest beyond the white,
> And art deceivd with forme of truth and shadow of the light.
> It is not easy for eche one the truth it selfe to know,
> Thys is the selfe same bow that doth amid the great wood grow,
> With trees of order thicke embraste, that misty errors hide,
> Nor ever might this golden twig of many men be spide,
> But only unto them, to whom the milke white Doves it show,
> But I of seede celestiall borne, the truth doe fully knowe [21]

Palingenius' trees "that misty errors hide" derive from the same
tradition out of which Spenser drew his forest of confusion.

A related arboreal image is presented in the second canto of the
Legend of Holinesse. St. George, in company with false Duessa,
seeks shelter from the fierce rays of the sun in the shade of two
goodly trees which cast "a calme shadowe far in compasse round."
Despite the cool pleasure of the place it is ominous ground, or so the
shepherds think:

> The fearefull Shepheard, often there aghast
> Under them never sat, ne wont there sound
> His mery oaten pipe, but shund th'unlucky ground.   (ii.28)

The trees, St. George discovers to his horror when he breaks a branch
of one of them, are the transformed Fradubio and Fraelissa, bewitched by Duessa and condemned to their evil plight until they are
bathed in a "living well."

The episode repeats in forms cunningly varied the situations and
problems the Knight has already encountered in the Wood of Error
and in Archimago's hut. The Wood is a shelter from storm, the
shade trees from the sun, and the attractive refuge, in both cases,
is a trap. When he is in the Wood St. George dares to enter the cave
of the monster despite the warnings of Una and the Dwarf; he thinks
that "Vertue gives her selfe light" and he is "full of fire and greedy

hardiment." When he is under the shade of Fradubio, that unfortunate, too, warns him to fly "Least to you hap, that happened to me heare," for he, like St. George, fell into error

> In prime of youthly yeares, when corage hot
>> The fire of love and joy of chevalree
>> First kindled in my brest (ii.35)

Both knights fall victim to the same evil spell. The magician Archimago soils Una in St. George's eyes by conjuring up a sprite in her likeness who first makes improper advances to the Knight and then is discovered in the arms of another airy creature, fashioned like a young squire,

> in a secret bed,
> Covered with darknesse and misdeeming night. (ii.3)

As Fradubio hesitates between the fair Fraelissa and the fair-seeming Duessa the witch besmirches her rival,

> raisd streight way
> A foggy mist, that overcast the day,
> And a dull blast, that breathing on her face,
> Dimmed her former beauties shining ray,
> And with foule ugly forme did her disgrace (ii.38)

Enraged by these delusions both St. George and Fradubio want to kill their lovely ladies. In the darkness of their spirits, they misdeem not only them but Duessa too, taking her to be as beautiful as she appears, deserving the devotion that her sad false tale inspires. It is hard to blame them, for Night herself, mother of falsehood, fails at first to recognize Duessa in her raiment of gorgeous gold:

> In that faire face
> The false resemblance of Deceipt, I wist
> Did closely lurke; yet so true-seeming grace
> It carried, that I scarse in darkesome place
> Could it discerne (v.27)

The error is theirs, nevertheless, and they suffer for it.

Like the Wandering Wood, the transformed Fradubio calls up

a multitude of associations. In addition to the obvious recollection of Vergil's tale of Polydorus (and Ariosto's imitation of it) Spenser here seems to allude to the biblical account of the fall of Adam and Eve. Fradubio is not Adam nor is Fraelissa Eve. But Fradubio's name appears to mean "in doubt" or "Brother Doubt" and Fraelissa's "frailty," [22] and it was the folly of Adam and the weakness of Eve that brought about the Fall. Although nothing in the story he tells justifies the explanation, Fradubio attributes his disaster to the same cause that led Adam to the first sin: "O too deare love, love bought with death too deare." And the release of this wretched pair from their imprisonment, like the release of mankind from its bondage to sin and death, must wait upon that miraculous bath which is, in one sense at least, baptism in Christ.

The human tree is a not uncommon figure for man captive to sin and therefore spiritually dead. Sir John Harington comments on Ariosto's version of the Polydorus story: "In Astolfos metamorphosis into a myrtle tree (which tree is said to be dedicated to Venus) we may note, how men given over to sensuality, leese in the end the very forme of man (which is reason) and so become beastes or stockes." [23] In the course of an entertainment at Woodstock in 1575 Queen Elizabeth heard the sound of voice and instrument issue from an oak tree. The singer called himself Despair:

> I am most sure that I shall not attaine,
> the onely good wherein the joy doth lye.
> I have no power my passions to refraine,
> but wayle the want which nought els may supply.
> > Whereby my life the shape of death must beare
> > that death, which feeles the worst that life doth feare.[24]

A painting by Mantegna portrays such a tree, its armlike branches raised in anguish while Minerva assails a horde of hideous monsters. About the tree is a scroll in Latin, Greek, and Hebrew praying for the expulsion of monstrous vice and for the return of heavenly virtue.[25] An engraving of the same period depicts a tree-man bearing the label "Virtus deserta."[26] And in a passage of biblical commentary, Bishop James Pilkington links together the metaphors of the worldly forest and the wood-bound spirit:

As long as we be wandering in the mountains and wild woods of this world, being highly minded and in great wealth or authority above others, as on an hill, we have froward proud minds, and not meet for God's house, until we be made lowly in our own sights, and fall flat down at Christ's feet, and have the rough bark of our old Adam pulled off.[27]

Bishop Pilkington's "bark of our old Adam" recalls a biblical tradition which provides authority for this figure of speech and suggests at the same time another connection between Spenser's story of Fradubio and Fraelissa and that of Adam and Eve. According to the Vulgate, when the disobedient pair heard the voice of God in the Garden they hid themselves "in medio ligni paradisi." The singular *ligni* is usually translated "of the trees" or "of the forest" but the interpretation which made Adam and Eve hide inside a *tree* or within the shade of it is a persistent one. St. Augustine takes the passage in this sense, understanding it to mean that they hid within themselves, divorcing themselves from the light of truth.[28] Sir Walter Ralegh reports (very skeptically) the conjecture of one Goropius Becanus (otherwise John Van Gorp, 1518–72) that the tree must have been a fig not only because it supplied the leaves to hide the errant couple but also because its trunk was big enough to accommodate them both. Despite his rejection of the idea (he had seen many fig trees and knew that they were only of "a mean size") Ralegh finds its proponent's allegorizing of the story "not unwitty":

The exceeding umbragiousness of this Tree he compareth to the dark and shadowed life of Man, through which the Sun of Justice being not able to pierce, we have all remained in the shadow of death, till it pleased Christ to climb the Tree of the Cross for our enlightening and redemption.[29]

Fradubio's unlucky shadow "far in compasse round" has, I think, the same significance as the "exceeding umbragiousness" of the tree in which or under which our ancestors hid themselves. Hugh of St. Victor explains that its leaves are the goods of this world, houses, vineyards, gardens, fishponds, gold, silver, jugs and pitchers, precious vessels of riches and pomp and glory. The delight of the shade which they provide, he goes on to say, is a delight in appearance, in the beauty of transitory things. And men who dwell in the shadow are unable to see the light of true sapience in comparison with which the knowledge of this world is folly.[30] The resemblance of such a tree to the Wood of Error is close indeed.

The diversity of the Wood, then, represents the rich variety of the mundane world. Because it titillates the senses it misleads, deposing reason from its rule. The Red Cross Knight enters it "with pleasure forward led/ . . . Led with delight." A similar bait leads to his desertion of Una. The first apparition of the counterfeit princess troubles his sleep with dreams of "bowres, and beds, and Ladies deare delight." When he is shown that counterfeit lady in the arms of the counterfeit squire

> he burnt with gealous fire,
> The eye of reason was with rage yblent   (ii.5)

In the prelude to his capture by Orgoglio he is carried away by the delightful song of the birds, drinks of a fountain presided over by a lazy nymph, and, disarmed, lies with Duessa "Pourd out in loosnesse on the grassy grownd." He is blinded, tricked, weakened by the temptations of the flesh, by pride, anger, lechery, sloth. But always he escapes. And Fradubio and Fraelissa, despite their doubt and frailty, are destined to escape too.

In the rescues of the Knight, reason plays a part. To Una's "No faith so fast . . . but flesh does paire" Arthur responds, "Flesh may empaire . . . but reason can repaire" (vii.41). The Dwarf makes possible the Knight's escape from the House of Pride by pointing out the heap of its victims, while his opposite, Ignaro, whose name "did his nature right aread," holds the keys that would open the locked doors of the palace of Orgoglio but is unable to use them. But a dwarf is a small man, and since the Fall the role of reason in man's salvation has been small, too. When Adam was created, Calvin declares, he was furnished "with an Understanding minde, whereby he might discerne good from evill, and right from wrong, and having the light of reason going before him, might see what is to be followed or forsaken." But as a result of the great transgression the powers of man are corrupted and he no longer enjoys the liberty to choose.[31]

A higher power must rescue benighted nature. The Knight is in desperate case in his encounter with monstrous Error in the Wandering Wood:

> God helpe the man so wrapt in Errours endlesse traine (i.18)

And God does help him, for Una cries out, "Add faith unto your force," and that new strength breaks the bands which hold him. As the literary character of the monster's spew makes clear, the Knight is here freed from the error of opinion or false belief, a kind of error which Tasso, in his exposition of the allegory of the *Gerusalemme Liberata,* distinguishes from the error of appetite, "that Temptation which layeth siege to the Power of our Desires."[32] But whether the error be emotional or intellectual—frailty or doubt—or both (for one leads to the other) man is incapable of saving himself. No ordinary means can unbind Fradubio and Fraelissa from their wooden prison.

Before the castle of Orgoglio in which the Red Cross Knight is held thrall Arthur's Squire blows his magic horn, a horn which disenchants and unmasks deceit, that unlocks the doors Ignaro is unable to open. When the Squire, poisoned by despair, falls victim to Duessa's purple beast, Arthur must come to his rescue. Arthur himself is laid low by Orgoglio's terrible club:

What mortall wight could ever beare so monstrous blow?   (viii.18)

The salvation of the Prince comes by "chance": the veil slips from his shield, the miraculous virtue of which is like that of the Squire's horn:

> all that was not such, as seemd in sight,
> Before that shield did fade, and suddeine fall   (vii.35)

Blinded by its light Orgoglio "hath no powre to hurt" and falls help-lessly at the first assault. At the end of his first day's battle with the Old Dragon the despairing Red Cross Knight stumbles into a brook flowing from the "well of life":

> For unto life the dead it could restore,
>   And guilt of sinfull crimes cleane wash away,
>   Those that with sicknesse were infected sore,
>   It could recure, and aged long decay
>   Renew, as one were borne that very day.   (xi.30)

From this immersion the Knight arises the next morning "As Eagle fresh out of the Ocean wave," strengthened for the encounter. But he is again forced back by the dragon to slip by chance ("eternall God that chaunce did guide") into a trickle of balm issuing from the Tree of Life:

> Life and long health that gratious ointment gave,
>   And deadly woundes could heale, and reare again
>   The senselesse corse appointed for the grave.   (xi.48)

And again the Knight rises fresh and strong for his last victorious battle.

I do not know whether Spenser intends us to distinguish between the water of the well of life and the balm flowing from the Tree of Life or whether these are different figures for the same thing. Revelation 22:1, 2 tells of "a pure river of water of life, cleare as chrystal, proceeding out of the throne of God, and of the Lambe. In the middes of the streete of it, and of either side of the river was the tree of life." The Geneva gloss interprets this river as "the ever-lasting grace of God." Others say that it represents "baptism, wisdom, true doctrine, *Christus irrigans,* Charity, or the Holy Spirit." [33] The "water of life" that Christ offers to the woman of Samaria (John 4:10) is explained in the Geneva edition: "This everlasting water, that is to say, the exceeding love of God, is called living, or of life, to make a difference betweene it, and the water that should be drawne out of a well." The balm is no doubt the oil of mercy that flowed, according to medieval legend, from the tree that was to bear Christ. Spenser's primary meaning is obvious: both the water and the balm are symbols of the freely given grace which saves men from the death which is damnation.

By a significant parallel, the poet enriches and complicates this theme of the rescuing power. It is Una who saves the Knight from Despair with her promise of heavenly reward:

> In heavenly mercies hast thou not a part?
> Why shouldst thou then despeire, that chosen art? (ix.53)

But when the Knight is at the point of defeat by Sans Joy, the agent of salvation is the false Duessa who cries out to his bitter enemy, "Thine the shield, and I, and all." The Knight mistakes this prom-ise as addressed to himself:

> Soone as the Faerie heard his Ladie speake,
> Out of his swowning dreame he gan awake,
> And quickning faith, that earst was woxen weake,
> The creeping deadly cold away did shake (v.12)

Deceit has duped herself and saved a soul for heaven.

Whatever the instrument, a faithful friend, a magical shield, the water of baptism, or Satan himself, it is divine grace that alone can preserve man from the consequences of his inevitable error:

> Ay me, how many perils doe enfold
> The righteous man, to make him daily fall?
> Were not, that heavenly grace doth him uphold,

> And stedfast truth acquite him out of all.
> Her love is firme, her care continuall,
> So oft as he through his owne foolish pride,
> Or weaknesse is to sinfull bands made thrall:
> Else should this Redcrosse knight in bands have dyde
> For whose deliverance she this Prince doth thither guide.   (viii.1)

For it is only through grace that the darkness of the soul can be lifted
and truth made manifest, evil seen as it is. When the Knight enters
the black cave of Error, his armor—his faith—makes "A litle glooming light, much like a shade" by which he can discern the horror of
the creature within. The monster seeks to flee

> For light she hated as the deadly bale,
> Ay wont in desert darknesse to remaine,
> Where plaine none might her see, nor she see any plaine.   (i.16)

By the light of Arthur's shield the giant Orgoglio is overthrown and
revealed to be nothing but a bladder stuffed with wind.[34] Duessa,
vanquished, is "so weake an enimy" that she may be allowed to fly,
stripped of her scarlet robe (viii.45). Even the Old Dragon who has
imprisoned Una's parents becomes in the light of St. George's victory only a bugaboo for children. At the sound of the Squire's horn,
"every dore of freewill open flew" (viii.5). By the light of Fidelia's
teaching—and only by that light—the truth which is in Scripture
becomes plain to see. His senses freed from the delusion of the forest,
from the pride and weakness that blind him, man, like Adam before
the Fall, has only to choose between beautiful reality and empty
ugliness.

Yet even after Arthur, here the emissary of grace, has torn open
the iron door in the castle of Orgoglio, the Red Cross Knight is not
free. He must be lifted up from the hellish pit in which he lies
despairing by

> constant zeale, and courage bold,
> After long paines and labours manifold   (viii.40)

He is wasted and weak, all his vital powers decayed, and the path to spiritual health is a long one. The course of treatment is described in the episode of the House of Holinesse. Brought to realization of his sinfulness by Fidelia's doctrine, the Knight desires to end his wretched days, and only Speranza is able to restore his hope of salvation. But the hope so given does not at once cure his "disease of grieved conscience." First, patience is needed, and then his "inward corruption and infected sin" must be extirpated by those "long paines and labours manifold" which drew him from Orgoglio's pit. Only when repentance has cleansed his spirit is the Knight ready for the instruction of Charissa, last and therefore youngest of the sisters:

> Full of great love, but Cupid's wanton snare
> As hell she hated (x.30)

Paradoxically, she is portrayed as a kind of Venus, sitting on an ivory throne with a pair of doves beside her, surrounded by a multitude of *putti*. Symbol of God's law, which is charity, and of His fruitful love, she is the polar opposite of Sans Loy, or Lawless Lust.

Not by charitable deeds but by God's mercy, which alone can save his soul, the Knight is led to "the highest Mount," the Mount of Contemplation from which he can see the New Jerusalem. "And hee caried mee away in the spirit to a great and an high mountaine, and he shewed me that great city, that holy Jerusalem, descending out of heaven from God" (Revelation 21:10). The poet compares this mountain with Parnassus, "On which the thrice three learned Ladies play/ Their heavenly notes"; with Sinai, on which Moses received the Law; and with the Mount of Olives, drawing his images from classical story and from the Old and the New Testaments (x.53–54). The home of the Muses is included because the highest reach of poetry is the divine vision, as Piers declares in the October eclogue, and because Plato and Vergil were able to glimpse the truth, however dimly. The hills of the Testaments are contrasted as death and life: on Sinai God wrote in bloody letters "The bitter doome of death and baleful mone," but Christ's sacred hill,

> Adornd with fruitfull Olives all arownd,
> Is, as it were for endlesse memory
> Of that deare Lord, who oft thereon was fownd,
> For ever with a flowring girlond crownd   (x.54)

As the instruction of Fidelia itself brings the Knight to the point of despair, so the glorious sight of the New Jerusalem fills him with a sense of his unworthiness:

> Unworthy wretch (quoth he) of so great grace,
> How dare I thinke such glory to attaine?   (x.62)

He begs to withdraw from life, either to spend his remaining days as a contemplative or to die at once

> That nothing may my present hope empare   (x.63)

for he knows that the joys of the earth are fruitless and its pitfalls inescapable. But now in another sense "death will never come, when needes require." Before he can attain his promised place among the saints in the holy city he must finish his appointed task on earth. And for the same reason the Knight may not accept the Sabbath of "ease and everlasting rest" offered him by Una's father after his victory over the dragon but must return to serve for six years his earthly office with the Faerie Queene.

In these passages, as in the debate between the Knight and Despair, Spenser echoes the interchange between the dreamer Scipio and his father in Cicero's *Somnium Scipionis*.[35] Scipio, who has just learned that mortal life is really death, pleads for release from it: "I pray you, most revered and best of fathers, since this is truly life, as I hear Africanus tell, why do I linger on earth? Why do I not hasten hither to you?" But his father answers, "Scipio, you and all other dutiful men must keep your souls in the custody of your bodies and must not leave this life of men except at the command of that One who gave it to you, that you may not appear to have deserted the office assigned you." The difference between the viewpoints of the pagan Cicero and the Christian Spenser is as striking as the similarity. Scipio has no sense of guilt; he merely wishes to free himself from the fetters of his body. Furthermore, as his father explains to him, an earthly life spent in service to the commonwealth is a "passport into the sky, to a union with those who have finished their lives on earth." Spenser's Christianity provides no heavenly reward for earthly work.

The Knight's immediate goal is Cleopolis, the city of mundane glory, not the New Jerusalem. In Spenser's philosophy the two cities are related as the beauty of the beloved lady to the beauty of heaven in Sonnet LXXII of the *Amoretti,* as the two first *Hymnes* to the two last: Jerusalem is heaven itself, while Cleopolis is

> for earthly frame,
> The fairest peece, that eye beholden can,

and its queen is "heavenly borne, and heaven may justly vaunt" (x.59). Since she is derived from heaven, she should be honored and served, but service to her is not a passport into the sky. Man can take no such step. When the Knight has performed his appointed task, when he has done his six years' work in this world, he must, the Hermit tells him,

> Thenceforth the suit of earthly conquest shonne,
> And wash thy hands from guilt of bloudy field:
> For bloud can nought but sin, and wars but sorrowes yield.
>
> (x.60)

Although the New Jerusalem is the sabbatical, the ultimate and sustaining vision, Cleopolis is the subject of *The Faerie Queene.*

During his absence from felicity, the Knight will sin and sin again, for blood can nought else. According to the ninth of the Thirty-nine Articles,

Original sin ... is the fault and corruption of the Nature of every man, that naturally is ingendered of the offspring of Adam; whereby man is very far gone from original righteousness, and is of his own nature inclined to evil, so that the flesh lusteth always contrary to the spirit; and therefore in every person born into this world it deserveth God's wrath and damnation. And this infection of nature doth remain, yea in them that are regenerated.

This inevitability is difficult to reconcile with a conception of the essential meaning of the Legend of Holinesse which makes of it a kind of *bildungsroman,* a story of education by experience. Such an interpretation is frequently proposed, however. The earliest example appears in a strange book by one Robert Salter which was published in 1626: *Wonderfull Prophecies from the Beginning of the Land.*[36] In biblical and apocryphal tales Salter finds a revelation of the four-fold state of man in Christ, the first being the state of nature originally derived from his parents and his conception in sin; the second, his adoption and childhood in Christ through grace; the third, his full growth and strength of manhood in Christ; the fourth, "the glory of the mans consumation" in which he rejoices "in the brightnesse of a good conscience." This "mystery" Salter says is represented in the first book of *The Faerie Queene:*

Hee there hath brought forth our Noble Saint George; at the first onely in the state of a Swayne, before his Glorious Queene cast downe on the ground [Uncouth, unkest] Unacknowne, uncared off as a dead trunke, and onely fit for the fire (as in our first Period).

But when hee had arrayed himselfe in the Armor of his Dying Lord, his presence is then become Gracious, and his person promising great things [as one for sad incounters fit]. Which hee first Passively (as in our second Period), and after Actively (as in our third Period) doth so victoriously passe through and finish; that at the length (as in our fourth Period,) hee is become altogether Impassible, whether of Assalts of the fraylety of Nature within, or Affronts of Adversaries without, as being fully possessed of that Kingdome, against which there is none to stand up.[37]

The interpretation gains some authority from Salter's claim to friendship with the poet: "The great contentment I sometimes enjoyed by his Sweete society, suffereth not this to passe me, without Respective mention of so true a friend." [38] Yet his directions provide no very clear guide to the meaning of the Legend of Holinesse. The first period which he describes takes place before the action of the book begins. Where one should draw the line between the passivity of the second period and the activity of the third I do not know; perhaps the battle with the dragon represents the latter and everything before it the former. Nor does Spenser make it clear that George is altogether "Impassible" at the close of the book.

Nevertheless, the text of the poem does provide some support for the idea that George's career represents a rising from sin to salvation, from earth to harvest. When the Knight encounters Error in the first canto, his armor casts "A litle glooming light, much like a shade"; as he prepares to do battle with the Old Dragon in Canto xi the armor fills heaven with light. At the beginning of Book II the Knight is too wary a fish for Archimago's hook; his wisdom has come by "triall of his former harmes and cares" (II.i.4). Under the instruction of Charissa,

> His mortall life he learned had to frame
> In holy righteousnesse, without rebuke or blame. (x.45)

In fact, the whole of the tenth canto, from the narrow entrance of the House of Holinesse to the height of St. George's vision at the pinnacle of the Hill of Contemplation, is the account of an upward progress, a movement reversing that from the wide gate of Lucifera's House of Pride to its deep dungeon crowded with wretched thralls.

But this upward progress is rather an analysis than a history. When Arthur raises the Knight from Orgoglio's pit he suggests the possibility of learning by experience:

> th'onely good, that growes of passed feare,
> Is to be wise, and ware of like agein.

If indeed men could be "ware of like agein" they might learn to
avoid sin and to live secure in the expectation of heaven. But Arthur's
very next words deny this optimism:

> This dayes ensample hath this lesson deare
> Deepe written in my heart with yron pen,
> That blisse may not abide in state of mortall men.   (viii.44)

The whole tenor of the Knight's adventures insists upon the point
that man is incapable of achieving his own salvation:

> Ne let the man ascribe it to his skill,
> That thorough grace hath gained victory.
> If any strength we have, it is to ill,
> But all the good is Gods, both power and eke will.   (x.1)

After his purgation by Penance, the Knight is indeed given over to
the charge of Mercy

> that he should never fall
> In all his wayes through this wide worldes wave,
> That Mercy in the end his righteous soule might save.   (x.34)

But Mercy in the form of God's grace has been at his side from the
beginning to save him whenever he stumbled. And in his final battle
with the Old Dragon he stumbles again, to be saved again.

The Knight may stumble but he will not in the end fall because
as Una tells him he is one of the chosen. It is the emphasis upon election (rather than adherence to the doctrine), the stress placed upon
human folly and weakness and divine omniscience and omnipotence,
that gives the story of the Red Cross Knight its Protestant cast and
makes it impossible to interpret in any profound sense as the history
of an education. Experience may strengthen man's reason and so
teach him to be aware of the nature of evil. But he will not always
be wary, and as the Knight admits even after his victory over the
dragon, Duessa's "wicked arts, and wylie skill" are "Too false and
strong for earthly skill or might" (xii.32). Had Spenser indeed in-

tended to represent the Red Cross Knight in the process of attaining a state of grace I can only wonder that he did not show him winning that armor of a Christian man piece by piece, the shield of faith in one episode and the breastplate of righteousness in another until, fully armed at last, he is equipped to overthrow the dragon. But the whole armor of God is already his in the first stanza of the first canto.

The Knight ends as he began, chosen for heaven, clad in the armor of Christianity, dedicated to the world's work, and prone to sin. The impression of movement in a direction remains, however, and not only because of the surface narrative pattern of knight's tale and saint's legend. The central theme gives rise to harmonics which constitute histories of accomplishment and conclusion: the story of the return of England to the true faith and the gospel of Christ's liberation of mankind.

Una is the faith of the Red Cross Knight, but she is also the daughter of the King and Queen of Eden and so the faith of mankind in its prelapsarian purity, the faith of the congregation of elected souls which is the "church" of Protestantism. Duessa is the falsehood which draws the Knight into sinful error, but she is also the daughter of the Emperor whose throne is set on the banks of the Tiber and the rider of Orgoglio's seven-headed beast, and so the false faith of Rome. The Knight is any righteous Christian, but he is also St. George the patron saint of Christian England. Archimago, the power which makes the false appear true, is in this sense the hypocrisy of Rome, a counterfeit contemplative dressed in "long blacke weedes," barefoot, knocking his breast, bidding his beads, entertaining with mock frugality, wearing the armor of the Knight and so pretending to a faith he has not. Corceca lacks divine illumination and is therefore "blind of heart"; she is a poor damned Roman Catholic wearing sackcloth, fasting incessantly, saying nine hundred paternosters and thrice nine hundred aves every day. The name of her daughter Abessa is constructed on the analogy of Duessa (*ab-*

esse) but it is also intended to suggest "abbess," unworthy recipient of the offerings made "for good intents" to the church and for the relief of the poor. Kirkrapine, the thief from whom Abessa receives these misappropriated goods, stands for the rapacity of those who take for themselves what is intended for charity; here he represents the greed of Rome.

This cast of characters plays a historical action. Its beginning is the beginning of Christianity in Britain—according to Protestant doctrine the true belief of the apostles, not the later distortion of the papacy, as Arthur learns in the House of Alma (II.x.53). St. George and England, seduced by falsehood, abandon the truth and wander in Duessa's evil ways. While St. George errs, Una must accept the "faithfull service" of the hypocrite Archimago because he pretends to be the Christian knight, and the true faith is forced to seek harbor in the hut of blind devotion. (Even Calvin does not deny to the Papists "such steps as it pleased the Lord to have remaining among them after the dissipation of the church," and Hooker is much more generous.[39]) At last, the forlorn Una and the imprisoned Knight are reunited through the agency of Arthur, instrument of God's grace and representative of the Tudor dynasty. For Una the victory over the Old Dragon which follows is the happy ending, since she is now restored

> To native crowne and kingdome late ygoe:
> Where she enjoyes sure peace for evermore,
> As weather-beaten ship arriv'd on happie shore.   (II.i.2)

The true faith will not again be exiled from England.

The victory over the dragon stands for more than the triumph of Protestantism in England. The monster holds mankind thrall, not merely one man or the English realm, and of the many who have tried to kill him only the hero succeeds. The Knight is a saint because his life is an imitation of Christ, and his wedding to Una is like the marriage of Christ and the faithful who are His Church, the marriage which is celebrated, according to the usual interpretation, in the Song of Songs. Since Christ freed the elect from their bondage to sin, the liberation of Eden from the Old Dragon is an end, though it is not the end which comes on Judgment Day.

The Church is safe home in England, and man is set free by Christ from his fleshly prison. Against the story of these achievements there moves the unremitting struggle of the chosen Christian against sin and confusion and self-doubt, stumbling constantly in the darkness, rescued as often by grace, a tale with only a promise for its ending.

The Legend of Temperaunce

PRAYS-DESIRE AND SHAMEFASTNESSE

THERE ARE NO DRAGONS, no giants in the story of the Knight of Temperaunce. Except for Acrasia's transformation of men into beasts there is little magic of any kind. The astounding illumination of Arthur's shield is replaced by the quality of his sword that keeps it from biting its owner. Archimago limits himself to telling Guyon and Braggadocchio false tales, stealing a weapon, and calming the furious Pyrochles. Darkness is gone from the atmosphere, though illusion persists: evil presents itself as desirable but the representation is artful rather than supernatural, the effect of cosmetics, not witchcraft. The glorious vision of the New Jerusalem and the promised union of St. George and Una have as their counterparts the conservative accomplishments of the defeat of Maleger and the restoration of humanity to the victims of Acrasia. The role of reason is reversed, for while the Dwarf lags after, the Palmer guides Guyon.

The change in tone is made evident by the change in the narrative matter. The Legend of Holinesse is the life of a saint, but the Legend of Temperaunce is the story of a hero like Aeneas. Not only are the episodes of the Cave of Mammon and the voyage to the Bower of Bliss obvious imitations of classical epic but the whole book is marked by Vergilian and Homeric allusion and reminiscence.

Amavia dies like Dido and a lock of her hair, like Dido's, is cut off as a token. At dinner with Medina, Guyon (like Aeneas) tells where he has been and where he is going. Trompart addresses Belphoebe in the words used by Aeneas to his mother Venus. Furor is bound with the hundred chains required to bind him in the *Aeneid*. Acrasia owes much to Ariosto's Alcina, Tasso's Armida, and Trissino's Acratia, but she, like her Italian models, is essentially Circe.

This classical ambience has a meaning similar to Dante's election of Vergil to guide him through the realms of Hell and Purgatory. The subject of temperance had been investigated and analyzed by the great "authorities" of the ancient world. Although their conclusions had been derived from a study of the laws of nature and without the aid of Christ's teaching and sacrifice, they were nevertheless valid in a limited way. The Christian virtues of faith, hope, and charity are of course essential to salvation, but the pagan virtues of justice, prudence, temperance, and fortitude are not only consonant with Christianity but its necessary adjuncts, as in effect the law of nature is part of the law of God. St. Augustine had declared Plato a great teacher, St. Thomas Aquinas had leaned heavily on the authority of Aristotle, even Savonarola and Calvin found lessons of value in the writings of the ancients. Renaissance interpretation made of the *Aeneid* and its Homeric models and indeed of the body of classical story a library of moral instruction from which the good man was to take what was useful to him, as the Jews took wealth from the plague-stricken houses of the Egyptians. To this library Spenser turned in his attempt to set forth the problem of the control of the complex human organism. But he turned to it as a Christian, giving to his principal character a guide who is a Palmer, one who has been to Jerusalem.

The name of the champion of this legend recalls Guy of Warwick of the chivalric romances, perhaps with reference to the Warwick associations of the family of Dudley. It also echoes the theme-word

"guide"—"God guide thee, Guyon," says the Red Cross Knight.[1]
Its choice seems to have been dictated by other associations as well.
Gehon, one of the four rivers of the Garden of Eden, was traditionally interpreted to signify the virtue of temperance since "it cleanses
the worthless body and quenches the fire of the vile flesh." [2] Even
more directly pertinent is the etymology of the word "gyon" which
appears in the *Golden Legend* life of St. George. Among the interpretations there given for the saint's name is the following: "George
may be sayd of gera: that is holy, and of gyon that is a wrasteler,
that is an holy wrasteler. For he wrasteled with the dragon." And
surely both Guyon and Arthur are wrestlers in the Legend of
Temperaunce: they wrestle as St. Paul says the armed Christian
must, not with flesh and blood, but with Furor, with Maleger, with
Impotence and Impatience, with their own natures.[3]

The scene of the struggle lies in the heart of man. In the "goodly
Parlour" which is the heart of the House of Alma, Prince Arthur
and Guyon meet a company of ladies engaged in a variety of
pursuits:

> Diverse delights they found them selves to please;
>   Some song in sweet consort, some laught for joy,
>   Some plaid with strawes, some idly sat at ease;
>   But other some could not abide to toy,
>   All pleasaunce was to them griefe and annoy:
>   This fround, that faund,[a] the third for shame did blush,
>   Another seemed envious, or coy,[b]
>   Another in her teeth did gnaw a rush:
> But at these straungers presence every one did hush.   (ix.35)

Although each of these ladies has her own quality, they are divided
by "But other some" into two categories, those who seek pleasure
and those who reject it. From among them the Prince and Guyon
select two damsels, both fair and both sad, though sad in different
ways. Arthur's choice holds in her hand a branch of the poplar,

---

[a] faund: cringed(?).   [b] coy: reserved, disdainful.

sacred to Hercules; she is dressed in purple and gold and her name is Prays-desire. To his blunt inquiry as to the nature of the trouble which clouds her beauty ("Or doen you love, or doen you lacke your will?") she answers, half-disdainfully, that her pensiveness, like that of Arthur himself, is caused by her "great desire of glory and of fame." The Prince, touched to the quick, changes color and turns hot and cold with passion. Meanwhile Guyon has been talking to the other lady who carries on her fist

> the bird, which shonneth vew,
> And keepes in coverts close from living wight   (ix.40)

She wears a blue garment "close round about her tuckt." Her beauty, too, is marred by strong passion, but she has no word of answer to the knight's query. Alma must explain:

> Why wonder yee
> Faire Sir at that, which ye so much embrace?
> She is the fountaine of your modestee;
> You shamefast are, but Shamefastnesse it selfe is shee.   (ix.43)

And like Arthur Guyon blushes in self-realization.

In the fortress of Medina, Sir Guyon has already met representatives of the two companies of Alma's parlor. One is Perissa, "poured out in pleasure and delight," excessive in wine, dress, and "of her love too lavish" (ii.36). Elissa, in contrast, scowls and frowns and enjoys nothing. Perissa's paramour is the bold Sans Loy; Elissa's is Sir Huddibras, an angry malcontent. Their names are significant. "Elissa" is derived from a Greek word meaning "deficient" (ἐλάσσων), and it is also a name for Vergil's Dido, the suicide whose dying speech is echoed by the suicide Amavia. Huddibras, according to Spenser's own history of ancient Britain, was a king who added nothing to his territories (x.25). "Perissa" is Greek for "excessive" (περισσός); Sans Loy is the lustful one of the Legend of Holinesse. These sisters and their mates are constantly at odds with each other and with

Medina who strives as constantly to keep them in order. She presides
over the dinner party to which Guyon is invited as guest:

> Betwixt them both the faire Medina sate
>   With sober grace and goodly carriage:
>   With equall measure she did moderate
>   The strong extremities of their outrage;
>   That forward paire she ever would asswage,
>   When they would strive dew reason to exceed;
>   But that same froward twaine would accourage,[e]
>   And of her plenty adde unto their need:
> So kept she them in order, and her selfe in heed.   (ii.38)

If there is no war at the table, it is only because Medina is an excellent
hostess.

Spenser's words "forward" and "froward" define the relationship
between Prays-desire with her poplar branch and dress of purple
and gold on the one hand and Shamefastnesse with her secretive
bird and close-tucked costume on the other. One is swayed by a
positive motive, a seeking for the goods of life; the other is impelled
negatively to retirement, avoidance, grief. The lust of Sans Loy, the
pleasure-seeking of Perissa, the soaring ambition of Arthur all belong
to the former category; the morose anger of Elissa and Huddibras
and the shamefastness of Guyon to the latter. The forward or outward tendency is consonant with human nature, for as Aquinas puts
it:

Man's life consists in a certain movement, which flows from the heart
to the other parts of the body: and this movement is befitting to human
nature according to a certain fixed measure.

. . . Consequently those passions that imply a movement of the appetite in pursuit of something, are not repugnant to the vital movement as
regards its species, but they may be repugnant thereto as regards its
measure: such are love, joy, desire and the like; wherefore these passions
conduce to the well-being of the body; though, if they be excessive, they
may be harmful to it.[4]

---

[e] accourage: encourage.

The froward, withdrawing tendency, in contrast, is inimical to life not only when it is excessive but in its very nature. Again Aquinas:

> On the other hand, those passions which denote in the appetite a movement of flight or contraction, are repugnant to the vital movement, not only as regards its measure, but also as regards its species; wherefore they are simply harmful: such are fear and despair, and above all sorrow. . . .
>
> . . . Nevertheless, fear and anger cause very great harm to the body, by reason of the sorrow which they imply.[5]

These are the ideas that Spenser expresses directly in the opening stanza of his sixth canto:

> A harder lesson, to learn Continence
>> In joyous pleasure, then in grievous paine:
>> For sweetnesse doth allure the weaker sence
>> So strongly, that uneathes it can refraine
>> From that, which feeble nature covets faine;
>> But griefe and wrath, that be her enemies,
>> And foes of life, she better can restraine;
>> Yet vertue vauntes in both their victories,
> And Guyon in them all shewes goodly maisteries.

This dichotomy of the passions [6] is one of the principal motifs of the Legend of Temperaunce. It appears in the pairing of Cymochles, addict of the Bower of Bliss, and his self-destructive brother Pyrochles; in Maleger's hag attendants, Impatience and Impotence; in lustful Dan Faunus and the fleeing nymph of Diana. The doors of Richesse and Sleep flank the gate of Hell in Mammon's realm. Of the souls suffering eternal punishment in the Garden of Proserpina only two are described: one is Tantalus, still coveting the drink and the fruit of the gods; the other is Pilate, still trying to wash the hands that by doing nothing delivered Christ to the crucifixion. In his last attempt at the virtue of Guyon, Mammon urges:

> Thou fearefull foole,
> Why takest not of that same fruit of gold,

> Ne sittest downe on that same silver stoole,
> To rest thy wearie person, in the shadow coole. (vii.63)

The golden bait is at once the fruit of the Tree of Knowledge, the prize of Hercules, the symbol of the victories of Atalanta and Cydippe, and the award of Paris whose judgment gained

> faire Helen for his meed,
> That many noble Greekes and Trojans made to bleed. (vii.55)

The stool represents the rock upon which Theseus sat bound forever, condemned to "endlesse slouth," as Spenser tells us in the Hell episode of Book 1 (v.35).

Although "vertue vauntes in both their victories" it is the froward tendency, that which goes counter to life's desires, which is the easier to restrain. Its unnatural, subversive quality Spenser figures in a variety of ways. Furor is described as "a man of mickle might" but unable to govern his power, so that

> oft himselfe he chaunst to hurt unwares,
> Whilst reason blent [d] through passion, nought descride

In fighting with him, Guyon furiously overthrows *himself*:

> Him sternely grypt, and haling to and fro,
> To overthrow him strongly did assay,
> But overthrew himselfe unwares, and lower lay. (iv.7, 8)

The burning Pyrochles (from $\pi\hat{v}\rho$, fire, and $'o\chi\lambda\acute{e}\omega$, disturb) is defeated by tactics which the poet compares to those used by a lion against a wrathful unicorn. The unicorn's own horn betrays him to his death:

> He slips aside; the whiles that furious beast
> His precious horne, sought of his enimies,
> Strikes in the stocke, ne thence can be releast,
> But to the mighty victour yields a bounteous feast. (v.10)

The self-destructiveness of Pyrochles and the unicorn is a fatal defect in battle, but it implies a more profound overthrow, that of the

[d] blent: blinded.

nobler element of the reason by the baser passions. Guyon lectures Pyrochles:

> Losse is no shame, nor to be lesse then foe,
> But to be lesser, then himselfe, doth marre
> Both loosers lot, and victours prayse alsoe.
> Vaine others overthrowes, who selfe doth overthrowe.   (v.15)

But Pyrochles will not be taught. He begs Guyon to release the hag Occasion though Guyon warns him that her "freedome shall thee turne to greatest scath." Inevitably, his passion leads him to suicide:

> I burne, I burne, I burne, then loud he cryde,
> O how I burne with implacable fire,
> Yet nought can quench mine inly flaming syde,
> Nor sea of licour cold, nor lake of mire,
> Nothing but death can doe me to respire.   (vi.44)

He can only respire—breathe again—by not breathing. And "in despight of life" Pyrochles finally dies at his own request.

As the froward passion ranges in its manifestations from modesty and inactivity to grief, wrath, and suicide, so the forward passion takes such various forms as hunger for money, power, and glory; desire for ease, beauty, and sexual satisfaction. Philotime or "love of honor" was created "most heavenly faire in deed and vew," the poet says, but fell from that high estate and must now rely for her attraction to mankind upon an artfully contrived beauty. She is a foil for Gloriana; the difference between them is manifest in the shouldering, unscrupulous crowd trying to climb aloft on her great golden chain of Ambition. Of Richesse Mammon says,

> Loe here the worldes blis, loe here the end,
> To which all men do ayme, rich to be made:
> Such grace now to be happy, is before thee laid.   (vii.32)

Cymochles (from κῦμα, wave, and 'ὀχλέω, disturb) is discovered in Acrasia's Bower of Bliss wading "in still waves of deepe delight," very like Antony entranced by Cleopatra. There is a pleasant grove in the Bower

> full of the stately tree,
> That dedicated is t'Olympicke Jove,
> And to his sonne Alcides, whenas hee
> Gaynd in Nemea goodly victoree   (v.31)

—the poplar, that is, emblem of Prays-desire and symbol of the "warlike prayse" this Cymochles has gained throughout the world. But the dominant features of the garden are found "on the other side," the entrapping "wanton Yvie," murmuring sounds of a gentle stream, delicious odors, loose ladies and lascivious boys. The temptations are ease, artificial beauty ("art striving to compaire/ With nature"), and sexual delight. Cymochles' temptress, Phaedria (the Greek means bright, glittering), is glossed by Spenser as "immodest mirth" leading to "loose desire"—she is therefore the servant of Acrasia (ἀκρασία, incontinence). At first sight there appears to be an irreconcilable opposition between the pursuit of warlike fame and delicious ease. But Phaedria proclaims herself kin to Philotime:

> Another warre, and other weapons I
> Doe love, where love does give his sweet alarmes,
> Without bloudshed, and where the enemy
> Does yeeld unto his foe a pleasant victory.   (vi.34)

Mars is Cupid's friend,

> And in Amours the passing houres to spend,
> The mightie martiall hands doe most commend.   (vi.35)

Cymochles' *dolce far niente* on Phaedria's pleasant island, like Mars's dallying with Venus, is not a denial of his hunger for renown but, according to the temptress, a fulfillment of it.

In the course of their final voyage to the beautifully evil Bower of Bliss Guyon and the Palmer encounter a whole range of those forward temptations to which Cymochles and his kind are prey. They pass the gulf which gorges itself on the greedy, the Rock of Reproach which wrecks those who spend their substance on wanton

joys and intemperate lusts, the delectable wandering islands where
Phaedria makes her home, an isle inhabited by a maiden who tries
to affect Guyon's heart "with fraile infirmity" by arousing a foolish
pity, and mermaids, so transformed because they strove for mastery
with the Muses themselves, who invite the weary travelers to their
port of rest from troublous toil. There are representatives of the
froward passion, too, like the "fatal birds"

> Such as by nature men abhorre and hate

But the dominant theme is the motive which appears to coincide
with man's nature.

The Bower itself is an artfully wrought snare for that nature:

> One would have thought, (so cunningly, the rude,
>> And scorned parts were mingled with the fine,)
>> That nature had for wantonesse ensude [e]
> Art, and that Art at nature did repine;
> So striving each th'other to undermine,
> Each did the others worke more beautifie;
> So diff'ring both in willes, agreed in fine: [f]
> So all agreed through sweete diversitie,
> This Gardin to adorne with all varietie. (xii.59)

In this strange world, nature and art are mingled in so unnatural
a fashion that nature seems to imitate art instead of the other way
about. Although the two are here essentially in conflict they are at
one in an effect of apparent harmony. Everything entices, embraces,
reaches out to trap,

> boughes and braunches, which did broad dilate
> Their clasping armes, in wanton wreathings intricate, (xii.53)

an ivy-vine, fashioned of purest gold, whose "lascivious armes" creep
low, the "locks and waves" of a maiden's hair. A wanton rises from
the fountain to display "her two lilly paps aloft"; soon after someone sings of the Virgin Rose,

[e] ensude: followed.   [f] fine: end.

> how sweetly shee
> Doth first peepe forth with bashfull modestee,
> That fairer seemes, the lesse ye see her may;
> Lo see soone after, how more bold and free
> Her bared bosome she doth broad display   (xii.74)

The verse itself winds in and out:

> For all that pleasing is to living eare,
> Was there consorted in one harmonee,
> Birdes, voyces, instruments, windes, waters, all agree.

> The joyous birdes shrouded in chearefull shade,
> Their notes unto the voyce attempred sweet;
> Th'Angelicall soft trembling voyces made
> To th'instruments divine respondence meet:
> The silver sounding instruments did meet
> With the base murmure of the waters fall:
> The waters fall with difference discreet,
> Now soft, now loud, unto the wind did call:
> The gentle warbling wind low answered to all.   (xii.70, 71)

These interwoven enticements are the web into which man is led
by his natural inclination.

He is led to his death as a man. The governor of the Bower of
Bliss has the name of Genius, man's tutelary spirit, the power which
generates and maintains his life. As such, he should be the representative of Nature in man, or Nature's priest, as Jean de Meun has
it. But this Genius is not the true god:

> this same was to that quite contrary,
> The foe of life, that good envyes to all,
> That secretly doth us procure to fall,
> Through guilefull semblaunts, which he makes us see.   (xii.48)

To be drawn into Acrasia's garden is not to follow a natural impulse
but to take a trick for the truth, to worship life's enemy in the guise
of its guardian. So Cymochles covertly watches the dissolute damsels,
and "them deceives, deceiv'd in his deceit." The lover of Acrasia,

stirred by his concupiscent nature, loses his manhood to become the beast into which that nature has been turned.

When it dominates, therefore, the forward passion loses its difference from the froward and becomes, as Aquinas says, repugnant to the vital movement. Its victims destroy themselves, as the froward Pyrochles does. Cymochles may not call for his own death, but resolved to "dye with honour and desert of fame" throws himself at Prince Arthur and is killed. Not only Impotence but Impatience also commits suicide. There is a dreadful fiend lurking behind Guyon, ready to tear him into a thousand pieces whether he reaches for the golden fruit or sits on the silver stool:

> If ever covetous hand, or lustfull eye,
> Or lips he layd on thing, that likt him best,
> Or ever sleepe his eye-strings did untye (vii.27)

For the consequence of surrender to either kind of passion is death.

The destructive nature of the passions appears most clearly in the story of Amavia and Mortdant, a tale which bears a relationship to the Legend of Guyon like that of Fradubio and Fraelissa to the Legend of St. George. Acrasia's deceitful charm identifies the unfortunate pair:

> *Sad verse, give death to him that death does give,*
> *And loss of love, to her that loves to live*
> *So soone as Bacchus with the Nymphe does lincke* (i.55)

Mortdant, whose name means "death-giving," is overcome by his lust and falls victim to the life passion. "Amavi[a]," I think, imitates Vergil's Amata, the suicide mother of Lavinia: "I have loved" for "the loved one." Like Amata, Amavia is overcome by the grief that torments her; she gives death to herself. As Sir Guyon explains, the paradox is the inevitable result of the spiritual insurrection in which raging passion "Robs reason of her due regalitie":

> The strong it weakens with infirmitie,
> And with bold furie armes the weakest hart;

The strong through pleasure soonest falles, the weake through
        smart.   (i.57)

The bold, forward male dies through weakness; the weak, retiring
female through bold fury. This weakening of the strong and strength-
ening of the weak is a deadly burlesque of Medina's wise management.

The same mockery is intended by the mysterious last line of
Acrasia's charm. Upton long ago noted a passage in the *Aethiopica*
of Heliodorus in which "Bacchus" means wine and "the nymphs"
water. Spenser no doubt learned the expression from that liveliest
of schoolbooks, Erasmus' *Colloquia* ("Convivium Profanum"): "Est
quidem igneus suapte natura Bacchus, sed adhibitis Nymphis red-
ditur temperantior." Spenser inverts the meaning. Acrasia's confusion of wine and water results not in temperance but in death,
for her name in Greek signifies not only "incontinence" but also
"bad mixture." When the strong spirit is made feeble or the weak
one inflamed the result is destruction.[7]

The "death" that follows the victory of the passions is multiple
in meaning. It is intended literally in the examples of Amavia and
of Phedon who, overcome by fury, kills his faultless beloved Clari-
bella. It is spiritual death in the instance of Gryll who prefers pig-
gishness to manhood. And it is a symbol of the consequence of
the sin of the flesh to which all men are heir. The inheritance of
Ruddymane, child of Amavia and Mortdant, is a mark of blood
which the pure spring will not wash off, token of God's hatred of
"bloodguiltinesse." The word is an uncommon one, the only precedent for Spenser's use listed in the *Oxford English Dictionary*
occurring in Coverdale's translation of the fifty-first psalm in which
David prays that his soul be cleansed of his guilt for the murder
which was the result of his lust. As Guyon buries Ruddymane's
father and mother, he "devoutly" swears:

> Such and such evill God on Guyon reare,
> And worse and worse young Orphane be thy paine,

If I or thou dew vengeance doe forbeare,
Till guiltie bloud her guerdon doe obtaine (i.61)

That "vengeance" is the destruction of Acrasia's Bower of Bliss and the restoration of their humanity to its victims—the subduing, therefore, of the passionate flesh.

In the opening lines of *Love's Labour's Lost* the King of Navarre addresses his friends as "brave conquerors"

That war against your own affections
And the huge army of the world's desires.

This is the war that Arthur wages against the forces of Maleger in defense of the House of Alma. The enemy's army is disposed into twelve companies, five to attack the senses, the openings into the soul, seven poised against the main gate. Perhaps the seven denote the seven sins, though there is nothing but their number to suggest it. Because they assail the castle directly they may represent the froward passions, the manifest "foes of life," in contrast to those that deceive the weakness of the sensitive flesh. But in the account of this army there is little emphasis upon the distinction between the two kinds of passion. The five companies attack Alma both with "open force" and with "hidden guile." "Lawlesse lustes" (the family of Sans Loy), here principally the desire for Beauty and Money, try to effect entry through the bulwark of the Sight. Hearing, Smell, and Taste are subjected to the assaults of reproach and flattery, foolish illusion and idle superfluity. The most terrible of the attackers are those who assail the sense of Touch,

Armed with darts of sensuall delight,
With stings of carnall lust, and strong effort
Of feeling pleasures

And the raising of this company to its bad eminence among the enemies of Alma foreshadows Guyon's conquest of Acrasia's Bower at the conclusion of the book.

In Alma's well-ordered house, which Maleger seeks to overthrow, the passions are not dead but obedient to control. The population of her parlor—her heart—pays homage to its mistress, as Elissa and Perissa submit themselves to the wise judgment of Medina. Spenser has little to say about how this state of things may be maintained. Guyon's Palmer is "his most trusty guide":

> when strong passion, or weake fleshlinesse
> Would from the right way seeke to draw him wide,
> He would through temperance and stedfastnesse,
> Teach him the weake to strengthen, and the strong suppresse.
>
> (iv.2)

This is more readily taught than done, since the passions are not easy to bridle. Like Guyon's horse, that

> despysed to tread in dew degree,
> But chaufd and fom'd, with courage fierce and sterne,   (iii.46)

they require a determined master. The rebellious horse will take advantage of every occasion to overthrow his rider. And Occasion is unavoidable. As the unfortunate Phedon says,

> what man can shun the hap,
> That hidden lyes unwares him to surpryse?   (iv.17)

Guyon himself is led into rash and furious attack upon the Red Cross Knight by the machinations of Archimago, and he is tricked into leaving the Palmer and sailing off with the frivolous Phaedria. The only advice that the Palmer can give is to fight down the passions before they grow unmanageably strong. In the early sixteenth century, somebody scribbled in the margin of a manuscript of Latin decretals, "yf Luste or anger do Thy mynde assaylle,/ Subdu ocasyon and Thou shalte sone prevaylle." [8] In obedience to this precept, Guyon binds Occasion in order to overcome Furor. His reason recovers its dominance before he comes to blows with St. George. Though Phaedria misleads him at first, his wisdom and wariness force her to ferry him back to firm land.

There is something of nobility in Pyrochles and Cymochles, so that one feels that if they had palmers to guide them they might have subdued Occasion and so escaped their fates. But Gryll and Braggadocchio are of a different quality. Even when Gryll's eyes are opened he prefers to remain a pig. Braggadocchio, who vaunts himself above the moon and withdraws into abject fear by turns, is by nature incapable of self-control. He is unfit to ride a horse:

> In brave pursuit of honorable deed,
>> There is I know not what great difference
>> Betweene the vulgar and the noble seed,
>> Which unto things of valorous pretence
>> Seemes to be borne by native influence;
>> As feates of armes, and love to entertaine,
>> But chiefly skill to ride, seemes a science
>> Proper to gentle bloud; some others faine
> To menage steeds, as did this vaunter; but in vaine. (iv.1)

What the poet means by "the vulgar and the noble seed" is a matter best left for discussion in connection with Book vi, where it looms large. For the present it is enough to recognize that there are natures such that they can no more govern a spirited horse than their own passions.

There is little in the argument up to this point that Aristotle or Plato would have found alien. The emphasis upon rational control of the complex human organism, the distinction between two kinds of passion depending upon pleasure and pain, the condemnation of extremes in human behavior, and the equation of manly self-government with nobility of character are all part of the stock of classical moral philosophy. Like Spenser, Aristotle asserts that "it is harder to fight with pleasure than with anger." [9] Both Plato and Aristotle agree that there are some, like Gryll and Braggadocchio, who cannot be taught virtue. Only those are capable of becoming Guardians of the Republic who after being brought "into terrifying situations and then into scenes of pleasure" resist every "enchantment" and remain guardians of themselves.[10] Aristotle concludes his *Ethics* by admitting that the "many" are unteachable because they live by passion and "do not by nature obey the sense of shame, but only fear, and do not abstain from bad acts because of their baseness but through fear of punishment."[11] Something of the doctrine of the mean appears in the Legend of Temperaunce: the general concept of moral excess and deficiency as well as the name Medina suggests it. Strictly Aristotelian is the narrow passage between the Gulf of Greed and the Rock of Reproach (the miser-glutton and the spend-thrift-wastrel) which Guyon must negotiate on his voyage to Acrasia's Bower. Plato's souls, like the victims of Mammon and Philotime, expiate their surrender to their passions in an afterlife. Even the bloody-handed babe, though he is not of the progeny of the Greek philosophers, would have seemed familiar to them, for not only the Bible but Euripides also says, "The gods visit the sins of the fathers upon the children."[12]

Nevertheless, what interests Aristotle in the *Nicomachean Ethics* does not, for the most part, concern Spenser.[13] He has nothing to say here about happiness as the goal of virtuous behavior or the contemplative life as the highest happiness. The subjects of justice and friendship have no place in this book, nor is any clear distinction made between the morality of voluntary and involuntary actions. Even the idea of the mean as the path to virtue receives little attention. Medina is rather a moderator of the passions and a peacemaker than a virtue lying between two vices, as courage lies between cowardice and foolhardiness. Perhaps her name derives from *medens,* healer, as well as from *medium*. Guyon is not the middle brother of Pyrochles and Cymochles, and Hell, not Heaven, is located between Richesse and Sleep. It is the rational way, rather than the middle way, to which the poet points. Furthermore, Spenser takes a number of positions directly contrary to Aristotle. The philosopher holds that "people who fall short with regard to pleasures and delight in them less than they should are hardly found, for such insensibility is not human," [14] but half the company of Alma's parlor belong to this category. He would have disapproved of Guyon's shamefastness, for he considers the sense of shame appropriate only to youth.[15] And he doubts Solon's doctrine that no one should be called happy while he lives and concludes, "Why then should we not say that he is happy who is active in accordance with complete virtue and is sufficiently equipped with external goods, not for some chance period but throughout a complete life?" [16] But, for Spenser, no man since Adam could conceivably live his life "in accordance with complete virtue." Herein lies the critical difference between the pagan philosophers and the Christian poet. The chosen spirits of the *Ethics* and the *Republic* are capable of learning to subordinate their passions and so to become their own guardians. Neither Guyon nor Prince Arthur is always able to do so.

Guyon's dark moment comes after his escape from the underworld. On reaching the surface he falls into a deathlike swoon, an easy prey to Pyrochles and Cymochles who are about to strip him of his armor when Arthur fortunately intervenes. The story of his rescue is introduced by the following stanza:

> And is there care in heaven? and is there love
> In heavenly spirits to these creatures bace,
> That may compassion of their evils move?
> There is: else much more wretched were the cace
> Of men, then beasts. But O th'exceeding grace
> Of highest God, that loves his creatures so,
> And all his workes with mercy doth embrace,
> That blessed Angels he sends to and fro,
> To serve to wicked man, to serve his wicked foe. (viii.1)

That this passage refers directly to Guyon is clear since we are next shown a blessed angel guarding the helpless knight. The angel turns over the charge of his safety to the Palmer but adds:

> Yet will I not forgoe, ne yet forget
> The care thereof my selfe unto the end,
> But evermore him succour, and defend
> Against his foe and mine   (viii.8)

Guyon then, like all of humanity, is a "wicked man."

But of what is he guilty? He has just won his way through a terrible adventure in the realms of Mammon and Philotime, steadfastly rejecting every temptation. It has been suggested that his error lies in visiting the underworld at all, in succumbing, that is, to the sin of idle curiosity.[17] But curiosity does not lead to the enticements of wealth, power, and worldly glory, the principal subjects of this episode. These, the bait of the forward passion, Guyon is constant in refusing. It is his very constancy in fighting off the temptations of Mammon and Philotime that has as its consequence the inglorious swoon which follows. For three days, he has been without

> food, and sleepe, which two upbeare,
> Like mightie pillours, this fraile life of man,
> That none without the same enduren can.   (vii.65)

Mammon is constrained to bring him back to the world of nature,

> But all so soone as his enfeebled spright
> Gan sucke this vitall aire into his brest,
> As overcome with too exceeding might,
> The life did flit away out of her nest,
> And all his senses were with deadly fit opprest.   (vii.66)

In rejecting wealth, power, and glory, he has denied himself food, sleep, and vital air. His victory over the ambitious forward passion has made him a victim of the ascetic froward, and he lies impotent and without hope, save for the intervention of the angel. The fault is human, but no less a fault. When Cymochles accuses Guyon of "guilt" Prince Arthur must admit the charge:

> Indeed (then said the Prince) the evill donne
> Dyes not, when breath the bodie first doth leave,

> But from the grandsyre to the Nephewes [g] sonne,
> And all his seed the curse doth often cleave,
> Till vengeance utterly the guilt bereave:
> So streightly God doth judge. (viii.29)

The evil done was Adam's, and no man can escape its consequence.

That this is the right interpretation of Guyon's fall is made clear by the fall of Arthur, which has precisely the same character, reversed. The Prince is able to resist the froward passion, for the magic of his sword keeps it from injuring its owner. His danger lies on the other side, in his attraction to Prays-desire. As Guyon can cope with the temptations of Mammon, Arthur is able to defeat Maleger (from *aeger,* sick), the power enveloped in symbols of death: "like a ghost he seem'd, whose graveclothes were unbound," his look as pale and wan as ashes, his skin "as cold and drery as a Snake,"

> Upon his head he wore an Helmet light,
> Made of a dead mans skull, that seem'd a ghastly sight. (xi.22)

The association of sickness and the froward passion is traditional. Cooper defines *aeger:* "Sicke: sorrowfull, pensiffe, or heavie." [18] Maleger fights while going away, deriving his strength from his weakness; like the suicide Amavia he is "most strong in most infirmitee." He is the power of Impotence. But as Arthur is occupied in binding a lame hag who is named Impotence, her mate Impatience catches hold of him and throws him over backward. The Prince is as helpless as Guyon was after his victory over the temptations of the underworld, and as desperately in need of divine aid:

> So greatest and most glorious thing on ground
>   May often need the helpe of weaker hand;
>   So feeble is mans state, and life unsound,
>   That in assurance it may never stand,
>   Till it dissolved be from earthly band.
>   Proofe be thou Prince, the prowest man alive,

---

[g] Nephewes: grandson's.

> And noblest borne of all in Britayne land;
> Yet thee fierce Fortune did so nearely drive,
> That had not grace thee blest, thou shouldest not survive.   (xi.30)

And to point the parallel with Guyon even more clearly, the rescued Arthur is compared to "one awakt out of long slombring shade." Since suppression of the forward passion implies dominance of the froward, it follows as a corollary that the converse is true. Man is therefore wicked because he cannot avoid wickedness, and his state remains unsound "Till it dissolved be from earthly band."

This is a far cry from the optimism which finds it possible for some men to achieve virtue by the exercise of their reason. Guyon must be rescued by Arthur, Arthur by the Squire. There is no conflict, then, between the teaching of the Legend of St. George and the Legend of Sir Guyon, as there is no conflict between the heroes themselves. Reason plays a greater part in the control of the passions than in the discovery of truth, but in neither is it decisive. If Arthur and Guyon are to win in the end it is because they, like St. George, are divinely graced. Nor is it possible to judge finally of their victory, for

> after death the tryall is to come,
> When best shall be to them, that lived best.   (i.59)

Under constant siege by the forces of Maleger, the House of Alma, goodly in its workmanship but built of that "Aegyptian slime" of which the ill-fated Tower of Babel was constructed, is also unsound of state. The analogy between the self-government of a virtuous individual and the management of a well-ordered commonwealth is one of the oldest ideas in political literature. The constitution of Alma's dwelling presents the figure of a community to illustrate the nature of the individual. It is first described as a geometric abstraction, part circle, part triangle, and part rectangle, the circle "set in heavens place" and "immortall, perfect, masculine," the triangle "imperfect, mortall, foeminine," the rectangle "twixt them both." Although much study has been devoted to the stanza in which this description occurs, its precise meaning and Spenser's source for it remain obscure.[19] For the present purpose it may suffice that in accordance with the traditional view the poet asserts man to be a composite of diverse faculties, the highest heavenly in its circular perfection, the lowest earthly in its triangular imperfection. The tour through the castle taken by Arthur and Guyon with Alma as guide shows that these faculties are to be identified with the rational, vegetative, and appetitive souls of classical analysis. Since the House is at peace within, however threatened by the evil powers without, each part of it fulfills its proper function, the cooks in the kitchen busily concocting, the ladies and gentlemen of the parlor displaying their various emotional tendencies, the counselors in the turret sagely advising. Spenser handles the description of the House and its workings lightly and wittily, though most of his commentators appear to have missed the humor: the portcullis (or nose) is "Neither unseemely short, nor yet exceeding long"; when the front gate is opened "no man might it close" (this is a woman's castle);[20] out of the rear gate the waste is thrown "privily." But the purpose of the description is serious enough. All of the inhabitants obey their mistress Alma and pay homage to her.

"Alma" means "soul" in Italian (from the Latin *anima*). In Hebrew, "Almah" is "virgin," as Spenser could have learned from Cooper's *Thesaurus,* and this meaning he seems to insist upon:

> Alma she called was, a virgin bright,
> That had not yet felt Cupides wanton rage   (ix.18)

The name is also associated with the Latin adjective *alma* (nourishing, fruitful).[21] In his imitation of Lucretius' hymn to Venus in the tenth canto of Book IV Spenser renders the words *alma Venus,* "Great Venus, Queene of beautie and of grace." The Alma of the castle has the same qualities:

For she was faire, as faire mote ever bee,
And in the flowre now of her freshest age;
Yet full of grace and goodly modestee,
That even heaven rejoyced her sweete face to see.   (ix.18)

As the beauty and grace of Venus make it possible for her to bind
together the disparate elements of this world so Alma's loveliness
gives her the power to make of man's complex body what it should
be according to its true nature, something "faire and excellent,/
. . . Whiles it is kept in sober government."

In the rear chamber of the topmost story of the House of Alma—
the chamber of Memory—Arthur and Guyon are given two great
volumes to read, the Prince an account of ancient Britain, the Knight
a history of Fairyland. These histories serve a double purpose. In
terms of the particular subject of the Legend of Temperaunce, they
show that firm control by the rightful governor of the diverse,
struggling constituents of the organism is as necessary for the commonwealth as it is for the individual. In terms of *The Faerie Queene*
as a whole, they make the point that a gentle man's striving for
honor is like Britain's quest for national fulfillment, and as the
trials of Aeneas reflect the struggle for Roman glory which cul-
minates in Augustus so the adventures of Arthur and his knights
mirror the troubled history of Britain and England to its high
achievement in Elizabeth.

The book of *Briton moniments* which Arthur reads recounts the
history of the island from its foundation by Brutus to the time of
Uther Pendragon, Arthur's father. Spenser draws his material chiefly
from Geoffrey of Monmouth, but he has consulted a number of
other historians and though he invents little he selects, combines,
and changes emphasis freely.[22] His story begins with the land a
savage wilderness inhabited by

hideous Giants and halfe beastly men,
That never tasted grace, nor goodnesse felt   (x.6)

After the conquest and pacification of Albion by the descendants of Aeneas the history becomes a medley of foreign and internecine warfare, treachery, turmoil, and rare intervals of peace. Many of the rulers are subject to the forward passions: Locrine falls victim to "vaine voluptuous disease"; the sons of Ebranck apply their minds "to praise, and chevalrous desire"; Bladud, expert in magic arts, attempts "to excell/ The reach of men." A climax is reached seven hundred years after the foundation when the dynasty of Brutus comes to an end, the realm torn into factions through discord. At this point, when there is left

> no moniment
> Of Brutus, nor of Britons glory auncient (x.36)

there arises Donwallo, "a man of matchlesse might," who reunites the shattered fragments of the kingdom, makes laws which keep secure

> the Traveilers high way,
> The Churches part, and Ploughmans portion (x.39)

and brings into civil government "Now one, which earst were many." Not long after the reign of Donwallo turbulence begins again, and the tale breaks off on that tragic note.

But it is not the end of the story in Spenser's conception. He tells us that Arthur's book

> of this lands first conquest did devize,
> And old division into Regiments,
> Till it reduced was to one mans governments. (ix.59)

A new Donwallo must appear, surely Arthur himself. And the promised resolution of the fragmented kingdom by the government of one foreshadows the conclusion of that other book, *Antiquitie of Faerie lond,* which Sir Guyon has been reading. This history is in the sharpest contrast to *Briton moniments.* There is no treason, no rebellion in it, only glorious achievement: the foundation of

Cleopolis and the building of the crystal palace Panthea, the golden
wall, and the bridge of brass.[23] The early rulers of Fairyland are
hidden in this unreal distance, but the mist is dispelled when "After
all these Elficleos did rayne." For Elficleos is unmistakably the first
of the Tudors, Henry VII, and the book ends with the succession
of his granddaughter, the reigning queen: "Long mayst thou Glorian
live, in glory and great powre." As long as Gloriana lives, the realm,
like Alma's house, preserves its God-given order and fulfills its
destined purpose.

Gloriana, Spenser tells us in the letter to Ralegh, stands for Queen
Elizabeth in her public person. In her private character as "a most
vertuous and beautifull Lady" the Queen is represented by Belphoebe—the beautiful Phoebe, or Diana. Like Diana the Huntress—
and like Vergil's Venus—Belphoebe bursts upon the scene a goddess
in beauty and nobility, graced with the finest gifts both of art and
of nature:

> And whether art it were, or heedlesse hap,
> As through the flouring forrest rash she fled,
> In her rude haires sweet flowres themselves did lap,
> And flourishing fresh leaves and blossomes did enwrap.   (iii.30)

Her elaborately pleated silken smock and her costly gilded buskins
clothe her beauty of body and spirit. Her dress falls below her "ham"
(the back of the knee) but leaves her legs free for nimble movement.
Here art and nature are in essential and perfect harmony, not the
superficial, false concord of the Bower of Bliss. Belphoebe's foils
are the empty vessels Trompart and Braggadocchio, Trompart who
dresses his speech in the words of the heroic Aeneas on his meeting
with his mother Venus, Braggadocchio who rides a hero's horse and
usurps the part of a most valiant knight. It is her task, therefore, to
distinguish between the true and the false paths to honor:

> Who so in pompe of proud estate (quoth she)
> Does swim, and bathes himselfe in courtly blis,

> Does waste his dayes in darke obscuritee,
> And in oblivion ever buried is
>
> Ne can the man, that moulds in idle cell,
> Unto her happie mansion attaine   (iii.40–41)

Neither the forward way of court life nor the froward way of retirement will serve:

> Abroad in armes, at home in studious kind
> Who seekes with painfull toile, shall honor soonest find.   (iii.40)

Belphoebe's every word speaks nobility, for she is in complete command of herself. She quells the savage beasts and masters passions. In her private as well as in her public person she is queen. And unlike Alma and the rest of humanity, her reign is secure.

The Legend of Chastitie

MAID AND WOMAN

THE ACTION OF the first canto of the *Orlando Furioso* has barely got under way when Ariosto breaks into the apostrophe: "Oh gran bontà de'cavallieri antiqui!" At a comparable point in the Legend of Chastitie Spenser echoes the exclamation: "O goodly usage of those antique times." Then the beautiful Florimell bursts on the scene, fearfully flying from a "griesly Foster" breathing out beastly lust, her hair like the tail of a comet signifying dread. She is Spenser's version of Ariosto's Angelica. The poet borrows from the *Orlando Furioso* elsewhere in *The Faerie Queene,* and there are other sources for the Legend of Chastitie, such as the pseudo-Vergilian *Ciris* I have already mentioned (p. 142). But the flavor of Ariosto is as pervasive here as that of classical epic in the Legend of Temperaunce. The narrative method itself imitates that of the Italian poem: the canvas is filled with characters, stories are broken off at their critical moments, no single hero is allowed to dominate the action.

"Mine author," writes Sir John Harington on the subject of the *Orlando,* "applyeth his whole worke, and referreth all the parts thereof to two principall heads and common places; namely *Armes* and *Love.*" [1] Ariosto begins his poem with a parody of Vergil; he

will sing "Of Dames, of Knights, of Armes, of loves delight." And
Spenser's book is of "dames" and of their love, whether delightful
or not: of Britomart, Florimell, Venus and Diana, Amoret and
Belphoebe, Malecasta and Hellenore. Although Britomart is absent
from many of the cantos she is properly the champion of the Legend
because what happens to others while she is off the stage concerns
the problems which this virgin-lover, or any true lover, must face.
For Britomart is the exemplar not only of chastity but of sexual love
also; she is both maid and woman, Diana and Venus, Belphoebe
and Amoret. She alone is unmoved by the attractions of Florimell
and Marinell; it is she who pierces the flaming barrier that separates
Amoret from Scudamour.

The qualities which make possible her victory are paradoxically
opposed:

> For she was full of amiable grace,
>   And manly terrour mixed therewithall,
>   That as the one stird up affections bace,
>   So th'other did mens rash desires apall,
>   And hold them backe, that would in errour fall;
>   As he, that hath espide a vermeill Rose,
>   To which sharpe thornes and breres the way forestall,
>   Dare not for dread his hardy hand expose,
> But wishing it far off, his idle wish doth lose.   (i.46)

These are precisely the qualities which characterize the lady of the
Amoretti:

> For with mild pleasance, which doth pride displace,
>   she to her love doth lookers eyes allure:
>   and with sterne countenance back again doth chace
>   their looser lookes that stir up lustes impure.   (xxi)

On the one hand she has the nature of woman-Venus: graceful,
amiable, gentle, mild; on the other the nature of maid-Diana: virtuous, strong, courageous, modest, desirous of honor. The Legend of

Britomart is concerned with a union of these opposed natures. Because a true love depends upon a joining of affection and chastity, Venus and Diana go together in search of the errant Cupid.

Although the maiden goddess scoffs at the ways of her sister and her "gay sonne," she is won by "sugred words and gentle blandishment" and agrees at last to help find him. They find, not Cupid, but twin girls newborn of Chrysogone who has been miraculously impregnated by the rays of the sun. Venus adopts the younger, Amoret; Diana the elder, naming her after herself:

> These two were twinnes, and twixt them two did share
> The heritage of all celestiall grace.
> That all the rest it seem'd they robbed bare
> Of bountie, and of beautie, and all vertues rare.   (vi.4)

Amoret is brought up by Venus in "true femininitee" and is taught "all the lore of love, and goodly womanhead" (vi.51). Diana entrusts Belphoebe to a nymph "To be upbrought in perfect Maydenhed" (vi.28). But the twins are not simple abstractions, just as Guyon is not Shamefastnesse nor Arthur Prays-desire. If Amoret's specialty is affection, it is "chaste affectione" (vi.52). Though Belphoebe is the paragon of chastity, hers is a "fresh flowring Maidenhead" (v.54), not a dry and barren one. She is not only chaste but also womanly:

> so curteous and kind,
> Tempred with grace, and goodly modesty,
> That seemed those two vertues strove to find
> The higher place in her Heroick mind:
> So striving each did other more augment,
> And both encrease the prayse of woman kind,
> And both encrease her beautie excellent;
> So all did make in her a perfect complement.   (v.55)

Belphoebe makes her home in a pleasant glade deep in the wooded mountains. It is planted with myrtle, sacred to Venus, and with laurel, the meed of heroes, and in these trees

> the birds song many a lovely lay
> Of gods high prayse, and of their loves sweet teene,
> As it an earthly Paradize had beene $\qquad$ (v.40)

A richly furnished pavilion set within it is fit to delight great princes. The two stanzas devoted to the description of Belphoebe's dwelling serve as a token balance to the elaborate portrayal of the Garden of Adonis, Venus' principal earthly resort and the scene of Amoret's upbringing.

This is a garden delightful to the senses, however thorny to the interpreter. Paradises of this kind are a standard device of the literature of the Middle Ages and the Renaissance, with a tradition reaching back to Homer's garden of Alcinous. Typically, there is a wall about them, with a gate and porter. There grow many flowers, gay and odoriferous, watered by a brook or a fountain, and many kinds of trees from whose branches sing many kinds of birds. It is forever spring, and a soft breeze blows. Often this delightful place, the *locus amoenus,* is identified with the Garden of Eden, or taken as a symbol for it. Whether for this reason, because of the fecundity and variety of its natural ornaments, because the classical god of gardens was Priapus, or because of the etymology which connected *amoenus* and *amor,*[2] the beautiful garden came to be especially associated with the theme of love and generation. Perhaps, too, the association depends upon the myth told by Diotima in Plato's *Symposium* of the conception of Love in the Garden of Zeus on the birthday of Aphrodite.

The most famous English representative of the genre before the time of Spenser is the garden of Nature in Chaucer's *Parlement of Foules*. Spenser knew it well, for he imitated from it the catalogue of diverse trees which opens the description of the Wood of Error in the Legend of Holinesse. Chaucer's garden has all the usual apparatus. Cupid lives there, accompanied by such attendants as perform the Masque of Cupid in Spenser's House of Busirane. There is a temple in the garden in which the god Priapus stands "in sovereyn place" holding his "sceptre" in his hand, and in a dark, private corner Venus and her "porter" Richesse disport themselves. The wall is decorated with broken bows "in dispit of Dyane the chaste." Presiding over all is the goddess Nature, in such array "as Aleyn, in the Pleynt of Kynde,/ Devyseth"—an evasion which Spenser imitates in the Cantos of Mutabilitie (vii.9). All this is prelude to the great debate as to who is to marry the "formel egle" that Nature holds on her hand. Since the parliament is made up of representatives of every ornithological estate, the problem of the individual lover is seen in the context of society as a whole, and, since Nature is president, of universal laws and forces.

When Spenser described the Garden of Adonis (and Acrasia's Bower of Bliss) he was making use of a figure anciently associated with sexual passion and the reproductive force of nature. The Mount of Venus which is in the middle of the Garden, like the temple in Chaucer, is full of sexual symbols:

> There stood a stately Mount, on whose round top
> A gloomy grove of mirtle trees did rise,
> Whose shadie boughes sharpe steele did never lop,
> Nor wicked beastes their tender buds did crop,
> But like a girlond compassed the hight,
> And from their fruitfull sides sweet gum did drop,
> That all the ground with precious deaw bedight,
> Threw forth most dainty odours, and most sweet delight.
>
> And in the thickest covert of that shade,
> There was a pleasaunt arbour, not by art,
> But of the trees owne inclination made,
> Which knitting their rancke braunches part to part,
> With wanton yvie twyne entrayld athwart,
> And Eglantine and Caprifole emong,
> Fashiond above within their inmost part,
> That neither Phoebus beams could through them throng,
> Nor Aeolus sharp blast could worke them any wrong.   (vi.43-44)

And there is "a strong rocky Cave . . ./ Hewen underneath that Mount." Spenser here imitates, of all things, Ovid's description of Gargaphie, the chaste retreat where Actaeon stumbles upon the naked Diana:

> There was a valley there, all dark and shaded
> With pine and cypress, sacred to Diana,
> Gargaphie, its name was, and it held
> Deep in its inner shade a secret grotto
> Made by no art, unless you think of Nature
> As being an artist. Out of rock and tufa
> She had formed an archway, where the shining water
> Made slender watery sound, and soon subsided
> Into a pool, and grassy banks around it.[3]

In Spenser's version, if not in Ovid's, *mons veneris,* the arbor, and the rock-bound cave beneath in which the boar is imprisoned are as anatomical as the scepter of Priapus.[4] In the Garden of Adonis, though not in the Bower of Bliss, this sexuality justifies itself because it is an essential element of Nature's grand scheme of maintaining the life of this world.

In a general sense, the subject of the Garden of Adonis is not dissimilar from that of the *Parlement of Foules.* But Chaucer's poem, perplexing though it may be for other reasons, does not present the philosophical tortuosities of Spenser's paradise. The interpretation of this philosophy is one of the principal cruxes of *The Faerie Queene.* Much of the attempt to elucidate it has been devoted to identification of its sources and the system to which it belongs. Here if anywhere such an effort is necessary to our understanding of the poem, for the myth of the Garden certainly depends upon some systematic theory of generation. Scholarship on the subject has revealed analogues to Spenser's philosophy in such various places as an allegorized Ovid, the *Zodiacus Vitae* of Palingenius, the poems of the twelfth-century Alain de Lille and Bernard Sylvestris, St. Augustine's literal commentary on Genesis, the writings of

Ficino, Leone Ebreo, Louis Le Roy, Boethius, Claudian, Lucretius, Empedocles, Plotinus, and Plato. This multiplicity of analogues is not mere chaos; it is proof that Spenser's ideas belong to an ancient tradition the roots of which reach into classical Greece, no doubt even deeper in time, its branches bearing fruit in Rome and in medieval and Renaissance Europe. It is not, I think, possible to identify Spenser's "source." Perhaps there was none in the usual sense of that term—one book or a few to which the poet turned as authority. But the accumulation of learning that has been expended on the subject allows at least an approximate understanding of the philosophy of Spenser's stanzas.[5]

In the interpretation that follows I shall make reference primarily to the *Enneads* of Plotinus and to *De genesi ad litteram* of St. Augustine, a work heavily influenced by Plotinus. Recognition of the significant relevance of these authorities is primarily the result of the researches of Professor Josephine Waters Bennett. Although attempts have been made to account for Spenser's meaning by reference to "easy" and popular works like Arthur Golding's translation of Ovid's *Metamorphoses,* they have, in my opinion, proved successful only in a vaguely general way. Whether or not Spenser himself waded deeply in neo-Platonic lore, the fact remains that the Plotinian tradition supplies the gloss which most clearly illuminates the meaning of the Garden of Adonis.

That Garden is "the first seminarie/ Of all things, that are borne to live and die,/ According to their kindes" (vi.30). These seedthings which generate all of animate nature are not souls in the Christian sense; they are "babes," "shapes," or "forms" which grow without tending, infinite in number, fit "t'indew" fish, fowl, beasts, men, and creatures unknown,

> And yet remember well the mightie word,
> Which first was spoken by th'Almightie lord,
> That bad them to increase and multiply   (vi.34)

Pondering upon the book of Genesis in which that injunction is given, St. Augustine found a way of accommodating the Mosaic account of creation and the Garden of Eden with a doctrine adumbrated by Plato and developed by the Stoics and the neo-Platonists, particularly by Plotinus. He wished to rationalize the biblical narrative of creation by a single act of all of this world, including life yet unborn: "The Lord God made the earth and the heavens. And every plant of the fielde, before it was in the earth, and every herbe of the field, before it grew" (Genesis 2:4-5). He had to explain, too, how living things might be spawned spontaneously by the action of the sun upon the mud of the Nile and how from time to time there appeared upon the earth monstrous creatures never seen before. And he had to account for the manifest fact of the continuity of species: somehow when God created the first pair of lions He must thereby have created the race of lions to the dissolution of the world.

The key to the solution of these difficulties Augustine discovered in what the pagan philosophers called "seminal reasons" (also translated "reason-principles"). An authority on the philosophy of Plotinus defines them: "La raison séminale, c'est la force qui contient à l'état indivisible tous les caractères qui se développeront séparément et successivement dans un être vivant; elle est comme la loi de développement de cet être." [6] These entities exist in a realm—Ficino's commentary on Plotinus calls it *seminarium mundi* [7]—intermediate between divine unity and rest on the one hand and mundane multiplicity and changefulness on the other:

That which resumes all under a unity is a Principle in which all things exist together and the single thing is All. From this Principle, which remains internally unmoved, particular things push forth as from a single root which never itself emerges. They are a branching into part, into multiplicity, each single outgrowth bearing its trace of the common source. Thus, phase by phase, there is finally the production into this world. [8]

Since these seminal reasons, which are generated by the One and generate the Many, include whatever has been, is, or will be on earth, Augustine was able to identify them with the unearthly plants and herbs that God made and so provide a rational explanation for the Mosaic narrative.[9]

The life of Spenser's Garden is free of the bitter darkness of the mundane:

> For here all plentie and all pleasure flowes,
> And sweete love gentle fits emongst them throwes,
> Without fell rancor or fond gealosie;
> Franckly each paramour his leman knowes,
> Each bird his mate, ne any does envie
> Their goodly meriment, and gay felicitie.   (vi.41)

Plotinus' realm of seminal reasons, too, is brighter and happier than our world, both because it is closer to the One and because it is free of Matter, "the fallen sediment of the Higher Order, bitter and embittering":[10]

And we must remember that what comes from the supernals . . . does not enter into the recipients as it left the source: fire, for instance, will be duller; the loving instinct will degenerate and issue in ugly forms of passion. . . . Any such quality, modified at best from its supreme form, deteriorates again within ourselves: things of any kind that approach from above, altered by merely leaving their source, change further still by their blending with bodies, with Matter, with each other.[11]

Spenser's "babes" are happy because they are not yet clothed with "sinfull mire"; they have not yet entered the world of "Fleshly corruption."

The presence of Time in the Garden proves that the creatures in it are not the immutable ideas of Plato. They "grow" in their seminary, though of their own accord, and without the help of a gardener. Although the world outside is described as "chaungefull" there is change in the Garden too; Time troubles its creatures:

> wicked Time, who, with his scyth addrest,
> Does mow the flowring herbes and goodly things,
> And all their glory to the ground downe flings,
> Where they doe wither, and are fowly mard (vi.39)

Yet Time's way in the Garden is not his way in the ordinary world, for

> There is continuall spring, and harvest there
> Continuall, both meeting at one time (vi.42)

and the trees blossom and fruit at once. It is inconceivable that a Platonic idea should beg for incarnation, yet "a thousand thousand naked babes" crowd around Genius, the porter of the Garden,

> which doe require
> That he with fleshly weedes would them attire:
> Such as him list, such as eternall fate
> Ordained hath, he clothes with sinfull mire,
> And sendeth forth to live in mortall state,
> Till they againe returne backe by the hinder gate. (vi.32)

Indeed, if the Garden is so delightful a place, why should they wish to leave it?

Plotinus explains their restlessness. In his scheme, the seminal reasons are the product of the radiation of unitary Intellect upon Soul, so that the Soul of the World, the *anima mundi* from which this terrestrial world derives, is conceived of as being filled with the multiplicity of forming ideas which give identity to material stuff. In this Soul resides the generative impulse, the nature-principle. Ficino's commentary describes the growth of the seeds: "Thus not with care, not with labor, but with effortless ease, just as the things of nature grow from nature itself, so the seeds of nature grow from intelligence." [12] As Plotinus says, the seed is stirred to unfold its potentialities, to separate itself, that is, from the unity which is its source:

For the Soul contained an unquiet faculty, always desirous of trans-lating elsewhere what it saw in the Authentic Realm, and it could not bear to retain within itself all the dense fullness of its possession.[13]

Spenser says of the "babes" in the Garden that Time is "their troubler." A modern student of the problem of time in Plotinus and St. Augustine uses the same term: "Ce trouble éternel, c'est précisé-ment le temps." [14] As the seminal reasons mediate between the One and the Many, so time in the *anima mundi* lies between the eternity of the unchanging and the mutability of the mundane:

Eternity, we have said, is Life in repose, unchanging, self-identical, always endlessly complete; and there is to be an image of Eternity—Time—such an image as this lower All presents of the Higher Sphere. Therefore . . . over against that Movement of the Intellectual Soul there must be the movement of some partial phase; over against that Identity, Unchangeableness and Stability there must be that which is not constant in the one hold but puts forth multitudinous acts; over against that One-ness without extent or interval there must be an image of oneness, a unity of link and succession.[15]

The seed of the individual gathers within it the entire life cycle. This is the "unity of link and succession" which Spenser suggests in making the time of the Garden, not the traditional perpetual spring, but a simultaneous spring and fall, growth and decay.

Despite the overpowering generative impulse which urges the "babes" to corporeal existence, they do not of themselves dictate the time of their incarnation. Spenser's Genius sends out into mortal state "Such as him list, such as eternall fate/ Ordained hath." Plotinus here refers to Plato:

According to Plato lots and choice play a part (in the determination of human conditions) before the Spindle of Necessity is turned; that once done, only the Spindle-destiny is valid; it fixes the chosen condi-tions irretrievably since the elected guardian-spirit becomes accessory to their accomplishment. . . . By the Lots (implying the unchosen element) we are to understand birth into the conditions actually existent in the All at the particular moment of each entry into body, birth into such and such a physical frame, from such and such parents, in this or that place, and generally all that in our phraseology is the External.[16]

The decision as to when a seminal reason enters the material world, according to Spenser and Plotinus, depends upon a collaboration of the inner generative impulse and outer circumstances determined, at least in part, by the fateful circuit of the heavens, and to this decision the "elected guardian-spirit"—Spenser's Genius—is accessory.[17]

The return of Spenser's "babes" to the Garden for "some thousand yeares" after they have run out their mortal lives is usually explained by reference to Plato's Myth of Er or to the Vergilian echo of that myth. But both Plato and Vergil make the between-life period one of reward or punishment for behavior in this world, and there is no expiatory motif in the replanting of the population of Spenser's seminary. There could not be, for the "babes" of the Garden are not rational souls but formal principles. Plotinus makes all as clear as Plotinus can:

The elements of this sphere change; the living beings of earth pass away; only the Ideal-form (the species) persists. . . . The Will of God is able to cope with the ceaseless flux and escape of body stuff by ceaselessly reintroducing the known forms in new substances, thus ensuring perpetuity not to the particular item but to the unity of idea.[18]

Furthermore, as the cosmos revolves, "The entire soul-period conveys with it all the requisite Reason-Principles [i.e., seminal reasons] and so too the same existents appear once more under their action." [19] For this reason, each cosmic year (the period required for the "fixed" stars to return to the same position, variously calculated from 6,000 to 36,000 years [20]) produces an identical reproduction of the individuals of the preceding one. Ficino comments:

Therefore your *anima* is able to bring forth few mutations of lives in a great year of the world, particularly because it lives, to be sure, a very short life on earth, above the earth a very long one. In the following year of the world, however, there will be not a mutation of lives but a resurrection of the very same people.

Elsewhere, Ficino reports the estimate that life above the earth lasts ten times as long as life on it.[21] Perhaps, when Spenser writes with apparent vagueness that after their return to the Garden the "babes" are clad "with other hew,/ Or sent into the chaungefull world againe," he is thinking of these two modes of reentry into the mundane, from time to time in "new substances" or every cosmic year in the identical substance.

Since the material substance is at the opposite pole from the Supreme, Spenser makes its home Chaos, "In hatefull darkenesse and in deepe horrore." Because it lacks quality of any kind, it becomes a "body" only "when as forme and feature it does ketch." It may "don" various forms (Spenser confuses the reader by using in the opposite sense the same metaphor he had used in clothing the "babes" in flesh), the forms fading in time as they do in the Garden itself. Despite its lack of quality, substance is nevertheless "conditioned" to accept forms "Meet for her temper and complexion." There is a similar ambiguity in Plotinus who finds it possible to conceive that the material substrate sometimes hinders the genetic principle which informs it: "Thus a lyre may be so ill-strung as to be incapable of the melodic exactitude necessary to musical effect." [22] To this occasional ineptitude of "substance" Spenser refers in his *Hymne of Beautie.*

Not only does Plotinus serve to explicate many of Spenser's ideas about the genesis of creatures, but he also makes use of a divine garden as a figure for the nexus of the formal and generative principles. In Plato's *Symposium,* Socrates repeats Diotima's story of the conception of Love on the occasion of the birthday of Aphrodite. In the course of the celebration Poros, or Plenty, overcome by an excess of nectar, went into the Garden of Zeus to sleep off his drunkenness. Penia (Poverty), who had come around to beg, lay down by his side and of this union love was born. Spenser alludes to the story in the first of the *Fowre Hymnes* (ll. 50–53). To the interpretation of this briefly told myth Plotinus devotes almost all of the fifth tractate of the third *Ennead*:

A garden is a place of beauty and a glory of wealth: all the loveliness that Zeus maintains takes its splendour from the Reason-Principle within him; for all this beauty is the radiation of the Divine Intellect upon the Divine Soul, which it has penetrated. What could the Garden of Zeus indicate but the images of his Being and the splendours of his glory? And what could these divine splendours and beauties be but the Reason-Principles streaming from him?

These Reason-Principles—this Poros who is the lavishness, the abundance of Beauty—are at one and are made manifest; this is the Nectardrunkenness. For the Nectar of the gods can be no other than what the god-nature receives from outside itself, and that whose place is after the divine Mind (namely, Soul) receives a Reason-Principle.

The Intellectual Principle possesses itself to satiety, but there is no "drunken" abandonment in this possession which brings nothing alien to it. But the Reason-Principle—as its offspring, a later hypostasis—is already a separate Being and established in another Realm, and so is said to lie in the garden of this Zeus who is divine Mind; and this lying in the garden takes place at the moment when, in our way of speaking, Aphrodite enters the realm of Being.[23]

The Renaissance philosophers of love—Ficino himself, Pico, Leone Ebreo—seized happily upon Plotinus' explanation of Plato's myth. Spenser's Garden seems to derive from it, too. Like the Garden of Zeus, that of Adonis is the dwelling place of the Plenty of seminal reasons: "here all plentie, and all pleasure flowes." The role of Poros Spenser assigns to Adonis. The poet describes him as "Father of all formes" and like those forms subject to time and death, yet

> he may not
> For ever die, and ever buried bee
> In balefull night, where all things are forgot;

> All be he subject to mortalitie,
> Yet is eterne in mutabilitie,
> And by succession made perpetuall,
> Transformed oft, and chaunged diverslie   (vi.47)

As the seed of the seeds of the Garden he is in a higher sense the unity of link and succession of which Plotinus speaks, at once subject to mortality and dominant over it. Venus, like the Soul of the World with which the Greek philosopher identifies her, seeks to take "her fill" of his "sweetnesse," to make herself pregnant,

> filled to satiety with Reason-Principles—the beautiful abounding in all plenty, so that every splendour become manifest in it with the images of whatever is lovely—Soul which taken as one all, is Aphrodite, while in it may be distinguished the Reason-Principles summed under the names of Plenty and Possession, produced by the downflow of the Nectar of the over realm.[24]

The anatomical reference of the Mount of Venus so becomes not only appropriate but inevitable, as the process of generation in the terrestrial world is the natural metaphor for the process by which that world is conceived. So it is used by the humanist Cristophoro Landino commenting on the meaning of that forest on the Carthaginian shore which Aeneas enters. Citing Trismegistus as his authority, he assigns to God the office of father, to the wood or matter that of mother, and to the *anima mundi* the seminal power "since it is instilled by God into the bosom of the wood." [25] And this Spenser says in another way in his tale of the impregnation of Chrysogone, sleeping after her bath:

> Miraculous may seeme to him, that reades
>   So straunge ensample of conception;
>   But reason teacheth that the fruitfull seades
>   Of all things living, through impression
>   Of the sunbeames in moyst complexion,
>   Doe life conceive and quickned are by kynd:
>   So after Nilus inundation,

> Infinite shapes of creatures men do fynd,
> Informed in the mud, on which the Sunne hath shynd.   (vi.8)

Although there is no Adonis in Plato's myth or in Plotinus' exposition of it, Spenser's election of him as the central figure of his garden of generation is easily justified. In ancient times the cult of women who worshiped Adonis prepared in his honor pots of quick-growing and quick-fading plants which were called "gardens of Adonis"—Shakespeare refers to them in *Henry VI, Part I:* "Thy promises are like Adonis' garden/ That one day bloom'd and fruitful were the next" (i.vi.6–7). Like the Babylonian deity Thammuz with whom he is often identified, Adonis spends six months of the year underground in the arms of Proserpina and six months above with Aphrodite. The popular Renaissance mythographer Natalis Comes cites the Orphic hymn as authority for the statement that Adonis is the sun "since he nourishes all things and is the author of germination." [26] He is therefore the appropriate symbol for the ambiguous nature of sexual love, the principal subject of the Legend of Chastitie. On the one hand he is the figure portrayed in the tapestry of Malecasta's castle, the unhappy victim of sexual passion, dead in the arms of the lascivious Venus. On the other he is the father of all forms, the divinely derived principle that keeps the world alive. The contrast between Malecasta's Adonis and that of this Garden is not unlike the contrast between Duessa's Christ and the Christ of the House of Holinesse.

In the Garden of Adonis there is no mud, no sinful mire. How this can be in a place which is somewhere on earth, Spenser does not explain. No doubt he thought of "Adonis" as a form of "Eden," [27] and the Garden therefore within this world yet without sin. When Cupid visits he lays aside his "sad darts"; he is the unarmed god of the age of innocence. Psyche's long troubles are here at an end:

> now in stedfast love and happy state
> She with him lives, and hath him borne a chyld,

> Pleasure, that doth both gods and men aggrate,
> Pleasure, the daughter of Cupid and Psyche late.   (vi.50)

The wild boar that wounded Adonis "with his cruell tuske" is now safely locked up. Imprisoned in the rocky cave beneath the Mount of Venus he is in his proper place.

The notion of a purer, more virtuous, and happier other world of which this earthly one is the gross image and from which it is derived attracted other Renaissance writers of imaginative literature. The *Zodiacus Vitae* of Marcellus Palingenius describes it:

> This same first framed world doth passe the world that senses see,
> As much as minde excelles the sense in perfecter degree:
> In which the chiefest life is God, where Saints as Starres appere,
> And therefore straunger things ar there, then are perceived heere:
> Sith it is perfecter by much. For nothing there doth dye,
> No time, nor motion, there hath rule, all fixed continually,
> As voide of place and safe from harme they all doe seeme to bee,
> There are the causes of each thing, and springs of all wee see.
> The world the senses may perceive: from this same world doth spring
> And seemeth here a figure sure, and shadow of that thing.
> All things more sound and perfect there, and all things whole appeare,
> We have but portions of the same which are increased here.
> By natures fault and great defect. So hartes a number be,
> For vertue one above, creates the hartes that here we see.
> By her the subtile Foxe is framed, by her the Lions live,
> And so of all the other beastes, that this our world doth give.[28]

The appearance of a similar concept in the third book of Bembo's *Gli Asolani* is directly relevant to Spenser's use of it since Bembo, too, is discoursing of love. Lavinello, the concluding speaker of Bembo's dialogue, resolves the conflict as to whether love is an evil or a good by repeating the words of a holy hermit whom he had met that morning on a hilltop, in obvious imitation of Socrates' report of the instruction of Diotima. The hermit urges Lavinello to turn from his concern with this world to the contemplation of another,

another world which is neither material nor evident to sense, but completely separate from this and pure; a world which turns around this one and is both sought and found by it, wholly divided from it and wholly abiding in each part of it; a world divine, intelligent, and full of light, itself as much beyond itself in size and virtue as it draws nearer to its Final Cause.

That world contains all that we have in this, but things as much more excellent than these as the heavenly are better than the earthly here. For just as this world has its earth, so that has its green earth too which puts forth plants and feeds its animals and has its sea to mingle with, its ambient air, its fire, its moon, its sun, its stars, its other spheres. But there the grass is never brown, the plants are never withered, the creatures never die, the seas are never rough, the air is never dark, the fire never parches, nor must its heavens and their bodies turn continually. That world has no need of any change, for neither summer nor winter, nor yesterday nor tomorrow, nor near nor far, nor large nor small confines it; but it rests contented with its state, having achieved the highest self-sufficiency and happiness, and being big with it, gives birth to this very world you see before you.[29]

In general conception, and especially in their agreement that the world of seminal reasons is a better one than this which it generates, Palingenius, Bembo, and Spenser are indebted to the same Plotinian tradition. But there are significant differences among these imagined realms. Palingenius locates the intelligible world vaguely "far away," Bembo in a sphere outside the terrestrial, Spenser somewhere on earth yet free of matter. Palingenius and Bembo exile Time from their worlds altogether; Spenser takes the harder (and more Plotinian) course of putting all Time into his Garden at once. Both Palingenius and Bembo avoid the tricky subject of reincarnation. Spenser, again confronting the problem directly, asserts the idea of reincarnation of "form" yet saves his Christianity by refusing to identify "form" with "soul." The only use of the word "soul" in these stanzas distinguishes it sharply from the "shapes" which are fit "t'indew it" (vi.35). It is worth noting that in the *Hymne of Love,* where the notion of reincarnation does not occur, Spenser does equate "form" and "soul": "For soule is forme and doth the bodie make."

But the most significant difference between Spenser and the others depends upon the didactic purpose to which the conception is turned. For Palingenius and Bembo, as indeed for Plato himself, the lesson to be learned from the pure world outside is that man can find true pleasure only by rising from earthly desire to the heavenly. For Spenser, as for Plotinus, the lesson is that earthly love is a reflection, however pale and distorted, of the generative power of the divine. Or as Venus puts it in her appeal to Diana to help in the search for Cupid:

> ill becomes you with your loftie creasts,
> To scorne the joy, that Jove is glad to seeke;
> We both are bound to follow heavens beheasts,
> And tend our charges with obeisance meeke.   (vi.22)

Sexual passion is part of the heavenly scheme of things, and obedience to heaven's behests can only be virtuous.

On earth, to be sure, where Cupid goes about armed, love may be the dead thing that the black inscription over the gate in Chaucer's *Parlement of Foules* describes: "Ther never tre shal fruyt ne leves bere." But the very barrenness of this aspect of love demonstrates that its evil is not the consequence of the procreative drive. It is flesh, the sinful mire so happily absent from the Garden of Adonis, not the desire for generation which is divine in origin, that poisons earthly love. In the *City of God,* Augustine considers the same problem in biblical rather than Platonic terms. Were it not for Adam's transgression, he believes, there would be no contention between chastity and sexual passion, for "the man, then, would have sown the seed, and the woman received it, as need required, the generative organs being moved by will, not excited by lust." [30] In Eden, as in the Garden of Adonis, there would be no shame in the sowing of the seed. And Milton's famous apostrophe to the wedded love of Adam and Eve is another declaration of the ideal purity of sexual intercourse.

The Garden of Adonis and Belphoebe's chaste dwelling, then, present love as it might be were man not what he is. In the school-room of the Garden, Amoret is taught that sexual love and the pleasure of sexual intercourse are good because they perpetuate the varied life of this world which reflects or imitates the eternal unity of the Supreme. The theme of generation is not absent from Belphoebe's education either, although for her a sexual love is impossible. However Timias suffers,

> that sweet Cordiall, which can restore
> A love-sick hart, she did to him envy;
> To him, and to all th'unworthy world forlore
> She did envy that soveraigne salve, in secret store. (v.50)

But her chastity is not barren:

> Eternall God in his almighty powre,
> To make ensample of his heavenly grace,
> In Paradize whilome did plant this flowre,
> Whence he it fetcht out of her native place,
> And did in stocke of earthly flesh enrace,
> That mortall men her glory should admire:
> In gentle Ladies brest, and bounteous race
> Of woman kind it fairest flowre doth spire,
> And beareth fruit of honour and all chast desire. (v.52)

The children of the love of Belphoebe are noble deeds.

The way of Belphoebe, or loving chastity, and the way of Amoret, or chaste love, correspond to the two kinds of human love of which Plotinus approves:

Those that love beauty of person without carnal desire love for beauty's sake; those that have—for women, of course—the copulative love, have the further purpose of self-perpetuation: as long as they are led by these motives, both are on the right path, though the first have taken the nobler way.[31]

The path into which the love of Belphoebe leads Timias may be the nobler of the two, but it is not full of delights, except perhaps for the most profound ones. When Belphoebe first meets him he is lying at the point of death from a wound in the thigh inflicted on him by the brother of that villain who chased Florimell breathing out "beastly lust her to defile" (i.17). The meaning of the wound is clear, for Belphoebe's attempt to cure him changes lust into love:

> O foolish Physick, and unfruitfull paine,
> > That heales up one and makes another wound:
> > She his hurt thigh to him recur'd againe,
> > But hurt his hart, the which before was sound   (v.42)

The prologue to this book, in which the reader is directed to identify Belphoebe with Queen Elizabeth, also portrays Sir Walter Ralegh as her "gracious servant"—a term calculated to allow the two meanings of obedient subject and lover (in the purest sense) of "His Cynthia, his heavens fairest light." The hint that Timias is to be thought of as Ralegh is reinforced by the divine Tobacco (made tactfully ambiguous by the alternatives "Or Panachea, or Polygony") which Belphoebe pounds into juice to cure him of his wounded thigh. But the personal reference, gracefully appropriate though it is, is not allowed to distort the moral teaching of the Legend of Chastity. Elizabeth becomes an instance of Belphoebe's nobility and maidenhood, Ralegh of the worship which a Belphoebe inspires. For Timias, the consequence of that worship is not pleasure, to be sure, but the resolution to spend his life in loyal service to his lady.

If Amoret's way is the less noble it is the more treacherous. Her sister is free; she must be rescued from her agony in Busirane's prison. That agony is the fear that gives wings to the fleeing Florimell; it is inflicted upon womanhood by the foul forester, by Proteus, by the beast like a hyena "That feeds on womens flesh, as others feede on gras" (vii.22), representatives of the unbridled ferocity of sexual passion, a ferocity which may manifest itself in brute force or in subtle deceit, too strong and too cunning for women's defenses. The fear is in Juliet's heart when she says to Romeo:

> Dost thou love me? I know thou wilt say "Ay,"
> And I will take thy word; yet, if thou swear'st,
> Thou mayst prove false. At lovers' perjuries,
> They say, Jove laughs. (ii.ii.90–92)

In the Garden of Adonis the wild boar is safe in his prison and "Franckly each paramour his leman knowes." But in this world the boar is loose and the course of sexual love full of peril. That boar is figured again in the Greedy Lust whom Spenser describes as "The shame of men, and plague of womankind" (iv.vii.18).

Plotinus concludes his praise of the "innocent frequenters of beauty" with the warning that they are not to be confused with the class "to whom it becomes an occasion of fall into the ugly—for aspiration towards a good degenerates into an evil often." [32] For the attraction of beauty is universal, but the effect of that attraction varies with the individual. The beauty that stirs love—or lust—is figured in this book by Florimell, the "flower-honey" that draws all in pursuit, old, young, rich, poor, noble, vile, beast, mortal, immortal. Arthur himself runs after her:

> Oft did he wish, that Lady faire mote bee
> His Faery Queene, for whom he did complaine:
> Or that his Faery Queene were such, as shee (iv.54)

Deplorable inconstancy, but not even Arthur can resist Beauty Herself. To be sure, Florimell has nothing to fear from Arthur, but she cannot know this. In essence, that "sacred fire, that burnest mightily/ In living brests" is different from the power that "doth base affections move/ In brutish minds, and filthy lust inflame" (iii.1), and they are different in their effects, as love stirs men to high endeavor while lust conduces to lewd sloth (v.1). But essence is not apparent, and effect need not manifest itself directly.

The threat is Protean in nature. One aspect of it is personified in the six knights who serve Malecasta:

> The first of them by name Gardante hight,
>   A jolly person, and of comely vew;
> The second was Parlante, a bold knight,
> And next to him Jocante did ensew;
> Basciante did him selfe most curteous shew;
> But fierce Bacchante seemd too fell and keene;
> And yet in armes, Noctante greater grew   (i.45)

The entertainment at Malecasta's castle, accordingly, is characterized by the glance of false eyes, flirtation, merriment, courteous kissing, wine, the "blacke vele of guilty Night." The seduction of Hellenore takes place on the kind of humid evening in which lust breeds. Again, there are "speaking lookes," charming talk, sweet song, the cup of wine, the cover of darkness. Hellenore is no difficult conquest, but woman's defenses are a flimsy protection against the determined attack of the sophisticated seducer:

> No fort so fensible, no wals so strong,
>   But that continuall battery will rive [33]   (x.10)

and the almost invariable success of the Squire of Dames is proof of their inadequacy.

So Florimell flies, making no distinction between the foul forester and Arthur himself. Sir John Harington comments on the flight of her prototype, Angelica: "Resist the divel, but fly fornication." [34] But Spenser's Beauty escapes from her pursuers only to fall into the hands of Proteus who woos her first with the techniques prescribed by the *Ars amatoria*—gentle words, flattery, gifts—and when these fail

> To dreadfull shapes he did himselfe transforme,
>   Now like a Gyant, now like to a feend,
>   Then like a Centaure, then like to a storme,

> Raging within the waves: thereby he weend
> Her will to win unto his wished end. (viii.41)

When we last see her in this book she is imprisoned in a dungeon deep beneath the sea. Rather than submit to lust in any of its Protean guises she prefers eternal thralldom and suffering.

In the Legend of Temperaunce, the division of the forces of Maleger which is directed against Sight is led by

> two then all more huge and violent,
> Beautie, and money, they that Bulwarke sorely rent. (II.xi.9)

Elsewhere in that legend the temptations of Beauty as the symbol of Fame and Money as the symbol of Power are linked together in the persons of Philotime and Mammon. Spenser did not lack authority for the association of Cupid and cupidity. In the *Romance of the Rose* Beauty leads Cupid's procession and "Biside Beaute yede Richesse." [35] The Renaissance philosopher of love, Leone Ebreo, distinguishes two Cupids, one the son of Mars and Venus who presides over "amorous delights," the other the son of Mercury and Diana who represents "the inordinate desire of riches and possessions." [36] Money, like Beauty, is desirable and hence an incitement to a kind of love. It is associated with love, too, in the Ovidian sense which makes it a powerful persuasive to womankind. In both senses money is also love's enemy, for it competes with love of woman, and unless it is spent the love of woman is difficult to obtain. Jean de Meun's Richesse refuses help to the Lover; in return the God of Love curses the wealthy, prophesying their submission to him and the loss of their riches. To these curses the friends of the Lover add the threat of cuckoldry. The fate of Malbecco fulfills these dire predictions. Arthur, of course, is Malbecco's opposite: he would rather find Florimell than have the "ransome of the richest knight,/ Or all the good that ever yet I gat" (v.7).

If Florimell is Beauty, her beloved Marinell of the Rich Strond is that other object of desire. Like Richesse in the *Romance of the Rose* he will suffer only those who submit to him to pass through his dominions. Fair ladies seek him as men seek Beauty:

> many Ladies faire did oft complaine,
>   That they for love of him would algates dy:
>   Dy, who so list for him, he was loves enimy.   (iv.26)

As his mother taught him, Marinell "ever from faire Ladies love did fly." But it is

> A lesson too too hard for living clay,
>   From love in course of nature to refraine   (iv.26)

His flight, like Florimell's, cannot save him, and in the last mention of him in the Legend of Chastitie he too is in a watery chamber, deep in the bottom of the sea, wounded almost to death in his encounter with Britomart.

As assailants of the House of Alma, Beauty and Money excite passion, perturbation of the soul. If love were merely a passion it would be amenable to rational control, at least in its initial stages. And so Britomart's nurse Glauce instructs her:

> But if thou may with reason yet represse
>   The growing evill, ere it strength have got,
>   And thee abandond wholly doe possesse,
>   Against it strongly strive, and yield thee not   (ii.46)

Similarly, Timias strives to rein his love for Belphoebe "with reason dew" (v.44). Neither succeeds. Though reason sometimes fails in the struggle with the passions generally, it is an altogether useless weapon against love: "love can higher stye/ Then reasons reach" (ii.36). For love is essentially different from the passions both in its genesis and in its nature and therefore in its problems. Guyon's victory over Acrasia cannot serve Britomart. Not the subjection of the passionate to the rational soul but the yoking together of affection and chastity is the central task of her legend.

The difference between Temperance and Chastity appears most

clearly in the story of Satyrane's conquest of that spotted beast that eats women. Like Maleger in his struggle with Arthur, the beast cannot be overcome by blows of the sword: "aye more fresh/ And fierce he still appeard, the more he did him thresh" (vii.32). When Satyrane grapples with the monster he "Rored, and raged to the under-kept." The attempt to master the sexual drive increases its power, as Scudamour finds when he attempts to pierce the wall of flame that separates him from Amoret "With greedy will, and envious desire":

> cruell Mulciber would not obay
> His threatfull pride, but did the more augment
> His mighty rage   (xi.26)

And in the Legend of Friendship, when Artegall strives to control his desire for Britomart, "the passion grew more fierce and faine,/ Like to a stubborne steade whom strong hand would restraine." Yet the struggle is not hopeless. For if the strong hand maintains its hold, the beast succumbs at last, and when Satyrane binds the hyena-like creature with Florimell's "golden ribband," the girdle of Venus, it

> trembled like a lambe, fled from the pray,
> And all the way him followd on the strand,
> As he had long bene learned to obay;
> Yet never learned he such service, till that day.   (vii.36)

Maleger cannot be tamed, but the horrid spotted beast, appropriately bound, can be taught to obey.

Because the beast has not yet been bound Amoret, like Florimell, suffers imprisonment. She is kept in "thraldome and continuall feare" (xi.16) by Busirane, whose name Spenser adapted from that of Busiris, legendary king of Egypt. Busiris was a bad man, as stories tell, who continued his practice of sacrificing visitors to his kingdom until Hercules put an end to it and him. The relevance of Spenser's allusion may depend upon another story about this king, his attempt to rape the chaste and beautiful daughters of Atlas, an attempt which

Hercules frustrated.[37] But it is chiefly as the type of tyranny that Busiris is known, an appropriate figure, therefore, for the tyrant Cupid. The outer chambers of Busirane's castle portray the metamorphoses of the amorous pagan gods, the "thousand monstrous formes" which false love wears. Within, there is played daily the Masque of Cupid, a procession led by Ease (as Idleness opens the garden door in the *Romance of the Rose*) followed by Fancy, Desire, Doubt, Danger, Fear and Hope, Dissimulation and Suspicion, Grief, Fury, Displeasure and Pleasance, Despite and Cruelty. This is the process of love in the world of men. Then after Amoret, her heart tortured and bleeding, and her triumphant captor, the tyrant Cupid, there come a rout of love's evil consequences ranging from Reproach, Repentance, and Shame to Poverty and Death "with infamie":

> There were full many moe like maladies,
>   Whose names and natures I note readen well;
>   So many moe, as there be phantasies
>   In wavering wemens wit, that none can tell,
>   Or paines in love, or punishments in hell   (xii.26)

The Masque is a distillation of unhappy love stories, like those which Chaucer lists of the deceived women whose names are soiled by "wikke Fame" because they succumbed to the passion of love: Dido, Phillis, Breseyda, Oenone, Isiphile, Medea, Dyanira, and Adriane.[38] The fear of joining this tragic throng cuts Amoret's heart and keeps her womanhood prisoner.

To win freedom for Amoret and happiness for her lover Scudamour it is necessary to overcome two related obstacles. The first is the terrible fear that binds her. The second is the fierce unruliness of the sexual passion that is the principal cause of that fear. Scudamour fails in his attempt to pierce the wall of flame that separates him from his beloved. He is thrown back "all scorcht and pitifully brent" (xi.26). The "huge impatience" arising primarily from his sor-

row that he cannot reach Amoret but also from the "burning torment"—the passion—within him reduces him to impotence; he can
do nothing but rage madly.

The terrible suffering of these two is not a retribution. Amoret
has committed no sin; the poet has for her only praise and compas-
sion. Even Scudamour's behavior is not truly reprehensible; his virile
impatience and her uncertain fearfulness are proper qualities of
noble young love in this corrupt world—though not in the purer air
of the Garden of Adonis. The bitter pang is as much a part of true
love as the fear of hell is of the hope of heaven. So Merlin instructs
Britomart:

> Most noble Virgin, that by fatall lore
> Hast learn'd to love, let no whit thee dismay
> The hard begin, that meets thee in the dore,
> And with sharpe fits thy tender hart oppresseth sore.
>
> For so must all things excellent begin   (iii.21–22)

Before Britomart is herself joined to her lover in some never-written
part of *The Faerie Queene* she must undergo the trials of the Masque
of Cupid: doubt, dissimulation, suspicion, jealousy. Yet she is ideally
suited by nature to conquer the obstacles to love.

Britomart combines in even balance the qualities of the womanly
and the maidenly twins, stirring up men's affections and at the same
time holding them in check. She does not "lightly" follow Beauty's
chase nor does she succumb to the charms of Marinell's wealth.
Florimell's anguished flight "As fearing evill" is directly juxtaposed
with Britomart's steady progress, "Ne evill thing she fear'd, ne evill
thing she ment" (i.16, 19). In Malecasta's castle, her innocent fear-
lessness becomes a defect in her defenses:

> Who meanes no guile, beguiled soonest shall,
> And to faire semblaunce doth light faith annexe;
> The bird, that knowes not the false fowlers call,
> Into his hidden net full easily doth fall.   (i.54)

Her vulnerability to "faire semblaunce" appears again in the wound
inflicted on her by the arrow of Gardante (i.65). She is able nevertheless to put her foes to flight and so to escape the danger. Though
she arouses passion in others and is capable of it herself, she is strong
enough to master it both in others and in herself.

Her true love, in fact, does not begin in the traditional way, as the
immediate effect of a blow through the eyes. In the *Hymne of
Beautie* the poet says that "love is not so light/ As streight to burne
at first beholders sight" (ll. 209–10). Britomart's falling in love appears to contradict this rule; actually it exemplifies it. Her enamor-
ment is made the subject of a fairy tale. In her father's closet she finds
a mirror, or rather a crystal ball "Like to the world it selfe," which
has the virtue of revealing to the observer

> What ever thing was in the world contaynd,
> Betwixt the lowest earth and heavens hight,
> So that it to the looker appertaynd   (ii.19)

At first she sees only herself, but then she begins to think of what
might "to her selfe pertaine"—that is, "Whom fortune for her husband would allot." The mirror returns a picture of "a comely knight"
bearing armor with the inscription "Achilles armes, which Arthegall
did win"—the armor which was awarded to Ulysses rather than to
Ajax because he was judged the most useful servant of the commonwealth. On the knight's shield is a crowned ermine, symbol of royal
spotlessness. And with this vision love strikes, as it strikes Arthur
himself in his dream of the Faerie Queene, and Britomart, like
Arthur, begins her search for the loved one she has seen only in
fantasy. As she scorns Marinell's wealth because she possesses that
of which it is only the shadow, power (iv.18), so she is moved not
by beauty of appearance but by its essence, beauty of spirit.

Despite its magical trappings, the process Spenser describes is real
enough. Love begins, he is saying, not at first sight, but with an
envisagement of what the beloved should be. This envisagement

depends, in turn, upon the nature of the lover himself and what "pertains" to that nature, or in the neo-Platonic language of the *Hymne of Beautie:*

> in your choice of Loves, this well advize,
> That likest to your selves ye them select,
> The which your forms first sourse may sympathize,
> And with like beauties parts be inly deckt   (ll. 190–93)

The ideal having been imagined, the lover must then find its fleshly counterpart.

In the prophecy of her offspring, too, Britomart is described as combining the qualities of a Belphoebe and an Amoret. The canto in which Merlin tells of her progeny begins with a stanza praising

> that sweet fit, that doth true beautie love,
> And choseth vertue for his dearest Dame,
> Whence spring all noble deeds and never dying fame.   (iii.1)

The generation of heroic actions, to which Belphoebe's pavilion is dedicated, is complemented by the account of Amoret's kind of generation, the "fruits of matrimoniall bowre" (iii.3), which links together through a succession of British rulers the virgin-lover Britomart and the "royall virgin . . . which shall/ Stretch her white rod over the Belgicke shore" (iii.49).

Britomart not only joins the qualities of womanly Amoret and maidenly Belphoebe but she is also at once feminine and masculine, virgin and knight, loving Artegall and inspiring Malecasta to lust. She recalls the figure of Venus in the armor of Mars, a favorite conception of Renaissance painters. Spenser was fascinated by the myth that made Venus a hermaphrodite: in *Colin Clouts Come Home Againe* he declares that "Venus selfe doth soly couples seeme," and in the Legend of Friendship she appears again as "Both male and female." For the purposes of his discourse such a figure was particularly appropriate, for the chaste love which Britomart exemplifies is a virtue of man and woman, and the obstacles which beset it oppose both sexes, though in different ways.

Where Scudamour fails, Britomart succeeds. She is wiser than to attempt the wall of flame "With greedy will and envious desire." She recognizes the "monstrous enmity" provoked by the effort to reach tormented womanhood, and she understands, too, that

> Daunger without discretion to attempt,
> Inglorious and beastlike is

With her sword pointing forward and her shield protecting her face, she passes through the fire "as a thunder bolt/ Perceth the yielding ayre." On one door in Busirane's castle she reads the words "Be bold, be bold," and on another, the iron door which opens into the inner chamber, "Be not too bold." She is mystified, but she need not have been. Her sword is her boldness, her shield restraint. Scudamour is only bold.

It remains for her to conquer Busirane. He turns his knife against the heroine, and

> Unwares it strooke into her snowie chest,
> That little drops empurpled her faire brest.   (xii.33)

But if Britomart is a woman she is also virginal in spirit. A fifteenth-century schoolmaster wrote this text for his students to translate into Latin:

Virginite, how may I extoll it! truly I cannot tell. it passeth eny manys wytt, not only myn, to expresse the bewty of it. ther is the floure that hath no spott, the floure of clennesse and honeste, the floure havyng the most swetest savor, passynge precious stonys in bewty, be they never so bright and oriant, a floure of hevyn growynge in the garthen of vertue, the which whosoever have it in his breste and kepith it he cannot be destroyde by noo maner of ways.[39]

Britomart may be wounded but she cannot be destroyed. So Florimell, powerless in the hands of the lustful old fisherman, cries out to heaven and

> See how the heavens of voluntary grace,
> And soveraine favour towards chastity,
> Doe succour send to her distressed cace:
> So much high God doth innocence embrace.   (viii.29)

The heroine smites Busirane with her sword and is about to kill him when Amoret

> Dernely unto her called to abstaine,
> From doing him to dy. For else her paine
> Should be remedilesse, sith none but hee,
> Which wrought it, could the same recure againe.   (xii.34)

And Britomart, her sword poised over Busirane's head "if ought he did offend," forces him to free Amoret from the chain that binds her. With the same chain she binds him, "more worthy to be so," for it is not womanhood but lust that should be fettered. Sexual passion must not die, for its death would end generation, but it must be tamed, or man becomes beast. The swift hyena-like creature that feeds on woman's flesh must be held by Florimell's girdle and taught to obey. The boar must be kept in his prison. Male violence must be tempered by restraint; maid and woman joined as "virgin wife" (iv.i.6). Only then is it possible for Amoret and Scudamour to unite in that pure, sensual embrace which crowns the end of the original version of the Legend of Chastitie:

> Had ye them seene, ye would have surely thought,
>   That they had beene that faire Hermaphrodite,
>   Which that rich Romane of white marble wrought,
>   And in his costly Bath caused to be site:
>   So seemd those two, as growne together quite

The Legend of Friendship

THE LEGEND OF CHASTITIE has for its subject the power of love; the Legend of Friendship is an anatomy of the relationship which love creates. The two books are frequently considered as one long one by commentators on *The Faerie Queene,* and the approach is tempting both because their subjects are linked and because the principal stories begun in the earlier book are carried forward in the later. But if Spenser's structure depends upon theme, as I assume it does, blurring the line between the books destroys a logical distinction which the poet was at pains to make.

That such a distinction was intended is manifest as soon as the two legends are set side by side instead of end to end. In Book III, Britomart seeks Artegall and Florimell Marinell; Timias lies heartsick and Scudamour cannot reach Amoret. The beautiful stanzas which join together the last pair Spenser deleted when he published the fourth book and the remainder of the poem in 1596, so that in its final version the Legend of Chastitie leaves all of the lovers still seeking, still under the domination of the tyrant Cupid, god of the masque. But in the fourth book, Britomart and Artegall and Florimell and Marinell are affianced, Timias and Belphoebe reconciled, and Scudamour assured of the faith of Amoret. The canceled conclusion of the Legend of Chastitie compares Scudamour and Amoret in their passionate embrace to a statue of a "faire Hermaphrodite." And it is the hermaphrodite Venus, sire and mother, begetter and conceiver, who stands as the symbol of the Legend of Friendship. Cupid, we are told, is absent when Scudamour comes to her temple. While the motto of the House of Busirane is "Be bold," that of the Temple of Venus reads, "Blessed be the man that well can use his blis" (x.8).

This Venus governs a realm which is larger than that of her son, for his is a province within it. Its boundaries may be known by the assault of Ate, mother of debate, who tries to destroy "borne brethren," "deare lovers," and "sworne friends" (i.24), or as the poet puts it elsewhere in this book, "deare affection unto kindred sweet," "raging fire of love to woman kind," and "zeale of friends combynd with vertues meet" (ix.1). Each of these attachments plays a part in the Legend of Friendship; they all appear in the story of its titular heroes, Cambel and Triamond.

The Cambel episode was inspired by Chaucer's unfinished *Squire's Tale,* and the influence of that story together with the one told by the Knight is felt throughout the book. Spenser begins the Cambel adventure with an unmistakable allusion to the first words of Chaucer's Knight: "Whylome as antique stories tellen us . . ." (ii.32). The tournament in which Palamon and Arcite contend for Emily provides the model for the tournament of the fourth canto, and Theseus' pavilions of Mars and Venus suggest the contrasting dwellings of Ate and Venus. The *Squire's Tale* supplies not only the matter of the Cambel episode but also the means by which Timias and Belphoebe are reconciled.

In addition to serving as mines of story and description, Chaucer's tales deal with themes directly relevant to the subject of the Legend of Friendship. The fragmentary beginning of the *Squire's Tale* announces that it will concern a father and his children, brothers fighting against a lover, the hard winning of a lady, and the warm

affection between a bird and a woman. The principal characters of
the *Knight's Tale* are both sworn friends and faithful lovers, their
friendship passing through the bitterest enmity before it is reestab-
lished, their love a purgatory of irrationality and suffering before
it leads to the heaven of Emily. When Spenser acknowledges his debt
to Chaucer,

> I follow here the footing of thy feete,
> That with thy meaning so I may the rather meete   (ii.34)

he refers particularly to the story of Cambel and Triamond but he
also intends the Legend of Friendship as a whole.

Of the three kinds of attachment with which this book is concerned, the natural bond of family is the first but the weakest:

> For naturall affection soone doth cesse,
>   And quenched is with Cupids greater flame:
>   But faithfull friendship doth them both suppresse,
>   And them with maystring discipline doth tame
>   Through thoughts aspyring to eternall fame.   (ix.2)

Spenser therefore pays little attention to the familial tie. It is illustrated by the heroic efforts of Marinell's mother to cure him of his
lovesickness, an example of maternal devotion which has its parallel
in Agape's expedition into the deep abyss of Chaos in her attempt to
lengthen the fated term of her sons' lives. More significant is the
union of Agape's sons in such firm affection

> As if but one soule in them all did dwell,
> Which did her powre into three parts divyde;
> Like three faire branches budding farre and wide,
> That from one roote deriv'd their vitall sap   (ii.43)

The oneness of Priamond, Diamond, and Triamond, which is like
the unity of the tripartite House of Alma, is represented in narrative
by the concession of the fates that allows Triamond to live out the
lives of his two brothers after their untimely deaths at the hands of
Cambel.

Since love of kin arises by nature, it differs essentially from sexual love and friendship, bonds which must be formed. Therefore the population of Venus' garden is of two categories, rather than three: "thousand payres of lovers" praising their god Cupid, and

> lovers lincked in true harts consent;
> Which loved not as these, for like intent,
> But on chast vertue grounded their desire, (x.26)

the examples of this second group including Hercules and Hylas, Jonathan and David, Damon and Pythias. Between these two kinds of lovers there are important differences, but they are alike in that they represent the achievement of concord.

The figure of Concord, "an amiable Dame" seated on the porch of the Temple of Venus, is flanked by two young men:

> Both strongly arm'd, as fearing one another;
> Yet were they brethren both of halfe the blood,
> Begotten by two fathers of one mother,
> Though of contrarie natures each to other:
> The one of them hight Love, the other Hate,
> Hate was the elder, Love the younger brother;
> Yet was the younger stronger in his state
> Then th'elder, and him maystred still in all debate. (x.32)

To find Concord assisted by Love is no surprise, but it is at first sight disconcerting to discover that Hate is also part of her train. The paradox disappears when it is realized that Concord is not a passive state but an active, resolving force:

> For strength and wealth, and happinesse she lends,
> And strife, and warre, and anger does subdew:
> Of litel much, of foes she maketh frends,
> And to afflicted minds sweet rest and quiet sends. (x.34)

If Concord subdues strife and turmoil she is related to the Love which is described in the first of the *Fowre Hymnes* as forming the world out of Chaos. Indeed, she has a similar function—similar but not identical, for the Love of the hymn is primarily a creator, while Concord's task is the preservation of that which is created:

> By her the heaven is in his course contained,
>   And all the world in state unmoved stands,
>   As their Almightie maker first ordained,
>   And bound them with inviolable bands;
>   Else would the waters overflow the lands,
>   And fire devoure the ayre, and hell them quight,[a]
>   But that she holds them with her blessed hands.   (x.35)

Since human affairs obey the same laws that apply to the universe as a whole, it follows that the union of man and woman or of friend and friend implies the overcoming of an initial antagonism. Before there is a resolution there must have been a conflict. That conflict is represented by Hate, who is therefore the elder, and the mastering power is his half-brother Love. But the victory of Love does not mean the end of Hate, for conflict is of the essence of the elements. Concord therefore joins the two hand in hand ("Albe that Hatred was thereto full loth") and strives to keep firm the state which results.

Hate, under the name of Ate and the guise of a foul hag, is introduced to the reader in the first canto. She is described as the servant of Duessa because her principal quality is her doubleness, a doubleness which is odd rather than even: she has squint eyes, a double tongue and a double heart, ill-matched feet and unequal hands (i.27-29). She is at odds with herself and therefore the sworn enemy of that even concord which Chaucer (following Boethius) describes as the work of Nature:

> Nature, the vicaire of the almyghty Lord,
> That hot, cold, hevy, lyght, moyst, and dreye
> Hath knyt by evene noumbres of acord [1]

In order to destroy this fair world and return it to the chaos from which it came she sows the seeds "of evill wordes and factious

---

[a] quight: requite.

deedes," seeds which in their ripeness brought down the towers of Babylon and Troy.

Conflict resolved is represented by a variety of symbols. The Venus who joins in herself both male and female is one such figure. Another is the snake which ties Venus' legs together, its head and tail "fast combyned." Cambina, bringing peace to the battling Cambel and Triamond, carries the caduceus:

> In her right hand a rod of peace shee bore,
>> About the which two Serpents weren wound,
>> Entrayled mutually in lovely lore,
>> And by the tailes together firmely bound,
>> And both were with one olive garland crownd,
>> Like to the rod which Maias sonne doth wield,
>> Wherewith the hellish fiends he doth confound.   (iii.42)

Some of Spenser's readers would have remembered that the caduceus was itself a token of Mercury's appeasement of a battle between two snakes. In Cambina's other hand is a cup of nepenthe,

>> a drinck of soverayne grace,
>> Devized by the Gods, for to asswage
>> Harts grief, and bitter gall away to chace,
>> Which stirs up anguish and contentious rage   (iii.43)

Her chariot is drawn by

>> two grim lyons, taken from the wood,
>> In which their powre all others did excell;
>> Now made forget their former cruell mood   (iii.39)

and those lions are of course figures for fierce Cambel and Triamond whose cruel mood Cambina is about to pacify. Britomart and Artegall, Florimell and Marinell, and the other pairs of lovers and friends whose anguish fills the pages of the Legend of Friendship all illustrate the workings of the same doctrine.

But the pacification of a quarrel does not of itself guarantee the formation of a true bond between erstwhile foes. Spenser draws the reader's attention directly to this when he compares the relation-

ship of Cambel and Triamond with that of Blandamour and Paridell
(iv.2). The latter knights, like the former, fight bitterly with each
other over a lady, or rather the appearance of a lady (for she is the
Snowy Florimell), and they are so evenly matched that they might
be fighting to this day were it not for the intercession of the Squire
of Dames. He ends the battle by suggesting that the contestants
should join forces to repel those who seek to take this Florimell away
from both of them. But the reconciliation so effected does not last,

> Ne certes can that friendship long endure,
> How ever gay and goodly be the style,
> That doth ill cause or evill end enure:
> For vertue is the band, that bindeth harts most sure.   (ii.29)

The Aristotelian argument which analyzes human relationships in
terms of the ends for which they are formed and the natures of those
that form them is evidently in Spenser's mind.

If virtue is the band, a Braggadocchio is incapable of friendship.
In fact, he is beyond the reach of hate, too. Reft of his Snowy Florimell and challenged to fight for her he finds an excuse so transparent
that he becomes the laughingstock of all,

> But naught he car'd for friend or enemy,
> For in base mind nor friendship dwels nor enmity.   (iv.11)

When the false Florimell is given her choice of suitors, it is Braggadocchio whom she elects, emptiness mating with emptiness. The
four whom she refuses are noble enough for anger, and when they
are rejected they turn upon each other:

> As when Dan Aeolus in great displeasure
>   For losse of his deare love by Neptune hent,[b]
> Sends forth the winds out of his hidden threasure,
>   Upon the sea to wreake his fell intent;
> They breaking forth with rude unruliment,
>   From all foure parts of heaven doe rage full sore,
> And tosse the deepes, and teare the firmament,

[b] hent: seized.

> And all the world confound with wide uprore,
> As if in stead thereof they Chaos would restore. (ix.23)

But although, inflamed by hate, they would restore Chaos, they cannot be bound by love, for Druon is by nature a solitary, Claribel
excessively passionate, Blandamour inconstant, and Paridell a rake.
Of "faint friends" they have become "cruell fomen," and though
Arthur abates their fury there is no hint that the enforced truce will
turn into a lasting friendship.

Virtue is the band, and it is also the root. It is Blandamour who
says,

> All things not rooted well, will soone be rotten (i.51)

and despite his own inconstancy the sentence is a true one. He utters
it when Scudamour is accused of ignobility on the ground that
Amoret has played him false. Somehow, the fact that Britomart
(who is thought to be a man) has kissed Amoret and slept with her
is taken as proof that Scudamour is no true knight:

> Fy fy false knight (then false Duessa cryde)
> Unworthy life that love with guile hast gotten,
> Be thou, where ever thou do go or ryde,
> Loathed of ladies all, and of all knights defyde. (i.51)

In Spenser's terms, the charge is not illogical. A relationship that
proves false must have been false at its beginning; since Amoret is
unfaithful she could not have been fairly won; he who wins a lady
by guile is no true knight. Duessa's testimony is perjured but her
reasoning is impeccable.

Without virtue no true bond can be formed. But there is a positive condition as well. Between those who can be united there must
exist an equality or matchableness of some kind; their natures must
be alike or complementary. One exemplification of this Aristotelian
teaching is the combat between Cambel and Triamond. Cambel,
protected by a magic ring which has the power "to staunch al

wounds, that mortally did bleed," overcomes and kills Priamond and Diamond. But Triamond, fortified by the "traduction" into his body of the souls of his dead brothers, proves a match for Cambel and fights him on even terms until Canacee comes upon the scene to resolve the conflict with her powerful wand. Jefferson Butler Fletcher, a teacher whose learning, wit, and kindliness I remember with admiration and affection, has argued against the usual interpretation of this story as demonstrating that only when Triamond has accumulated virtue by a concentration of three souls does he become the spiritual match of Cambel and fit for his friendship. He points out that Triamond loses two of those three souls before the end of the fight, and adds, "We might say a cat with nine lives equals (in fight) one able dog, but I question if that is the kind of equality that would make for cat and dog friendship." [2] The point is fairly made. But the narrative of *The Faerie Queene* often appears silly when it is translated literally into didactic statement, and it is rarely if ever self-consistent. Spenser is careful to show that each of the three sons of Agape has a particular knightly excellence but not all of the excellences which a knight might have (ii.42), and immediately after this statement he compares the three to a single soul whose power is divided into three parts. The figure seems to have been inspired by Vergil's King Erulus "whom at his birth his mother Feronia had given (awful to tell!) three lives with threefold armour to wear—thrice had he to be laid low in death" (*Aeneid*, VIII.563–66). Servius comments on this passage: "In this place by the three lives (*animas*) he proclaims a great and complete man." [3] The battle with Cambel is therefore a combat between one and three who are one, and the result is a draw. The magical assistance supplied to one side by a mother and to the other by a sister further emphasizes the parity between them. It is this parity, I think, that Spenser expected his readers to consider.

Other examples of friends and lovers in Book IV widen the conception of fittingness in union. Amyas and Placidas look marvelously much alike, so that each can take the place of the other. The bond between Timias and the dove depends upon their common misfortune in love, and their mutual solace eases their suffering. A similar link holds together Amoret and Britomart.

These are friends; among lovers another principle operates:

> It hath bene through all ages ever seene,
> That with the praise of armes and chevalrie,
> The prize of beautie still hath joyned beene;
> And that for reasons speciall privitie:
> For either doth on other much relie.
> For he me seemes most fit the faire to serve,
> That can her best defend from villenie;
> And she most fit his service doth deserve,
> That fairest is and from her faith will never swerve. (v.1)

For this reason, the fourth canto presents a tournament designed to discover the most worthy knight, and in the fifth,

> fitly now here cometh next in place,
> After the proofe of prowesse ended well,
> The controverse of beauties soveraine grace (v.2)

Neither contest, however, produces a valid result. That for male valor is won by Britomart and her enchanted spear, that for feminine beauty by the Snowy Florimell. Evidently such competitions, dependent as they are upon gross human judgment, cannot be relied upon. The true test, in contrast, is to be found in the desperate encounter between Britomart and Artegall. Despite her magic weapon, he proves able to overcome her in battle and so establishes himself as the real champion. If she conquers him at the end it is because of her beauty, not her valor. And if the prize for manly prowess in arms should go to Artegall rather than to Britomart, that for womanly beauty should be awarded to Amoret, not to the Snowy Florimell.

That prize, the girdle of Venus which Amoret can wear and the Snowy Florimell cannot, has two virtues:

> to bind lascivious desire,
> And loose affections streightly to restraine [4]   (v.4)

These two qualities (for Spenser is not being redundant) suggest the particular dangers which assail the relationship of lovers, unbridled passion and "lightness" or inconstancy. The theme is treated comprehensively in the story of the noble lady Aemylia and Amyas, the Squire of Low Degree. Neither the difference in their station nor the objection of Aemylia's father keeps them apart. Their assignation is prevented by two terrible antagonists. One is Greedy Lust, a monster who snatches Aemylia away to his cave where he rapes women and eats them, like the spotted beast that Satyrane overcame in the Legend of Chastitie. The poet calls him "The shame of men, and plague of womankind" (vii.18). Meanwhile, Amyas is made prisoner by a son of Corflambo, the giant who casts "secret flakes of lustfull fire/ From his false eyes" (viii.48). Corflambo's daughter, the fair Poeana, falls "lightly" in love with the captive Amyas. The modifier is significant, for though Poeana is outwardly so fair that like Florimell she attracts Arthur,

> But ah, she given is to vaine delight,
> And eke too loose of life, and eke of love too light.   (viii.49)

Like other lovelorn ladies, she complains of her cruel paramour,

> singing all her sorrow to the note,
> As she had learned readily by rote.   (ix.6)

She and Greedy Lust, therefore, correspond to the two tendencies restrained by the girdle of Venus, both expressions of lust but one typically the feminine, the other the masculine, form. Before Aemylia and Amyas can be united in an enduring marriage, the frivolity of the woman and the fierce passion of the man must be subdued.

In a more complicated way, these two obstacles to the successful union of lovers are exemplified in the stories of Amoret and Florimell. Like Aemylia and Amyas, both are prisoners. As Amoret is womanly, her tormentor is the woman-eating monster who abducts Aemylia. As Florimell is beautiful, her tormentor is the shape-shifting Proteus, symbol of inconstancy.

Amoret's imprisonment inevitably recalls her torture at the hands of Busirane in the final episode of the Legend of Chastitie. The reader of the 1590 edition of *The Faerie Queene* would have known that torture only as the pain of love under the domination of the armed Cupid; now in the fourth book he learns for the first time that Busirane's rape takes place on the night of Amoret's marriage to Scudamour. Why is Busirane able to prevent the consummation of their marriage? Its roots are sound. In winning her Scudamour has proved his nobility: he has overcome twenty knights, gone through the Gate of Good Desert, and forced his way past Delay and Danger. Amoret's fitness is made known by the ladies who surround her: Womanhood, Shamefastness, Cheerfulness, Modesty, Courtesy, and Obedience. As she sits in the lap of Womanhood, arrayed in lily white, Scudamour steps forward boldly, "shaking off all doubt and shamefast feare," and takes her by the hand:

> Thereat that formost matrone me did blame,
>   And sharpe rebuke, for being over bold;
>   Saying it was to Knight unseemely shame,
>   Upon a recluse Virgin to lay hold,
>   That unto Venus services was sold. (x.54)

The rebuke echoes the warning of the House of Busirane, "Be bold . . . be not too bold." But neither Womanhood's protest nor the tears and importunities of Amoret can win her "wished freedome" from him. The Shield of Love, for which he is named, serves as his warrant. Emblazoned with Cupid's "killing bow/ And cruell shafts" it terrifies Womanhood, and the lover leads his unwilling prize out through the gates of the temple.

Only by boldness can Scudamour tear the reluctant Amoret from the lap of Womanhood. But the victory carries within it the seeds of disaster. The fear which it inspires is redoubled by the boisterous festivities of the wedding night,

> whilest every man
> Surcharg'd with wine, were heedlesse and ill hedded,
> All bent to mirth before the bride was bedded   (i.3)

and by the Masque of Cupid with its prophecy of the pains and misfortunes which attend upon the tyrant Love. In the *Knight's Tale,* Emily too shudders away from the thought of marriage, praying to Diana:

> Chaste goddesse, wel wostow that I
> Desire to ben a mayden al my lyf,
> Ne nevere wol I be no love ne wyf.
> I am, thow woost, yet of thy compaignye,
> A mayde, and love huntynge and venerye,
> And for to walken in the wodes wilde,
> And noght to ben a wyf and be with childe.
> Noght wol I knowe compaignye of man.[5]

And when she sees the omen of her fate,

> so soore agast was Emelye
> That she was wel ny mad, and gan to crye,
> For she ne wiste what it signified;
> But oonly for the feere thus hath she cried;
> And weep that it was pitee for to heere.[6]

No doubt, every well-bred maiden of the Middle Ages and the Renaissance had a similar horror of the "compaignye of man." Even Chaucer's Criseyde, no maiden but a widow, quakes like an aspen leaf when Troilus takes her in his arms. Like Amoret, she has been won already:

> "Ne hadde I er now, my swete herte deere,
> Ben yold, ywis, I were now nought heere!" [7]

But the winning does not subdue Criseyde's womanly fear. She is "quyt from every drede and tene" only when she finds it in her heart to trust Troilus, "Whan she his trouthe and clene entente wiste." Then,

> as aboute a tree, with many a twiste,
> Bytrent and writh the swote wodebynde,
> Gan ech of hem in armes other wynde.[8]

This is the canceled conclusion of the third book of *The Faerie Queene*.

Amoret and Scudamour are not brought together in the Legend of Friendship. Indeed, the poor girl vanishes from the story in the middle of the ninth canto, just before Arthur, with whom she has been traveling, meets her long-lost lover. The narrative stumbles awkwardly here, but there is no reason to suppose that Spenser intended a final happy reunion for this book. The other principal love stories, of Britomart and Artegall and of Florimell and Marinell, culminate in pledges of faith, not in consummated marriages. And for the purposes of this legend it is sufficient that Amoret be rescued from the fear of lust and Scudamour convinced of her constancy:

> So all that ever yet I have endured,
> I count as naught, and tread downe under feet,
> Since of my love at length I rest assured,
> That to disloyalty she will not be allured. (x.2)

That assurance comes hard to Scudamour. As Amoret suffers because of her fear of passion, so Scudamour suffers because of his fear that she has succumbed to it. He is so taken in by the slanderous report of Amoret's dalliance with Britomart that in his fury he almost kills Glauce. He is in agony waking and sleeping; the hammers of the House of Care beat incessantly and the crowing cock and shrieking owl add their cacophony to the pounding. When his weary eyes close at last, the master smith nips at his heart with red-hot tongs. Only the chance discovery that Britomart is a woman can teach him that his mistrust is groundless.

The blacksmiths of the House of Care are a symbol of a chaotic order: "For by degrees they all were disagreed." Spenser alludes here to the often repeated tale of Pythagoras' discovery of the relationship of numerical proportion to musical harmony. The philosopher chanced one day to pass an open blacksmith's shop where hammers of different weights striking hot iron in alternate and regular succession produced an effect of perfect concord. By changing the weights of the hammers he was able to destroy the harmony and to determine that the effect depended upon the degrees of difference of the various weights. He found too that of the many possible numerical combinations only six produced harmony—no doubt, Spenser's six discordant blacksmiths parody this conclusion.[9] The "orderly" succession of hammer strokes in the House of Care is therefore a burlesque of the true order of the Temple of Venus, just as the apparent agreement of art and nature in the Bower of Bliss mocks their real concord in the person of Belphoebe. Chaos —*discordia concors*—rules in Scudamour's heart.

For Florimell and Marinell, too, "lovers heaven must passe by sorrowes hell" (vi.32). Spenser matches Florimell's suffering with that of Amoret:

> Of lovers sad calamities of old,
> > Full many piteous stories doe remaine,
> > But none more piteous ever was ytold,
> > Than that of Amorets hart-binding chaine,
> > And this of Florimels unworthie paine   (i.1)

Busirane keeps Amoret prisoner for seven months; Proteus holds Florimell thrall for the same length of time. Book iv begins with the freeing of the one and ends with the freeing of the other. The

girdle of Venus fits them both. But the two heroines are not inter-
changeable. Amoret's "hart-binding chaine" is the chain that binds
"lascivious desire"; she smarts "because his sinfull lust she would not
serve." Florimell's imprisonment is caused by the manifold temptation which her beauty creates: her single devotion to Marinell is
assailed by gifts and graces, cruelty and threats, so that she must
straitly restrain "loose affections." Her pain is "unworthie" because
in this degenerate world beauty, representative of "The great Crea-
tours owne resemblance bright"

> Unto abuse of lawlesse lust was lent,
> And made the baite of bestiall delight (viii.32)

But in innocent antiquity,

> Then loyall love had royall regiment,
> And each unto his lust did make a lawe,
> From all forbidden things his liking to withdraw. (viii.30)

Neither Florimell nor Amoret would then have suffered, for in that
world lust was always bound by law and love was always constant.

The lust which Amoret arouses creates the fear and mistrust which
hold her apart from Scudamour. The universal attractiveness of
Florimell's beauty creates the rejection of womankind which separates her from Marinell. For the Marinell of the Legend of Friendship is not quite the same character as the Marinell of the preceding
book. There, his principal attribute is his riches; here it is his ob-
duracy. His heart, we are told, is rock-hard, stony, stubborn, like
Florimell's unyielding prison, and it must be hard indeed to resist
the beauty which captivates all. As it is not enough for Amoret to
be chaste so it is not enough for Florimell to be constant. Again the
solution comes by chance: Marinell overhears Florimell's bitter
complaint and so comes to realize the unwavering truth of her who
"had refusde a God that her had sought to wife" (xii.16). Love
humbles his pride,

> Into his mouth his maystring bridle threw,
> That made him stoupe, till he did him bestride   (xii.13)

and Marinell is brought

> To damne himselfe by every evill name;
> And deeme unworthy or of love or life,
> That had despisde so chast and faire a dame   (xii.16)

So sorely is he grieved by this sickness that he can be saved from death only by the sight of that once despised beauty. And now it is he who shows his love for his lady while she, no less "in secret hart affected," masks her feelings for fear that she be accused of "lightnesse" (xii.35).

The obstacles which beset the union of lovers are summed up in the story of Britomart and Artegall. Her virginal defenses are overcome by his chivalric virtue. He in turn, though in the past he has despised all women (vi.28), is conquered by her beauty. The proud woman is humbled and the "salvage knight" tamed. But although they have won each other, the enduring bond remains to be formed. Love does not so easily master his half-brother Hate:

> Yet durst he not make love so suddenly,
>   Ne thinke th'affection of her hart to draw
>   From one to other so quite contrary:
>   Besides her modest countenance he saw
>   So goodly grave, and full of princely aw,
>   That it his ranging fancie did refraine,
>   And looser thoughts to lawfull bounds withdraw;
>   Whereby the passion grew more fierce and faine,
> Like to a stubborne steede whom strong hand would restraine.
>
>   (vi.33)

Not by sudden incursion but by "Continuall siege unto her gentle hart," "With faire entreatie and sweet blandishment" he brings her at length "unto a bay," like the gentle deer of the *Amoretti* who is at last "with her owne goodwill . . . fyrmely tyde."

Lovers such as these are subject to the disrupting power of pride, passion, fear, and mistrust. But even relationships free of sexual appetite and grounded on virtue alone may be broken, at least for a time. Belphoebe has accepted Timias as her servant and they hunt leopard and bear together, nobly eschewing idleness. During such a hunt, Timias comes upon the fleeing Amoret as she is about to be recaptured by Greedy Lust. In the ensuing battle Amoret, whom the villain uses as a shield, is wounded by Timias. While Belphoebe chases the churl to dispatch him, Timias nurses the stricken lady:

> From her faire eyes wiping the deawy wet,
> Which softly stild, and kissing them atweene,
> And handling soft the hurts, which she did get. (vii.35)

That this is more than appropriate solicitude is suggested by the "argument" that precedes the canto: "The Squire her loves." When Belphoebe returns to the scene, she is so angered that she almost kills them both, but she restrains herself and

> drawing nigh, ere he her well beheld;
> Is this the faith, she said, and said no more,
> But turnd her face, and fled away for evermore. (vii.36)

Timias forsakes the company of man and lives in the wilds with his sorrow until Belphoebe is brought to him by the mediation of a turtle dove (adapted from the falcon in the *Squire's Tale*) and at length, moved by his miserable state, restores him to her favor. Evidently the devotion of a Timias must be an exclusive one—in the long and happy life which he leads thenceforward he even forgets Arthur:

> all mindlesse of his owne deare Lord
> The noble Prince, who never heard one word
> Of tydings, what did unto him betide (viii.18)

If this desertion is reprehensible, it must find its excuse in the exalted nature of the object of Timias' devotion. For Belphoebe's

wrath is "the displeasure of the mighty" (viii.1); she is not only
Amoret's virginal twin but Queen Elizabeth herself. The relationship
is therefore no ordinary friendship but a special kind of bond, that
between subject and sovereign, a bond which for Spenser super-
sedes all others. Indeed when the poet wishes to sing the praises
of his own lady, he feels it necessary to apologize to Gloriana. The
story of Belphoebe, Amoret, and Timias so becomes an illustration
of the conflict between the calls of patriotic service and private emo-
tion. In terms of this conflict Spenser here unmistakably refers to
Elizabeth's anger because of Ralegh's love affair with her maid of
honor, Elizabeth Throckmorton, an anger which resulted in his
imprisonment in the Tower and his banishment from the court.

The bond which unites a land under its sovereign also provides
the theme for the wedding of the Thames and the Medway which
is celebrated in the eleventh canto of this book. The nation becomes
the poet's subject as it does in his accounts of St. George's victory
for true religion, Arthur's book of *Briton moniments,* and the prophetic vision of Merlin. The bridegroom wears upon his head a
strange coronet set with towers and castles:

> That was to weet the famous Troynovant,
> In which her kingdomes throne is chiefly resiant.^e   (xi.28)

All the rivers of England bow low to this symbol of British power,
honoring him as their "principall." They bear to the wedding their
various associations of wealth, beauty, heroic tradition, learning, and
poetry. The rivers of Ireland are present too:

> Sith no lesse famous then the rest they bee,
> And joyne in neighbourhood of kingdome nere,
> Why should they not likewise in love agree,
> And joy likewise this solemne day to see.   (xi.40)

---

^e resiant: abiding.

This union in love and homage is attended also by the famous rivers of the earth, the Nile, the Rhone, Scamander, the Ganges, Roman Tiber,

> Rich Oranochy, though but knowen late;
> And that huge River, which doth beare his name
> Of warlike Amazons, which doe possesse the same   (xi.21)

Their presence raises Britain to the stature of the most famous nations of all time and provides the spur to Englishmen to win immortal glory (and "endlesse gaines") through the conquest of the golden lands of the new world.

But the widest view is not merely national. In the Temple of Venus a lover sings to the goddess the great hymn with which Lucretius opens his *De rerum natura*. The marriage celebrated by so numerous and so distinguished a company in Proteus' hall becomes a symbol of cosmic harmony and plenitude, the work of Venus:

> O what an endlesse worke have I in hand,
>   To count the seas abundant progeny,
>   Whose fruitfull seede farre passeth those in land,
>   And also those which wonne ^d in th'azure sky?
>   For much more eath to tell the starres on hy,
>   Albe they endlesse seeme in estimation,
>   Then to recount the Seas posterity:
>   So fertile be the flouds in generation,
> So huge their numbers, and so numberlesse their nation.
>
> Therefore the antique wisards well invented,
>   That Venus of the fomy sea was bred;
>   For that the seas by her are most augmented.   (xii.1, 2)

She is the binding, generative power that holds together mother and child, man and woman, friend and friend, subject and sovereign, the diversity of a nation, the great globe itself.

^d wonne: dwell.

The Legend of Justice

THE IDOL AND THE CROCODILE

THE APPEAL TO golden antiquity as a standard by which to measure the life of this world is a recurrent theme in *The Faerie Queene*. It is nowhere given greater emphasis than in the Legend of Justice, the Proem taking its departure from the age of Saturn:

> For during Saturnes ancient raigne it's sayd,
>> That all the world with goodnesse did abound:
>> All loved vertue, no man was affrayd
>> Of force, ne fraud in wight was to be found:
>> No warre was knowne, no dreadfull trompets sound,
>> Peace universall rayn'd mongst men and beasts,
>> And all things freely grew out of the ground:
>> Justice sate high ador'd with solemne feasts,
> And to all people did divide her dred beheasts. (Proem.9)

The action of Artegall's story is set in the generation following this happy age, a time when virtue still flourished but "then likewise the wicked seede of vice/ Began to spring." When Artegall was a child, Astraea, goddess of justice, lived on earth and it was she who trained him in her ways. But as men waxed wicked she returned to her heavenly home leaving to the hero her iron groom Talus and the golden sword Chrysaor as legacy. He is her heir, and his moral qualities as administrator of justice are the subject of his legend. His task is to imitate—not to restore—the natural justice of the age of Saturn.

Appropriately, therefore, Artegall appears in the guise of a hero of ancient myth, a founder of civilization like the euhemerized gods of the *Library of History* of Diodorus Siculus. He is introduced as the peer of Bacchus and Hercules whom the poet describes as the civilizers and lawgivers of the East and the West, and he is compared to Osiris, father of Hercules according to the genealogies of Spenser's time.[1] His conquest of the Souldan is likened to Hercules' slaying of the tyrant Diomedes; he is enslaved and dressed in woman's clothing by Radigund as Hercules by Omphale. Arthur shares this Herculean character by virtue of his victory over Geryoneo, son of the three-bodied giant that Hercules slew. And as Hercules conquers the shape-shifter Achelous so Talus masters the shape-shifter Malengin.

Artegall's name, like that of his beloved Britomart, is full of meanings. He is the equal of Arthur, in a sense his alter ego since he fathers the line of British kings culminating in Arthur reborn as the Tudor dynasty. "Art-egall" suggests his role as the knight of equity. But the primary allusion is to an ancient king of Britain whose history is recorded by Geoffrey of Monmouth. Geoffrey's Arthgallo began his rule as a very bad king indeed:

He made it his business everywhere to smite down the noble and upraise the base; to take away from the rich that which was their own, and to heap up untold treasure for himself.

The barons found this intolerable and deposed him, setting his brother Elidur in his place. The loyal Elidur managed at length to restore the crown to Arthgallo, who by this time had learned to distinguish right from wrong:

Arthgallo, accordingly, reigned ten years, and did so amend him of his former misdeeds, as that now he did begin to abase the baser sort and to exalt the gentler, to allow every man to hold his own, and to do right justice.[2]

This kind of justice, however it may disturb modern conceptions, is fundamental to the teaching of the Legend of Artegall.

The egalitarian giant whom Artegall encounters in the second canto is an advocate of the program of Arthgallo's first reign. He rests his case upon the admitted fact of the progressive worsening of the state of the world:

> Seest not, how badly all things present bee,
> And each estate quite out of order goth?
> The sea it selfe doest thou not plainely see
> Encroch uppon the land there under thee;
> And th' earth it selfe how daily its increast,
> By all that dying to it turned be?
> Were it not good that wrong were then surceast,
> And from the most, that some were given to the least?   (ii.37)

He then announces his program of reform: he will pull down the mountains and make them level with the plains; he will destroy the distinctions of power and wealth that obtain among men. Evidently he is a follower of those Hebrew and Christian scholars who held that the earth was created smooth and round, like a ball or an egg, and that its rugged deformation was the result either of God's curse after the Fall or of the action of the Flood.[3] He presumes to fulfill Isaiah's prophecy that in the last days God will make low the high mountains (2:12–14). His program derives from the assumption that the balance of the golden age—golden precisely because it was close to the perfection of the created universe—was a balance of equalities. This state of things he undertakes to restore "In sort as they were framed aunciently."

The giant is wrong on two counts, in his understanding of the nature of the golden age and in his effort to return to it. It is true, of course, that the world is degenerate. In the Proem, the poet complains,

> Me seemes the world is runne quite out of square,
>   From the first point of his appointed sourse,
> And being once amisse growes daily wourse and wourse.

The stars and the planets move "at randon"; men are now "transformed into hardest stone." But the harmony of the golden age was not one which gave equal weight to heaven and hell, fire and air, king and peasant. Rather it depended upon the fulfillment of its proper task by each part of the universe:

> For at the first they all created were
>   In goodly measure, by their Makers might,
> And weighed out in ballaunces so nere,
>   That not a dram was missing of their right.
>   The earth was in the middle centre pight,
> In which it doth immoveable abide,
>   Hemd in with waters like a wall in sight;
>   And they with aire, that not a drop can slide:
> Al which the heavens containe, and in their courses guide.   (ii.35)

The balance is one of order and function, no part lacking its "right." It is associated with the idea that everything in creation by its essential quality has a "natural place" which it seeks. By means of this doctrine Aristotle accounted for the free fall of heavy objects, the rising of fire, and all other motions which are apparently not enforced by the violence of an external power. Beatrice explains to Dante at the end of the first canto of *Paradiso* that all the natures of the world tend to move toward the stations assigned to them by the divine plan and that it is for this reason that he rises effortlessly toward the empyrean. And since the natures of this world are infinitely diverse the giant's desire to set all at the same level is contrary to the way of justice.

Nature has made a difference between man and woman and given to each different powers. Therefore the roles they justly play in this world are different. Spenser makes the point by contrasting two encounters between knight and lady similar in every respect except their conclusions. After a fierce battle, Artegall succeeds in over-throwing the Amazon queen Radigund. He is at the point of delivering the final blow when he is overcome by the beauty of her face, bathed though it is in sweat,

> At sight thereof his cruell minded hart
>> Empierced was with pittifull regard,
>> That his sharpe sword he threw from him apart,
>> Cursing his hand that had that visage mard:
>> No hand so cruell, nor no hart so hard,
>> But ruth of beautie will it mollifie.   (v.13)

As he is now disarmed, Radigund is able to impose her will upon the hero and to enslave him, dressing him in woman's clothing and setting him to the female tasks of spinning and carding. His "wilfull defeat" by the Amazon almost precisely parallels his fight with Britomart in the sixth canto of Book IV. This too is a terrible battle in which Artegall at last gains mastery. He lifts up his hand, ready "to worke on her his utmost wracke," but the sight of her angel's face (marred with sweat like Radigund's) numbs his arm and the sword falls to the ground from his slack fingers. Scudamour comments:

> Certes Sir Artegall,
>> I joy to see you lout so low on ground,
>> And now become to live a Ladies thrall,
>> That whylome in your minde wont to despise them all.   (IV.vi,28)

The beauty of Britomart, like that of Radigund, tames the "salvage knight" and makes him "thrall." Yet the result of this encounter we must deem a good and that of the other an evil.

It is just both that man should excel woman in strength and that feminine beauty should vanquish the heart of a gentle man. But when she has won her battle, Britomart's "wrathfull courage gan appall,/ And haughtie spirits meekely to adaw." [a] At last, after his long suit,

---

[a] adaw: daunt.

> she yeelded her consent
> To be his love, and take him for her Lord,
> Till they with marriage meet might finish that accord.   (iv.vi.41)

But the Amazon is of another metal, and she does not take Artegall
for her lord. Having made the mistake of accepting her condition
that the loser in battle must forever obey the victor, Artegall is
forced to subject himself to her lordship:

> Tho with her sword on him she flatling strooke,
> In signe of true subjection to her powre,
> And as her vassall him to thraldome tooke.   (v.18)

The relationship is torment for both, for Artegall because he must
fill "A sordid office for a mind so brave," for Radigund, now
enamored of him, because she cannot bring herself

> To serve the lowly vassall of her might
> And of her servant make her soverayne Lord   (v.27)

Such a state is unjust because it is against nature:

> Such is the crueltie of womenkynd,
>   When they have shaken off the shamefast band,
>   With which wise Nature did them strongly bynd,
>   T'obay the heasts of mans well ruling hand,
>   That then all rule and reason they withstand,
>   To purchase a licentious libertie.
>   But vertuous women wisely understand,
>   That they were born to base humilitie,
> Unlesse the heavens them lift to lawfull soveraintie.   (v.25)

The last line, of course, is intended to justify the reign of Elizabeth
as a legitimate exception to the general rule. It need not be taken
as mere timeserving, for Sir Thomas Elyot in the *Defence of Good
Women,* written in the reign of Henry VIII, and Calvin in a letter
dated 1554 make the same exception.[4] Apart from that line, however,
the two stories taken together constitute Spenser's comment on the
theme of marital sovereignty in its relation to the justice of nature.
    The giant is wrong also in his desire to restore the golden age.

For if the world is mutable, it is so in accordance with God's behest. In the Cantos of Mutabilitie, Spenser undertakes to resolve the paradox of the changeful creation of an unchanging creator. Here, as in the episode of the Garden of Adonis, he is content to say that change is servant, not master:

> the earth is not augmented more,
> By all that dying into it doe fade.
> For of the earth they formed were of yore,
> How ever gay their blossome or their blade
> Doe flourish now, they into dust shall vade.[b]
> What wrong then is it, if that when they die,
> They turne to that, whereof they first were made?
> All in the powre of their great Maker lie:
> All creatures must obey the voice of the most hie.   (ii.40)

Without venturing to question the inscrutable ways of that Maker, the knight of Justice must imitate the law of nature as best he can. By so doing he obeys the laws of reason. Such as keep those laws, Richard Hooker declares, "resemble most lively in their voluntary actions that very manner of working which Nature herself doth necessarily observe in the course of the whole world. The works of Nature are all behoveful, beautiful, without superfluity or defect; even so theirs, if they be framed according to that which the Law of Reason teacheth."[5] The giant denounces as unjust the advantage gained by a hungry ocean on the kingdom of the shore. But Artegall finds nothing inequitable in the ocean's transfer of land from the island belonging to Bracidas to that of his brother Amidas, for though it is change it is change adjudged by nature. It is equally right, therefore, that Bracidas should possess the treasure which the sea took from Amidas to give to him.

Although the giant's scales cannot erase the difference among kinds or annul the decisions of nature, they do have a proper function. Artegall urges him to use them to weigh against each other two

[b] vade: pass away.

"wrongs" or "falses" in order to discover which of the pair is the greater. Spenser has here in mind the Aristotelian argument concerning the just distribution of goods. A transaction is unjust when one party has too much and the other too little. Justice is the mean between these two wrongs or defects since it gives to each party not what is absolutely equal but "equal in accordance with proportion." Wrong may be balanced against wrong, while right sits "in the middest of the beame alone."

When the giant tries to counterpoise wrong and right, however, he finds that his scales will not work. False slides off the weighing pan; all the wrongs that he can lay together will not weigh down a little right. The principle is given dramatic demonstration when the false Florimell is set in the balance with the true in the presence of the knights invited to Marinell's wedding. To men's eyes they are equally beautiful, but

> Streight way so soone as both together met,
> Th'enchaunted Damzell vanisht into nought:
> Her snowy substance melted as with heat,
> Ne of that goodly hew remayned ought,
> But th'emptie girdle, which about her wast was wrought.   (iii.24)

The astonished assembly must conclude, with the giant, that "by no meanes the false will with the truth be wayd." In the light of truth, falsehood is negative, unreal. This is no longer Aristotle.

In the age of gold, while Astraea dwelt on earth, "all loved vertue," force and fraud were unknown, and justice resided in men's hearts. When she departed at the coming of brazen times, according to Spenser's favorite mythographer Natalis Comes, she left as her legacy the written law, written because in the decaying world men no longer obeyed the unwritten precepts of natural justice.[6] A written law requires power to enforce it:

> For vaine it is to deeme of things aright,
> And makes wrong doers justice to deride,

Unlesse it be perform'd with dreadlesse might,
For powre is the right hand of Justice truely hight.   (iv.1)

This power Spenser identifies with the goddess's gift to Artegall
of the iron man Talus whom classical story described as regularly
making the rounds of Crete armed with the laws inscribed upon
tablets of brass:

His name was Talus, made of yron mould,
Immoveable, resistlesse, without end.
Who in his hand an yron flale did hould,
With which he thresht out falshood, and did truth unfould. (i.12)

The hunt for truth is one of Talus' functions; he is also responsible
for the punishment and exposure of those judged guilty. He pursues
relentlessly the guileful villain Malengin who tries to escape first
by running and then by turning himself successively into fox, bush,
bird, hedgehog, and snake. When Munera hides from justice,

Talus, that could like a limehound winde her,
And all things secrete wisely could bewray,
At length found out, whereas she hidden lay
Under an heape of gold.   (ii.25)

In his role as executioner he chops off her hands and feet (not as
brutal as it sounds for they are made of gold and silver) and nails
them on high for the edification of all. The punishments which he
and Artegall administer are regularly made public for their deter-
rent effect: Sanglier must carry about the head of the lady whom
he has killed, Pollente's severed head is pitched upon a pole, Braggadocchio is hung by the heels, Trompart's face is "deform'd with
infamie."

Although he is invulnerable and irresistible, Talus has his limitations. When Radigund subdues Artegall he makes no move to
rescue his master, for he must obey the judging intelligence and not
act on his own. Nor is his flail suitable for use in war (ix.44). When

Arthur engages in his perilous fight with the Souldan Talus awaits
the outcome:

> by his stirrup Talus did attend,
> Playing his pages part, as he had beene
> Before directed by his Lord; to th'end
> He should his flaile to final execution bend.   (viii.29)

This quarrel between the Prince and the Pagan lies outside his
province. Only the flashing brilliance of Arthur's shield, the revelation of truth by the grace of God, can decide it. When that decision
has been made human justice can play its part.

There are other attributes besides power necessary to make the
administrator of justice feared and obeyed. It seems at first inappropriate to endow the just man with cunning, but if criminals are
guileful, the keepers of order must be clever enough to catch them.
"Craft against vice I must apply," says the Duke in *Measure for
Measure.* Solomon cunningly decided the parentage of a child, and
Artegall follows his example in proving a lady to belong to one
and not to another claimant. The wily Malengin falls into a snare
set by Arthur and Artegall. As so often in *The Faerie Queene,* the
point is that the morality of an action lies in the nature which per-
forms it and in its purpose, not in itself. For a knight to let go
of his shield and to waver in battle appears to be shameful, and it
is indeed so in the case of Sir Burbon, despite his excuse:

> when time doth serve,
> My former shield I may resume againe:
> To temporize is not from truth to swerve,
> Ne for advantage terme to entertaine,
> When as necessitie doth it constraine.
> Fie on such forgerie (said Artegall)
> Under one hood to shadow faces twaine.
> Knights ought be true, and truth is one in all:
> Of all things to dissemble fouly may befall.   (xi.56)

Yet in his own fight with Grantorto, Artegall also lets go of his shield and stoops his head before his enemy's blows. But he is no timeserver. He looses his shield in order to encumber his opponent whose axe is caught in it; he shuns his strokes, but

> No shame to stoupe, ones head more high to reare,
> And much to gaine, a litle for to yield   (xii.19)

Since Artegall's end is good, only Detraction can accuse him of treachery and unmanly guile.

But Justice does not consist merely of a hunt for the truth, punishment of the guilty, and insistence upon reverence for authority and the code of law. These attributes of terror, mortality, and force represent only half of the charge which Duke Vincentio gives over to his deputy Angelo at the beginning of *Measure for Measure:*

> we have with special soul
> Elected him our absence to supply,
> Lent him our terror, dress'd him with our love

> Hold therefore, Angelo:
> In our remove be thou at full ourself.
> Mortality and mercy in Vienna
> Live in thy tongue and heart.

> Your scope is as mine own,
> So to enforce or qualify the laws
> As to your soul seems good.[7]

Love, mercy, the qualification of the law are part of Justice too. At the feet of Queen Mercilla, as she sits in sovereign majesty, there lies a sword

> Whose long rest rusted the bright steely brand;
> Yet when as foes enforst, or friends sought ayde,
> She could it sternely draw, that all the world dismayde.   (ix.30)

That rusted weapon, like the rusted armor which Piers calls on Cuddie to celebrate in the October eclogue, is the sign of power so great that it is rarely used. So too is the huge lion beneath her feet

> With a strong yron chaine and coller bound,
> That once he could not move, nor quich ͨ at all;
> Yet did he murmure with rebellious [8] sound,
> And softly royne,ͩ when salvage choler gan redound. (ix.33)

The potentiality of the sword and the lion create the majesty and dread of temporal authority. But the sword is not drawn, and the lion is chained.

The queen who restrains this power is called Mercilla, and she holds a scepter in her hand, "The sacred pledge of peace and clemencie." Her maids of honor are the Litae, a bevy of white-clad virgins, daughters of Jove,

> those they say
> Upon Joves judgement seat wayt day and night,
> And when in wrath he threats the worlds decay,
> They doe his anger calme, and cruell vengeance stay.
>
> They also doe by his divine permission
> Upon the thrones of mortall Princes tend,
> And often treat for pardon and remission
> To suppliants, through frayltie which offend. (ix.31–32)

Jove's threat to destroy the world recalls the wrath of Jehovah, and the calming of that wrath the mercy of Christ.

In the opening stanzas of the tenth canto, immediately following the episode of the trial at the court of Mercilla, the poet raises and avoids the question as to whether mercy is a part of justice or derived from it. He is content to say that mercy, like justice, was bred in the Almighty's seat and "From thence pour'd down on men, by influence of grace." He then weighs their roles:

> For if that Vertue be of so great might,
> Which from just verdict will for nothing start,

ͨ quich: stir.   ͩ royne: growl.

> But to preserve inviolated right,
> Oft spilles the principall, to save the part;
> So much more then is that of powre and art,
> That seekes to save the subject of her skill,
> Yet never doth from doome of right depart:
> As it is greater prayse to save, then spill,
> And better to reforme, then to cut off the ill.   (x.2)

The one "virtue" is concerned with keeping inviolable the statutes of law. It forbids Portia to do what Bassanio asks:

> Wrest once the law to your authority:
> To do a great right, do a little wrong

The written "part" must be saved, even if the human "principal" spills, for otherwise

>   many an error by the same example
> Will rush into the state [9]

The other "virtue," however, begins with the individual whom the generality of statute ignores. Spenser associates it with "equity." The French political philosopher, Jean Bodin, describes the relationship of law and equity in terms very like those used by the poet of justice and mercy:

> For that to say truely, the law without equitie, is as a bodie without a soule, for that it concerning but things in generall, leaveth the particular circumstances, which are infinit, to be by equalitie sought out according to the exigence of the places, times, and persons: whereunto it behoveth the magistrat or judge so to apply the laws, whether it be in tearmes of justice, or in matter of estate, as that thereof ensue neither any inconvenience nor absurditie whatsoever. Howbeit yet that the magistrat must not so farre bend the law, as to breake the same, although that it seeme to be right hard: whereas it is of it selfe cleere enough.[10]

Since it deals with individuals rather than with codified abstractions equity may be understood as the legal equivalent of the quality of mercy, and so an English judgment of the year 1589 describes its function: "to soften and modify the extremity of the law."[11] The innocent and upright judge therefore stands, as Bodin puts it, "in the middle betwixt the law and the equitie thereof: but yet to bee himselfe in the power of the law, so as is equitie in the power of the magistrat: yet so as nothing be by him deceitfully done, or in prejudice of the law." In the course of the development of the English legal system equity itself became institutionalized and the problem of reconciling it with the code became a constant plague. But for Spenser as for Bodin justice and mercy, law and equity are opposed only in the sense that life and death are opposed in the Legend of Holinesse, and they are at one in that sense also. Although "it is greater prayse to save, then spill," the merciful judge "never doth from doome of right depart."

The strange vision which Britomart sees in the Temple of Isis, goddess of equity, sets sword and scepter, rigor and clemency, against each other and resolves their opposition. Like Mercilla with the lion at her feet is the silver statue of Isis, her foot upon a sleeping crocodile. The dream begins with the transformation of Britomart into a monarch, her moonlike miter changed into a crown of gold, her linen stole into a red robe. Her state of beauty and felicity is broken by a hideous tempest which blows the holy fire about and is at the point of destroying the temple and all within it. In this crisis the crocodile wakes and devours both flames and tempest. Grown great and proud in his power he threatens to consume the goddess herself. But he is beaten back by Isis' rod, his pride turning to humility, and he sues for grace at the idol's feet,

> Which she accepting, he so neare her drew,
> That of his game she soone enwombed grew,
> And forth did bring a Lion of great might;
> That shortly did all other beasts subdew. (vii.16)

When Britomart wakes, understandably dismayed by her experience, the priests of the temple explain to her that the crocodile represents "The righteous Knight that is thy faithfull lover," and is really Osiris,

That under Isis feete doth sleepe for ever:
To shew that <u>clemence</u> oft in things amis,
Restraines those sterne behests, and cruell doomes of his.   (vii.22)

Her vision, then, is a universalized form of such a story as Shakespeare tells in *Measure for Measure*. Sleeping law—Shakespeare compares it with a sleeping lion and again with "an o'ergrown lion in a cave" [12]—invites chaotic disorder and the destruction of the realm. Stern force is required to suppress the turmoil but unchecked becomes itself destructive. Only when law is restrained by clemency, when a union of the two occurs, does majesty show itself stable, victorious, and fruitful.

This ideal union is illustrated by the trial of Duessa before the court of Mercilla. The episode is colored throughout by obvious reference to the trial of Mary Queen of Scots, but the topical meaning only slightly affects its function as an integral part of the exposition of the theme of the book. The guilt of Duessa is hidden behind her "great countenance and place" and the rare beauty of her appearance. The appeal for mercy depends upon these qualities and also—here the historical occasion dictates—upon

> Daunger threatning hidden dread,
> And high alliance unto forren powre   (ix.45)

Prince Arthur, sitting on one side of Mercilla, is deeply affected by the lady's unhappy state, while Osiris-Artegall, on the queen's other side, is constant against her. When Zeal, attorney for the prosecution, proves her guilty of murder, sedition, incontinence, adultery, and impiety, even Arthur repents of his "former fancies ruth" and joins in the unanimous verdict of the court. Now the court, which is the law, calls upon "Mercilla myld" to punish the prisoner,

> But she, whose Princely breast was touched nere
>   With piteous ruth of her so wretched plight,
> Though plaine she saw by all, that she did heare,
> That she of death was guiltie found by right,

> Yet would not let just vengeance on her light;
> But rather let in stead thereof to fall
> Few perling drops from her faire lampes of light;
> The which she covering with her purple pall
> Would have the passion hid, and up arose withall. (ix.50)

The death of Duessa is relegated to a sidelong mention in the following canto, the emphasis falling on the "strong constraint" which required Mercilla "With more then needfull naturall remorse" to allow the sentence to be carried out. Insofar as the episode refers to the historical trial of Mary the poet is justified in the way he tells the story since Queen Elizabeth was indeed strongly urged by Parliament and her Council to remove the Marian threat, and although she signed the death warrant she at least pretended to be angered by its execution. But for the central purpose of the Legend of Justice the conclusion to be drawn is that "it is greater prayse to save, then spill."

If Mercilla presiding over the trial of Duessa is prefigured by Isis with the crocodile under her foot, Grantorto at the trial of Irena has as his symbol the idol Geryon [13] and the fiend under the altar. The contrast between Isis and Geryon is emphatic and detailed. For the beautiful silver goddess there is the monstrous golden god. For the openly terrifying male crocodile there is a fiend with the face of a maid,

> To hide the horrour, which did lurke behinde,
> The better to beguile, whom she so fond did finde. (xi.23)

Isis restrains her terror; Geryon calls his forth. Her priests are devoted ascetics who drink no wine not only because it addles the brains but also because it is, or represents, blood. The guardians of the chapel of Geryon are a strong garrison led by a seneschal "That by his powre oppressed every one," and to the idol is sacrificed

> The flesh of men, to Gods owne likenesse framed,
> And powring forth their bloud in brutishe wize,
> That any yron eyes, to see it would agrize. (x.28)

The chapel of Geryon stands for the reverse of justice, or tyranny.

One such tyrant is Geryoneo, son of Geryon and builder of the chapel. He guilefully takes advantage of the widow Belge and once he has won her confidence shows his true nature by "tyrannizing, and oppressing all," and sacrificing her children, one by one, to the fiend in the chapel. It is given to Arthur to rescue her and the last two of her offspring and to destroy both the idol and the fiend. As in the trial of Duessa, the political intention is transparent, the lady Belge and her children representing the Low Countries and the provinces into which that realm was divided, Geryoneo the Empire, and Arthur the righteous power of England.

Artegall's final task is the saving of Irena. He is himself in part responsible for her plight, because the delay occasioned by his "thraldome" to Radigund has brought the captive lady whom Gloriana assigned him to rescue into the direst jeopardy. The effeminacy of that imprisonment so takes on a new meaning. It illustrates not only the unnaturalness of the subjection of man by woman but also the enfeeblement of justice held in fetters by pity, and more generally the diversion of the gentle man from his proper work in the world by the power of feminine beauty. The poet cites Antony, Samson, and Hercules as other examples of great warriors who failed in the performance of their duty because they allowed themselves to be tied by women. In order to fulfill Gloriana's behest Artegall must harden himself against the attraction of Britomart and go sternly on his way, accompanied only by Talus. If Osiris must never be unbridled, neither must he be emasculated.

"Irena" in Greek means "peace," and a "myld Eirene" has already been numbered among the Litae, or Hours, attending Queen Mercilla. Peaceful femininity imprisoned by Grantorto makes a double contrast with righteous Artegall enchained by the warlike Amazon. Righteousness must be governed by clemency, not pride, so that Britomart must overcome Radigund to set matters right.

And mild peace is in dire jeopardy when injustice rules, so that Artegall must conquer Grantorto. But even this comparison does not exhaust the complexity of Spenser's web of parallels and contrasts. Irena's predicament is the foil of Duessa's. Duessa is of "great countenance"; Irena a "tender rose." Duessa comes to Mercilla's realm with the treasonable intention of killing the queen; Irena, relying on Artegall's promise to fight for her,

> Did thither come, where she afrayd of nought,
> By guilefull treason and by subtill slight
> Surprized was, and to Grantorto brought,
> Who her imprisond hath, and her life often sought.   (xi.39)

Duessa is tried by legal process, Irena by a parody of the law, in effect by brute force. It is striking evidence of the primacy of Spenser's moral intention, I think, that a partisan of Mary Queen of Scots might find reason to identify her with pitiful, oppressed Irena rather than with proud, treacherous Duessa.

When Artegall defeats Grantorto, we know by their names and by their histories that right has conquered wrong. But an ignorant world looking only upon the superficialities of the action cannot know. When Talus inflicts grievous punishment is he just or cruel? When a knight lets go of his shield is he a coward or a skillful warrior? How can one distinguish between clemency and weakness? As Artegall comes away from the scene of his last victory he is assailed by Envy, Detraction, and the Blatant Beast who rail at him

> Saying, that he had with unmanly guile,
> And foule abusion both his honour blent,
> And that bright sword, the sword of Justice lent,
> Had stayned with reprochfull crueltie,
> In guiltlesse blood of many an innocent:
> As for Grandtorto, him with treacherie
> And traynes having surpriz'd, he fouly did to die.   (xii.40)

Slander is a crime, and the slanderous poet who abused Queen
Mercilla is properly punished by having his tongue nailed to a post.
But defamation is part of the necessary burden of the righteous
hero. So Shakespeare:

> No might nor greatness in mortality
> Can censure scape; back-wounding calumny
> The whitest virtue strikes. What king so strong
> Can tie the gall up in the slanderous tongue? [14]

Artegall forbids Talus to chastise Detraction:

> So much the more at him still did she scold,
> And stones did cast, yet he for nought would swerve
> From his right course   (xii.43)

For the law cannot justify a just man; his justification must lie
within himself, in his certainty of his own righteousness. Artegall
knows himself "from perill free."

In the circumstances of the summoning of Artegall to Faerie
court before he has completed his task of reforming Irena's "ragged
commonweal" there is a clear reference to the recall of Lord Grey
from Ireland in 1582. Detraction's charge of "reprochefull crueltie"
had in fact been made against Grey and appears to have been the
principal reason for the Queen's dissatisfaction with his government. This matter of Ireland, taken together with the account of
Arthur's rescue of Belge, his aiding of the wavering Sir Burbon (the
Bourbon, Henry of Navarre), his Armada-like battle with the
Souldan, and the trial of Duessa-Mary, constitutes a kind of history
of the chief political events in England of Spenser's own times. It
fills that place in the Legend of Justice which is taken by the marriage of the Thames and the Medway in the fourth book, by
Merlin's prophecy and the volume of *Briton moniments* in the third
and second, and by the account of England's return to true religion
in the first.

Although allusion to the affairs of the nation plays a larger part in the Legend of Justice than in the other books of the poem, the principal concern remains "ethice" rather than "politice." The discourse deals with the nature of those who act justly rather than with the nature of just action. The latter theme is not absent: it appears, for example, in Artegall's debate with the giant who would level the mountains and in his restoration of male sovereignty to the land of the Amazons. Even in these instances, however, the moral problem is central. The vulgar who flock about the giant support him "In hope by him great benefite to gaine," not because they find his arguments convincing. And the Amazon women reject rule, reason, and the authority of man "To purchase a licentious libertie." The dominant interest of the book is in the moral qualities and moral dilemmas of a righteous man, and this is true even when the poetic figure is drawn from the realm of politics. The point of the episode of Sir Burbon is not that he did a wrong thing but that he did it for "love of lordship and of lands," that he served the time. Mercilla pronouncing sentence at the end of the trial of Duessa would have been Queen Politic. Since she sheds a tear instead she is Queen Natural.

The Legend of Courtesie

IN THE FINAL CANTO of the Legend of Courtesie, the shepherdess Pastorella after her terrible ordeal as prisoner of the brigands is nursed to health by the friendly care of Sir Bellamour and his wife Claribell. As the handmaid Melissa dresses her, she notices a rosy mark upon Pastorella's breast which she recognizes as the birthmark of the lost infant daughter of her master and mistress, a

> litle purple mold,
> That like a rose her silken leaves did faire unfold   (xii.7)

Because Claribell's father had angrily disapproved of her match with Bellamour, the child was for safety's sake left by Melissa behind a bush in the wilderness. Found and brought up by the shepherds, Pastorella grew to young womanhood until happy chance brought her to the home of her parents and revealed her identity.

This story motif goes back at least to the recognition of Odysseus. It is an especial favorite with the writers of such late Greek romances as *Daphnis and Chloe,* the *Aethiopica,* and *Leucippe and Clitophon,* a body of narrative extraordinarily popular in Renaissance times and a principal inspiration for Montemayor's *Diana Enamorada* and Sidney's *Arcadia.* This tradition and the example of the *Arcadia* produced rich and varied fruit in England, ranging from prose narratives like Greene's *Menaphon* and Lodge's *Rosalind* to Shakespeare's *As You Like It, Pericles,* and *The Winter's Tale.* The genre is marked by its frequent use of the devices of infant exposure (in these stories babies are safer in the forest than in the cradle), separation of families and lovers, obscure oracles always misunderstood and always fulfilled, moments of happiness destroyed by the incursion of beasts and beastly men, imminent death or loss of virginity, last-minute rescues, startling coincidences, recognitions and happy resolutions. Although a pastoral setting is used by the Greeks only in *Daphnis and Chloe* it becomes usual in English narratives of this kind, probably because of Sidney's influence. Most of the ingredients of the genre—a tiger, brigands, infant exposure, and a recognition scene—appear in Spenser's story of Calidore and Pastorella which is the principal subject of the last four cantos of the Legend of Courtesie. Its characteristics are also evident elsewhere in the book, for example in Calepine's fortunate arrival in time to save Serena from the priest's knife and in the strange tale of his rescue from the jaws of a bear of the infant whom he later pawns off on one Sir Bruin as Bruin's own in accordance with a riddling prophecy.

It is particularly the theme of hidden or unknown identity that makes this book an imitation of the *Arcadia* and Greek romance. Besides Pastorella and the bear baby the reader encounters a variety of other characters the circumstances of whose birth are at odds with their worldly states. The insolent Mirabella

> was a Ladie of great dignitie,
> And lifted up to honorable place,
> Famous through all the land of Faerie,
> Though of meane parentage and kindred base (vii.28)

The Squire Tristram, true heir of Meliogras, king of Cornwall, hides in exile from his usurping uncle and spends his time hunting wild beasts, like the young princes in Shakespeare's *Cymbeline.* The Salvage Man who befriends Serena cannot even speak, and yet

> though he were still in this desert wood,
> Mongst salvage beasts, both rudely borne and bred,
> Ne ever saw faire guize, ne learned good,
> Yet shewed some token of his gentle blood,
> By gentle usage of that wretched Dame.
> For certes he was borne of noble blood,
> How ever by hard hap he hether came;
>   As ye may know, when time shall be to tell the same.   (v.2)

The time never is, in that part of *The Faerie Queene* which exists.
But on the surface it seems plain that the lesson of these instances
is that blood will out, that whatever the circumstances of fortune
or upbringing, man's nature is determined by his inheritance. Or,
in the words which Spenser applies to the Salvage Man:

> O what an easie thing is to descry
>   The gentle bloud, how ever it be wrapt
> In sad misfortunes foule deformity,
>   And wretched sorrowes, which have often hapt?   (v.1)

The plain meaning is not, I think, the important one, though
Spenser's commentators generally so take it. If Spenser really believed that true gentility derives exclusively from inheritance he
would have run quite counter to almost every Renaissance and
medieval writer on the subject with whose work I am familiar.
Most of those writers do assert that gentle birth usually provides
favorable opportunities for the growth of a gentle spirit, and some
suggest that since titles of nobility were originally granted in recognition of noble deeds the descendants of gentry are more likely than
others to inherit noble dispositions and to emulate the actions of
their ancestors. But this is very different from saying that character
depends upon birth alone. It is impossible to argue from the opinions
of others to those of Spenser. But it is remarkable that in a passage
that seems to express most clearly the thesis of inherited gentility,
the poet claims to approve a most explicit denial of it:

True is, that whilome that good Poet sayd,
　The gentle minde by gentle deeds is knowne.
For a man by nothing is so well bewrayed,
　As by his manners, in which plaine is showne
　Of what degree and what race he is growne.
　For seldome seene, a trotting Stalion get
　An ambling Colt, that is his proper owne:
　So seldome seene, that one in basenesse set
Doth noble courage shew, with curteous manners met.

But evermore contrary hath bene tryde,
　That gentle bloud will gentle manners breed　　　　(iii.1, 2)

The "good Poet" is Chaucer, and in the passage referred to Chaucer
himself leans upon the testimony of

　　　the wise poete of Florence,
That highte Dant [1]

There can be no question as to Chaucer's meaning, nor Dante's:

Looke who that is moost vertuous alway
Pryvee and apert, and moost entendeth ay
To do the gentil dedes that he kan;
Taak hym for the grettest gentil man.
Crist wole we clayme of hym oure gentillesse,
Nat of oure eldres for hire old richesse.
For thogh they yeve us al hir heritage,
For which we clayme to beene of heigh parage,
Yet may they nat biquethe, for no thyng,
To noon of us hir vertuous lyvyng,
That made hem gentil men ycalled be,
And bad us folwen hem in swich degree.[2]

And Chaucer goes on to point out that if gentility were the preroga-
tive of particular blood lines, the descendants of noble families
would always be gentle, which experience proves false. Therefore,

　　he that wole han pris of his gentrye,
For he was boren of a gentil hous,

And hadde his eldres noble and vertuous,
And nel hymselven do no gentil dedis,
Ne folwen his gentil auncestre that deed is,
He nys nat gentil, be he duc or erl;
For vileyns synful dedes make a cherl.[3]

When Spenser borrows a story he does what he likes with it, but is it possible that he here turns head over heels the meaning of the very authority whom he summons as witness?

A clue to the mystery may be found in a book which Spenser knew and recommended to others in a poem published with its English translation: *Nennio, or a Treatise of Nobility: Wherein Is Discoursed What True Nobilitie Is, with Such Qualities as Are Required in a Perfect Gentleman*. The English version by William Jones was published in 1595, but the Italian had appeared in 1532 and Spenser seems to have read it in the original since he comments on the correctness of the translation. His commendatory sonnet describes the work:

Who so wil seeke by right deserts t'attaine,
   Unto the type of true Nobility,
And not by painted shewes and titles vaine,
   Derived farre from famous Auncestrie,
Behold them both in their right visnomy
Here truly pourtray'd, as they ought to be

In the course of this treatise Domenico, who speaks for those who would have nobility go by families, cites David as evidence: "We are to praise no man before his death, because he is knowne in his children, intending thereby, that the honor and glorie of man, remaineth with his posteritie after his departure out of this life." But Fabricio, who believes that true nobility is attained by "right deserts," invokes the spiritual sense:

In like sort ought we to understand the last authority alleadged by you, which seemeth to intende, that man is known in his children: for hardly shal we know him that departeth this world, without leaving any issue.

We shal know him indeed in his children, that is to say, by his fruits, for if he hath sowne good fruite, in this mortall life, we may certainly judge, that he shall receive better fruite in the life to come.[4]

For Fabricio, then, the children are the works and the father is the spirit which produces them. I suggest that this is Spenser's meaning also. As he says in the Proem:

> vertues seat is deepe within the mynd,
> And not in outward shows, but inward thoughts defynd.

"Degree," "race," "blood" are figures of speech for the essential nature of man, the nature which is "bewrayd" by the actions which proceed from it.[5] Manners and deeds are the offspring of the mind; if they are truly gentle their source must be also. Pastorella, Tristram, and the Salvage Man are noble because they do gentle deeds; Mirabella must be of low birth because she acts badly. Arthur calls Turpine "basely borne" for no other reason than that his behavior is base (vi.36). The bear child supplies a crucial illustration. Nothing is known of his parentage, but Calepine has high hopes for his future:

> And certes it hath oftentimes bene seene,
>   That of the like, whose linage was unknowne,
>   More brave and noble knights have raysed beene,
>   As their victorious deedes have often showen,
>   Being with fame through many Nations blowen,
>   Then those, which have bene dandled in the lap.
>   Therefore some thought, that those brave imps were sowen
>   Here by the Gods, and fed with heavenly sap,
> That made them grow so high t'all honorable hap.   (iv.36)

Since these of no renowned lineage are heroic indeed, they must be heroes in essence, and therefore are they fabled the children of the gods.

It is by the unfolding rose that the real Pastorella is known. The same image describes the revelation of Tristram's self when he is dubbed a squire and enters upon his proper profession of arms:

> Full glad and joyous then young Tristram grew,
> Like as a flowre, whose silken leaves small,
> Long shut up in the bud from heavens vew,
> At length breakes forth, and brode displayes his
>   smyling hew.   (ii.35)

Although the kind of genesis that makes explicit what was implicit is logical rather than biological, I would not argue that Spenser denies the relevance of ancestry to gentility. Even though the spiritual intention is primary and the literal secondary, the fact that throughout the Legend of Courtesie discovered ancestry is so often the key to demonstrated worth is evidence that Spenser associated noble birth and virtuous character. He is at pains to point out exceptions, however. Sir Aladine, though meanly born, is nevertheless full of valor (iii.7). The shepherd Melibee is a truly gentle man. On the other hand, Sir Turpine and the nameless knight whom young Tristram overthrows "wrought knightlesse shame"; their actions deny their gentility. It is pertinent here to recall the episode in the Legend of Temperaunce in which Braggadocchio steals Guyon's horse and attempts to ride it. The valiant courser "despysd to tread in dew degree" and tries to throw his rider. The poet observes,

> skill to ride, seemes a science
>   Proper to gentle bloud; some others faine
> To menage steeds, as did this vaunter; but in vaine.

No doubt this reflects the traditional opinion that only gentlemen born can ride horses properly. But the primary meaning of the episode is made clear in the lines that follow:

> But he, the rightfull owner of that steed,
>   Who well could menage and subdew his pride,
>   The whiles on foot was forced for to yeed   (ii.iv.1, 2)

The horse that Braggadocchio cannot manage is pride; the "gentle bloud" that alone can keep pride under control is nobility of spirit.

In the opening words of this book, Spenser defines the virtue which is its subject as the "ground" of all goodly manners, the "roote" of civil intercourse among men. It is not manners or civility, therefore, but that which produces them that constitutes the matter of the legend. Throughout *The Faerie Queene,* of course, Spenser is much concerned with the distinction between appearance and essence. Since "courtesy" as the poet understands it refers to that human quality which determines a man's behavior toward his fellows, the distinction is of particular importance here. How is one to know a noble or gentle man from a base and shameful one?

Actions which men call ignoble constantly recur in the Legend of Courtesie, and the word "shame" and its derivatives echo through the book. Women are stripped naked and they are discovered dallying with their lovers; men do cruel and underhanded things, lie, carry burdens like porters, and hide behind women's skirts in battle. If some of these shameful acts are performed by the villains of the story, others are done by its heroes and heroines. Calepine is the author of the plan by which Sir Bruin is tricked into accepting the bear baby as his own. When Calidore returns Priscilla to her father (she and Aladine had been enjoying their forbidden love in a covert glade when they were discovered and attacked by a "proud discourteous knight"), his explanation for her absence is a masterpiece of tergiversation:

> There he arriving boldly, did present
> The fearefull Lady to her father deare,
> Most perfect pure, and guiltlesse innocent
> Of blame, as he did on his Knighthood sweare,
> Since first he saw her   (iii.18)

The clause "since first he saw her" technically preserves the sanctity of his oath but Calidore's intent is surely to deceive. Arthur pretends to be wounded and helpless; Pastorella pretends some show of favor to the robber chief; Calidore pretends friendship for the cowardly Coridon.

The problem of distinguishing between acts essentially and apparently shameful is set forth most clearly in a pair of episodes, the first of which has puzzled many of Spenser's readers. Calepine's beloved Serena is wounded by the Blatant Beast as she wanders unsuspiciously about the fields. The knight sets the bleeding lady on his horse and goes with her in search of harbor. Sir Turpine, who has the advantage of being mounted, runs at him with his spear, and when Calepine tries to evade the blow,

> Yet he him still pursew'd from place to place,
>> With full intent him cruelly to kill,
>> And like a wilde goate round about did chace,
>> Flying the fury of his bloudy will.
>> But his best succour and refuge was still
>> Behind his Ladies backe   (iii.49)

Fortunately, the Salvage Man appears at this juncture and stops the "craven" Turpine from "Chasing the gentle Calepine around." But is it possible to call a man who hides behind his lady's back "gentle"?

The match to this story is that in which Prince Arthur, having gained entry to Sir Turpine's castle by feigning weakness, chases the villain from room to room until he flees at last for refuge to the chamber of his wife Blandina. There the Prince knocks him senseless to the ground and is about to deliver the mortal blow,

> Which when the Ladie saw, with great affright
>> She starting up, began to shrieke aloud,
>> And with her garment covering him from sight,
>> Seem'd under her protection him to shroud   (vi.31)

Surely Spenser means the reader to consider the two cases together. We are certain that Calepine is a very brave man: he thrusts a stone into the mouth of a fierce bear. And we are equally certain that Turpine is a coward: when the Salvage Man chases him he

> Gan cry aloud with horrible affright,
> And shrieked out, a thing uncomely for a knight.   (iv.8)

Although both are protected by women from superior force, their actions are only superficially the same. To know the noble from the base, one must inquire as to the spirit, not the deed.

Blandina herself is an example proving the fallaciousness of appearance. At the very beginning of Book vi we are told that Calidore's gentleness of spirit, mild manners, comely appearance, and gracious speech "did steale mens hearts away." Blandina seems to have the very same ability to please. She entertains the Prince

> With all the courteous glee and goodly feast,
> The which for him she could imagine best.
> For well she knew the wayes to win good will
> Of every wight, that were not too infest,
> And how to please the minds of good and ill,
> Through tempering of her words and lookes by wondrous skill.
> (vi.41)

The graciousness of Calidore and of Blandina are very different, however. His springs from his nature; hers is

> false and fayned,
> To some hid end to make more easie way (vi.42)

Yet she is skillful enough to pacify the wrathful Arthur and save her husband's life for another day.

Is it disgraceful for a woman to be seen naked? Poor Serena, captured by cannibals and stripped of her clothing, is rescued by Calepine just as she is about to be sacrificed on the altar. She is so ashamed of her "uncomely case" that she cannot say a word to her rescuer. "Shame would be hid," the poet remarks elsewhere (viii.5). Yet round about Colin dance a hundred maidens, lily white, and their nakedness represents the opposite of shame, for they

> naked are, that without guile
> Or false dissemblaunce all them plaine may see,
> Simple and true from covert malice free (x.24)

It may be agreed that Serena's lack of clothing should be taken primarily in the literal sense and that of Colin's entertainers in the figurative. It is also true that Serena's nakedness has been the object of the lustful admiration of savages while the troupe about Colin dance for him alone—they disappear the moment that Calidore intrudes on the scene. The point remains, nevertheless, that nakedness is not of itself shameful, and the poet insists upon it by describing Serena's body in a manner at once sensual and reverent (viii.42–43).

Chief of the damsels who dance about Colin are Jove's daughters, the three Graces:

> These three on men all gracious gifts bestow,
>   Which decke the body or adorne the mynde,
>   To make them lovely or well favoured show,
>   As comely carriage, entertainement kynde,
>   Sweete semblaunt, friendly offices that bynde,
>   And all the complements of curtesie:
>   They teach us, how to each degree and kynde
>   We should our selves demeane, to low, to hie;
> To friends, to foes, which skill men call Civility.   (x.23)

Spenser shows them to us in the pose in which they were traditionally pictured in classical times and which reappears frequently in Renaissance painting, hands joined in a dance, two facing in one direction and one in the other.[6] The haunt of these Graces is a *locus amoenus,* not one like the Bower of Bliss in which nature and art are essentially at odds or like the Temple of Venus in which art complements nature, but a purely natural one, the work of the artist Nature:

> For all that ever was by natures skill
> Devized to worke delight, was gathered there,
> And there by her were poured forth at fill,
> As if this to adorne, she all the rest did pill.   (x.5)

The Graces are the natural endowment of Calidore, as his name signifies, and they come unasked to fortunate people:

> For some so goodly gratious are by kind,
> That every action doth them much commend,
> And in the eyes of men great liking find (ii.2)

Others, who may have stronger mental powers, try to achieve such graciousness, and although they are never fully successful, "praise likewise deserve good thewes, enforst with paine." Even the naturally endowed, however, may learn from experience and training. Calidore makes errors when he first enters the society of the shepherds: he offers money to Melibee for his keep and courts Pastorella in a manner appropriate to delicately bred ladies. He is not aware that "Those that are good manners at court are as ridiculous in the country as the behavior of the country is most mockable at the court." [7] Educated by his rejection, he adapts himself readily, drops his "loftie looke," dresses himself in shepherd's clothing, and while retaining his essential generosity of spirit takes on the ways of his companions.

Some Renaissance writers who delineate the nature of the gentleman emphasize strongly the importance of education, both for the mind and for the body. Sir Thomas Elyot, for example, is concerned in the first part of *The Book of the Governor* with the way the twig is bent, and he therefore prescribes proper nurses, competent tutors, a course of study, appropriate recreation and physical exercise, and moral training. But Spenser cares less about the bending of the twig than about the seed from which it springs because gentility, he believes, depends upon inherent nature. Some savages and some courtiers are gentle in spirit; others are not. The view is compatible, of course, with the Calvinist doctrine of election. Education therefore becomes a secondary matter. Calidore may learn to behave himself properly among peasants and the lady Briana to leave her cruel customs. Even Mirabella, though meanly born, may be taught by suffering to pity the suffering of others, though whether or not she will thus retroactively ennoble her birth Spenser does not

say. The use of education is most clearly defined in the episode of
the bear baby. Calepine presents the infant to Sir Bruin's wife with
the following injunction:

> Lo how good fortune doth to you present
> This litle babe, of sweete and lovely face,
> And spotlesse spirit, in which ye may enchace
> What ever formes ye list thereto apply,
> Being now soft and fit them to embrace;
> Whether ye list him traine in chevalry,
> Or noursle up in lore of learn'd Philosophy.   (iv.35)

The spirit is still soft, so that it may be molded into the form of
a knight or a learned man—or a learned poet. But it is spotless, as
the lovely face demonstrates, so that whatever form it assumes will
be gentle.

By virtue of the three Graces men's hearts are won and civil
intercourse maintained; the work of the three brothers Despetto,
Decetto, and Defetto is to destroy harmonious human relations. Of
Despetto's family is the Disdain which Mirabella has used and now
abuses her. He is sib to Orgoglio, the poet tells us, like Orgoglio
huge and powerful, and like him also in his basic weakness, for
both are brought down by blows at the leg. The disease which he
represents is contagious, for Crudor's "high disdaine/ And proud
despight of his selfe pleasing mynd" (i.15) communicates itself to
the disdained Lady Briana and from her to her seneschal Maleffort
"Who executes her wicked will, with worse despight" (i.15),
Despetto breeding Despetto. The principal client of Decetto is Sir
Turpine. As Crudor establishes the custom of robbing passing
knights of their beards and ladies of their locks, so Turpine mulcts
them of their arms and upper garments, but as Arthur points out

> Yet doest thou not with manhood, but with guile
> Maintaine this evill use   (vi.34)

Deceit is also contagious, for Turpine's hatred of errant knights
began when someone wrought him "fowle despight" (iii.40) and

he in turn suborns two otherwise innocent knights to a traitorous attack on the Prince.

The third of the brothers of disruption, Defetto (Detraction), has neither the mock strength of Despite nor the mock wisdom of Deceit, but is the most spiteful and indeed the most dangerous. He is one aspect of the Blatant Beast, the object of Calidore's quest:

> A wicked Monster, that his tongue doth whet
> Gainst all, both good and bad, both most and least,
> And poures his poysnous gall forth to infest
> The noblest wights with notable defame:
> Ne ever Knight, that bore so lofty creast,
> Ne ever Lady of so honest name,
> But he them spotted with reproch, or secrete shame. (vi.12)

The Beast is not merely slanderous, for that would imply that he attacks only those who are blameless. Nor may he be limited by the term "reproach" unless it be understood to include self-reproach as well as the reproach of others. He stands for shame, deserved or not, public or private.

Calidore's pursuit of the Blatant Beast takes him from courts to cities and the countryside, through all estates and even to the clergy where the fiend, regardless of religion, wreaks much destruction. Spenser does not say whether the clergy is being slandered or justly blamed. In the world of the monastery, however, matters are plain enough, for the Beast's fouling of it is described as a work of supererogation.

Sometimes the reason for the Beast's attack is clear. Serena is wounded as she wanders carelessly about the pleasant fields,

> as liking led
> Her wavering lust after her wandring sight (iii.23)

The "heedlesse" Timias is bitten "the whiles he was thereof secure" (v.16). No medicine will cure the poisonous sting which infamy infixes in the name of a gentle man, "such hurts are hellish paine." The Hermit's advice to Serena and Timias prescribes a ceaseless watchfulness, a reining in of eyes, ears, and tongue, a subduing of desire and a bridling of delight, an avoidance of secret dealings and, in general, of the occasion for blame. It is the best that he can recommend both for the prevention and for the cure of the disease. The value of the treatment seems to be denied by Serena's profound sense of shame when her body is exposed to the cannibals, but Spenser may expect his readers to think of this predicament as a delayed retribution for her carelessness in solacing herself in "covert shade" with Calepine. Those who follow the Hermit's advice may be defamed, indeed, but they do not suffer from feelings of guilt. The lady Briana accuses Calidore of brutality, but he answers,

> Not unto me the shame,
> But to the shamefull doer it afford.
> Bloud is no blemish; for it is no blame
> To punish those, that doe deserve the same   (i.26)

And though the Beast barks at Artegall, in his righteousness that knight knows himself "from perill free" (i.9).

Although the word "courtesy" derives from "court," as the poet explains at the beginning of the Legend of Sir Calidore, and although its derivation is justified by the virtuous condition of the court of Gloriana, the Blatant Beast is not unknown in princes' palaces. Melibee, who has spent ten years serving as royal gardener, observes that he could never imagine such vanity as he saw there. Wearied by his arduous quest, Sir Calidore envies the peaceful life of the shepherds, free of "warres, and wreckes, and wicked enmitie," and free too, so the peasants say, of the poisonous Beast. He asks permission of Melibee to rest his bark on the pastoral shore, leaving undecided for the time being whether he will return after a brief vacation to his assigned task or remain among the shepherds. Before long, the attractions of pastoral life and the delightfulness of Melibee's adopted daughter Pastorella bring him to the determination to resign his quest and to dwell thenceforth among "the rustick sort." He has forgotten that his pursuit of the Beast has taken him to these very cottages, and he does not realize or has yet to learn that the pastoral world is subject to the wars, wrecks, and wicked enmity from which he is trying to escape. If there is a Melibee among the shepherds there is also a cowardly and envious Coridon, one who like Sidney's Dametas, Greene's Menaphon, and Shakespeare's Audrey gives the lie to the dream of an ideal Arcadia. Calidore's error is that of Basilius in Sidney's romance who brings on the misfortunes he seeks to avoid by deserting his royal duty for pastoral seclusion.

More important, it is wrong for Calidore to put on shepherd's clothing and to wield a shepherd's hook because his calling is of another kind. When he eulogizes the shepherds' life and wishes

> th'heavens so much had graced mee,
> As graunt me live in like condition;
> Or that my fortunes might transposed bee
> From pitch of higher place, unto this low degree   (ix.28)

Melibee answers that happiness does not depend upon riches or poverty, high or low station, but upon the use made by the individual of the fortune which heaven allots to him. Therefore,

> fittest is, that all contented rest
> With that they hold: each hath his fortune in his brest.   (ix.29)

Calidore misinterprets this doctrine to mean that each man is at liberty to fashion "his own lyfes estate," so that he may elect whatever station pleases him, as though a budding rose might choose to bloom a violet. The Hermit, it is true, has chosen to hang up his arms and retire from knighthood, and the poet obviously approves of his decision to do so. But his retirement comes only when age has made it impossible for him to wield his sword. Calidore deserts his duty in the prime of his life:

> Who now does follow the foule Blatant Beast,
> Whilest Calidore does follow that faire Mayd,

> Unmyndfull of his vow and high beheast,
> Which by the Faery Queene was on him layd,
> That he should never leave, nor be delayd
> From chacing him, till he had it attchieved?   (x.1)

In the role of a peasant he is as unnatural as the effeminated Artegall
and as useless for the work of the state.

Calidore may be pardoned, or at least not "greatly blamed." His
abandonment of the quest is not only compatible with his character
but results from the very qualities that make him the knight of
courtesy. As the antithesis of Despetto, Decetto, and Defetto, he
hates the vanities of court life and loves

> the perfect pleasures, which doe grow
> Amongst poore hyndes, in hils, in woods, in dales   (x.3)

for which Pastorella stands as a symbol. Keeping sheep would have
no attractions for Crudor or Turpine, Blandina or Mirabella.
Furthermore, the pursuit of the Blatant Beast is an endless, dis-
couraging task. In *Mother Hubberds Tale* Spenser urges the toil-
weary courtier to escape for a time from his dutiful exercises into
the recreative delights of music, "Or els with Loves, and Ladies
gentle sports" (l.757). But though we may excuse Calidore's error,
it is error nevertheless, and he comes at length to recognize it:

> Tho gan Sir Calidore him to advize
>   Of his first quest, which he had long forlore,
>   Asham'd to thinke, how he that enterprize,
>   The which the Faery Queene had long afore
>   Bequeath'd to him, forslacked had so sore;
>   That much he feared, least reprochfull blame
>   With foule dishonour him mote blot therefore;
>   Besides the losse of so much loos [a] and fame,
> As through the world thereby should glorifie his name.   (xii.12)

He has failed to subdue his desires and is therefore fair game for
the Blatant Beast, the enemy whom he is charged to suppress.

[a] loos: praise.

On the theme of escape or digression from duty Spenser rings a variety of changes in the final cantos of the book. If the attractions of Pastorella have led Sir Calidore astray, so too has the pastoral episode diverted the poet from his principal purpose. Like a ship encountering contrary winds, however, the temporary stay does not mean that he has lost sight of his goal, for it has served to display his hero's courtesy "Even unto the lowest and the least" (xii.1–2). During this digression, the poet appears under his pastoral name of Colin, piping to the dancing Graces. These Graces are themselves the daughters of a vacation: they were begot by Jove of fair Euronyme while "In sommers shade him selfe here rested weary" (x.22). The scene is Mount Acidale, significantly the resort where the goddess Venus reposes and rests herself, preferring it to royal Cithaeron in which she transacts her business as a sovereign majesty. "Acidalia" is indeed a surname of Aphrodite and a spring or brook in which the Graces bathe. But Spenser may have been thinking also of the medieval Latin *accidia,* the sin of sloth.[8] Colin diverts himself, then, on the pleasant mountain where Venus rests from her labors in the course of an episode in which the hero of the book has forgotten the task which he must perform.

Colin's diversion is itself a failure of duty. The Legend of Courtesie, alone of the books of *The Faerie Queene,* contains no celebration of the Queen, her ancestry, or the country over which she rules. Instead, the poet pipes to a country lass so peerlessly lovely that she deserves to be another grace. The beauty of this simple peasant girl has distracted him from the fulfillment of his obligation to Gloriana. Like Calidore, he is aware of his error and apologizes for it:

> Sunne of the world, great glory of the sky,
>> That all the earth doest lighten with thy rayes,
>> Great Gloriana, greatest Majesty,
>> Pardon thy shepheard, mongst so many layes,

> As he hath sung of thee in all his dayes,
> To make one minime of thy poore handmayd,
> And underneath thy feete to place her prayse,
> That when thy glory shall be farre displayd
> To future age of her this mention may be made.   (x.28)

And like Calidore, he may be pardoned.

One of the sonnets of the *Amoretti* plays with this idea:

> After so long a race as I have run
>   Through Faery land, which those six books compile,
>   give leave to rest me being halfe fordonne,
>   and gather to my selfe new breath awhile.
> Then as a steed refreshed after toyle,
>   out of my prison I will breake anew:
>   and stoutly will that second worke assoyle,
>   with strong endevour and attention dew.
> Till then give leave to me in pleasant mew,
>   to sport my muse and sing my loves sweet praise:
>   the contemplation of whose heavenly hew,
>   my spirit to an higher pitch will rayse.
> But let her prayses yet be low and meane,
>   fit for the handmayd of the Faery Queene.   (LXXX)

But the optimistic prophecy of the sonnet is at odds with the conclusion of the Legend of Courtesie. The book ends on that ambiguous note which characterizes the endings of the other legends of *The Faerie Queene,* a compromise between the storyteller's demand for a resolution and the moralist's conviction that the world stands irresolute. St. George must fulfill his duty to Gloriana, Gryll will still be Gryll, Scudamour has not yet won his Amoret, Marinell and Florimell are affianced but not wed, Artegall is called away before he can complete his task. So Calidore at last conquers the Blatant Beast and binds him with an iron chain, but the end is not an end. Since that time the Beast has escaped and now ranges the world, grown great and strong,

> Ne spareth he most learned wits to rate,
> Ne spareth he the gentle Poets rime,
> But rends without regard of person or of time. (xii.40)

Wearied and discouraged by his long hunt, Sir Calidore betrayed his purpose by seeking safe contentment among the shepherds. Wearied and discouraged by the slanderous attacks made on his "former writs" and without hope that this new work will fare better, Spenser too resolves to escape from his duty:

> Therefore do you my rimes keep better measure,
> And seeke to please, that now is counted wisemens threasure.
>
> (xii.41)

"And seeke to please," for Spenser, is as much as to say that he has abandoned his task. And only the fragmentary Cantos of Mutabilitie—if indeed they were written after these lines—remain to suggest that he made any more of *The Faerie Queene*.

Cantos of Mutabilitie

THE EVER-WHIRLING WHEEL

ALTHOUGH NO ONE, I think, has questioned Spenser's author-
ship of the posthumously published fragment entitled "Two Cantos
of Mutabilitie" (actually two cantos numbered vi and vii and two
stanzas of Canto viii) some scholars have found it impossible to
understand how a Legend of Constancie built around it could
conform to the method of the other books and therefore have
doubted that it was ever planned as the "core" of a seventh book
of *The Faerie Queene*.[1] I cannot with any security guess how the
rest of a Legend of Constancie would have been written—who the
champion would have been, what episodes would have been included, how such a book would have ended or been linked with
the others. It seems to me quite certain, at least, that it would have
differed from the books we have, as each differs from the next, for
Spenser rarely if ever builds twice alike. But if the basic approach
of this study is valid, we should expect to find those characteristics
in any new book of *The Faerie Queene* which serve to bind the
others together and so constitute the unity of the whole. The
attempt to demonstrate this for the Cantos of Mutabilitie becomes,
in effect, a restatement of the conclusions drawn in the preceding
chapters concerning the structure and philosophy of the poem.

Each book of *The Faerie Queene,* I have tried to show, announces itself as an "imitation" of a particular literary model appropriate to its meaning. Each defines a moral problem by reference to an ideal world in which the problem does not exist, investigates it in terms of the oppositions and paradoxes which create it, and expresses those oppositions and paradoxes in a wide variety of ways, among them a political dimension. Each presents its resolution in a central episode which portrays the goodness, harmony, and fruitfulness of which this world is capable. And each recognizes that since such a resolution is of this world it must be tentative only.

In modeling his Legend of Constancie, Spenser turned inevitably to the classical work on the subject of mutability, Ovid's *Metamorphoses:*

> In nova fert animus mutatas dicere formas
> Corpora

From the *Metamorphoses* he derived not only his resolving symbol, the goddess Natura, but also the inspiration for each of the three sections that make up the cantos, Mutabilitie's challenge to the gods, the episode of Faunus and Diana, and the pageant of the changeful world. These parallels have been known to Spenser scholarship for many years.[2] They require examination here both because they sharply illuminate Spenser's way with his literary models and because they suggest the particular emphasis he wished to give to the theme of his new book.

Ovid begins with the beginning, the forming of the world out of chaos by god or nature (a passage Spenser echoes in his *Hymne of Love*) and its progressive degeneration from an age of gold to the age of iron. Spenser's equivalent in these cantos is a brief account of the perversion of "all which Nature had establisht first/ In good estate" by the Titaness Mutabilitie who not only "wrong of right, and bad of good did make" but also in biblical rather than pagan terms "death for life exchanged foolishlie." Then Ovid tells of the

attempt of the giants to scale the heights of heaven by piling Pelion
on Ossa and of their destruction by Jove's thunderbolt. Yet the
enemy of the gods is not altogether destroyed:

> the bulk of those huge bodies
> Lay on the earth, and bled, and Mother Earth,
> Made pregnant by that blood, brought forth new bodies,
> And gave them, to recall her older offspring,
> The forms of men. And this new stock was also
> Contemptuous of the gods, and murder-hungry
> And violent. You would know they were sons of blood.[3]

Spenser's Jove makes this earthy, bloody tradition the genesis of
Mutabilitie. He reminds the assembly of gods of the attempt upon
heaven of "Earths cursed seed":

> But how we then defeated all their deed,
> Yee all doe knowe, and them destroied quite;
> Yet not so quite, but that there did succeed
> An off-spring of their bloud, which did alite
> Upon the fruitfull earth, which doth us yet despite.

> Of that bad seed is this bold woman bred   (vi.20, 21)

And in his narration of Mutabilitie's ascent to the sphere of the moon
and the resulting chaos Spenser conflates the gigantomachia of Ovid's
first book with the tale of Phaeton's wild ride in his father's chariot
of the second.

Ovid describes the council of the gods at which Jove, angered by
the threat posed to the order of the world by human evil (a threat
particularized in the wolflike impiety of Lycaon), shakes his awful
locks, at which earth, sea, and sky tremble, and ponders the annihilation of humanity. The gods assent, though they are troubled by the
prospect of an earth empty of mankind. But as Jove's thunderbolt
is poised for destruction he stays his hand and decides to use the
weapon of deluge instead. The story follows of the universal flood
from which Deucalion and Pyrrha alone are saved. Spenser's Jove,

too, consults with the heavenly assembly as to how the threat to cosmic harmony may be met. The allusion to the Ovidian model is unmistakable:

> With that, he shooke
> His Nectar-deawed locks, with which the skyes
> And all the world beneath for terror quooke,
> And eft his burning levin-brond in hand he tooke. (vi.30)

But he stays his hand,

> and having chang'd his cheare,
> He thus againe in milder wise began;
> But ah! if Gods should strive with flesh yfere,[a]
> Then shortly should the progeny of Man
> Be rooted out, if Jove should doe still what he can (vi.31)

Having required his readers to recall the *Metamorphoses,* however, Spenser at the same time makes sure that they recognize the difference between the classical treatment of the challenge to the gods and his own.

For nothing redeems the ugliness of Lycaon's sin; there is no shadow of right on his side; his end and that of evil humanity are justly decreed by an all-powerful Jove. If Ovid's god refrains from incinerating the world it is because he finds virtue in Deucalion and his wife. But the new Jove is disarmed by Mutabilitie's beauty. Though she has brought evil into the world, she is

> of stature tall as any there
> Of all the Gods, and beautifull of face,
> As any of the Goddesses in place (vi.28)

Nor is there any suggestion that this beauty is a magical or cosmetic appearance like that of Duessa and the false Florimell. Furthermore, Mutabilitie's claim is not without justice, and Jove is unable to deny it. She bases it on the blood—literal and figurative—which gave her

[a] yfere: together.

birth, blood nobler and more ancient than that of the Olympian gods. On her mother's side she derives from Earth, child of Chaos; on her father's from Titan, whose younger brother Saturn thrust him from his right. Jove cannot be arbiter here; however he may "inly grudge" he must allow the appeal to the god of Nature.

The hearing of that appeal is deferred while the poet tells the story of Diana and "foolish God Faunus." Like the tale of Mutabilitie's assault upon heaven, this episode is not a borrowing from the *Metamorphoses* but a kind of parody of it. In Ovid's version the noble youth Actaeon stumbles unawares upon Diana's grotto; he is the helpless victim of fate and his transformation into a deer and the tearing of his flesh by his own hounds punish no sin that he has wilfully committed. But Spenser's Faunus (so called because Vergil's annotator Servius derives Faunus and Fatuus, the Foolish One, from the same root[4]) brings about his own disaster and with it the destruction of the paradise of Arlo Hill. With obvious reference to the temptation of Eve he corrupts the nymph Molanna with "Queene-apples, and red Cherries from the tree" and, fool that he is, having achieved the forbidden sight breaks out into loud laughter. Yet though he brings his punishment upon himself, it is not the tragic end of Actaeon; he is merely dressed in a deerskin and chased for a while by the dogs. His discomfiture, in fact, is comic, like that of Falstaff in *The Merry Wives of Windsor*. The river-nymph Molanna is let off lightly too: her stream bed is "whelmed with stones" but she is allowed to join with her beloved Fanchin. And although Diana deserts Arlo Hill and plagues it with wolves and robbers, it is still covered with fair forests, feeds delicious brooks, and overlooks a fruitful plain.

The trial scene at Nature's court which is described in Canto vii is also indebted to the *Metamorphoses,* the principal inspiration being the long speech of Pythagoras in Ovid's last book. Like the philosopher's oration, the pageant which Mutabilitie summons has the purpose of demonstrating the changefulness of the world. The adaptation is free: Spenser expands some parts of the testimony and changes or suppresses others. The Pythagorean plea for vegetarianism becomes merely a reference to

> The beasts we daily see massacred dy
> As thralls and vassalls unto mens beheasts (vii.19)

If the idea of metempsychosis appears at all it is in the form of the proposition that matter is indestructible:

> out of their decay and mortall crime,
> We daily see new creatures to arize;
> And of their Winter spring another Prime,
> Unlike in forme, and chang'd by strange disguise (vii.18)

Pythagoras' long catalogue of changes in the geography of the earth Spenser omits altogether, perhaps with the intention of using it elsewhere in the book.

But it is the contrast between Ovid's conclusion and that of Spenser that particularly illuminates the central concern of these cantos. Ovid is not satisfied, at least for his literary purposes, to accept as ultimate the idea of an uncertain, degenerating world. He assigns to Jove a final speech which qualifies the long history of mutable fortunes. For Julius Caesar and Augustus there are thrones in heaven; the former is a star that burns forever and the latter outshines even his father's glory. And in an epilogue the poet claims that despite a wrathful Jove, or war, or fire, or flood, or venomous time, the book of *Metamorphoses* and the name of its author will endure as long as Rome remains the Eternal City. Although in *The Ruines of Time* and elsewhere Spenser responds to the challenge of mutability in ways similar to these of Ovid, he elects another kind of resolution to be uttered by the goddess Nature. Here he has posed the problem in different terms, and these terms demand a different answer. The altercation between the Titaness, born of blood and earth, and the heavenly gods inquires into the relationship between the mortal and the divine, the created and the creator. Nature's decision must be a cosmic one.

The cosmos before Mutabilitie's foolish exchange of wrong for right and death for life, and Arlo Hill before Faunus' fatuous pursuit of forbidden knowledge, provide the standard by which the state of the present may be known. Similar reference points are to be found in each of the books of *The Faerie Queene,* realms free of the evil and darkness which perturb and obscure this life. The unsullied state is Eden before the Old Dragon besieged it, the golden world in which Astraea dwelt, Belphoebe's pavilion and the Garden of Adonis, the glorious history of Fairyland about which Guyon reads in the House of Alma, the Acidalian mount, or, vaguely, that "antique age yet in the infancie/ Of time" when "loyall love had royall regiment" (IV.viii.30). The happy states may be biblical, chivalric, poetic, or philosophic in inspiration; they are alike in that they are neither the unchanging serenity of heaven—that is, the New Jerusalem—nor the dark confusion of the mundane. They belong to the category to which the French humanist Guillaume Budé assigns More's *Utopia:* "a state . . . leading a kind of heavenly life, on a lower level indeed than heaven, but above the defilements of this world we know," [5] the world of nature, that is, as it would be were evil absent.

The folly of Mutabilitie has fouled the pure world with sin and death, that of Faunus with wolves and robbers. Elsewhere in *The Faerie Queene* these evil consequences are given horrible shapes: they are dragons, monsters, spotted beasts, hideous women, and repulsive giants. Their attributes are simple ones: they destroy, disrupt, bind, render sterile. But the dark powers do not reign over the world they have invaded, for poised against them are opposing simplicities, Una's lamb, Britomart's virginal spear, Artegall's sword Chrysaor. In the Cantos of Mutabilitie the purely dark and the purely bright appear only on the fringes as Mutabilitie's ancestor Chaos and the ultimate pillars of eternity. The poet's principal concern is less with these polar abstractions than with the real world lying between them.

Since Arlo is an Irish hill, it is a metaphor not only for an Eden decayed but also for a fertile and beautiful country tormented by rebellion and lawlessness. As we have seen, political analogy of this kind appears frequently throughout the poem. In these cantos, as elsewhere, the reference is not merely a separable meaning communicated to an inner circle. Ireland and France, Queen Elizabeth, Mary of Scotland, and Sir Walter Ralegh are appropriate to *The Faerie Queene* because they are instances of the real world which is its subject.

That world is not, for Spenser, a Manichaean battleground on which light and dark, good and evil, battle for supremacy. Rather, it is at once both light and dark, good and evil. In it, Una's black stole is as necessary to her as the sunny brightness of her face, Alma's house may be the most fair and excellent of dwellings or the most foul and indecent, Venus is both the mistress of the fruitful Garden of Adonis and the Acrasia-like temptress portrayed in the tapestry of Malecasta's Castle Joyeous, Concord is flanked by Love and Hate, Osiris threatens the state and preserves it. These are not superficial paradoxes; indeed the whole structure of Spenser's moral philosophy and the poem he wrote to express it is based upon them. Faith and Doubt do not contend for the soul of St. George; faith engenders his sense of guilt and fear of damnation is evidence of his faith. The drive to satisfy human aspirations leads to the loss of humanity. Love of beauty, the necessary motive to generation, turns instead to agony and sterile lust. The union of friends and lovers is rooted in antagonism, and the bond so formed arouses the fear and jealousy which tend to disrupt it. Law may be cruel and mercy partial; because of his justice the righteous man is thought unjust. The same qualities that make civilized society possible move toward a rejection of society. Whatever is good is not simply good but by its very nature potentially evil.

These ambiguities and self-contradictions are the stuff of *The Faerie Queene*. The simple solutions of the sin-free world are not available in this one. Light and dark are both omnipresent; whatever exists in the mundane partakes of both. Either may dominate, but neither is absent. Duessa is beautiful, at least superficially, and her claim upon the Red Cross Knight is not without justice; Una's beauty is shadowed and she is capable of despair. The shrine of Geryon is not a realm other than the Temple of Isis; it is the same temple upside down, a reciprocal rather than a negative. In Chaucer, too, the one gate to the palace of Venus bears two inscriptions, one of gold and the other of black.

Like Chaucer's gate, Mutabilitie is a figure of this mixed kind, the resultant of Steadfastness and Confusion. Jove is her foil; he claims to be above change but he cannot deny that he and all other heavenly bodies move and "all that moveth doth mutation love." But if Steadfastness does not rule alone, neither does Confusion. For the evidence that Mutabilitie presents in support of her claim to universal dominion is conclusive proof that the world is not a congeries of random motions: the multitude of living creatures that comes to the great trial before the bar of Nature is disposed by the sergeant Order; the orderly succession of seasons, months, hours, of life and death demonstrates not only the variety but also the coherence of the created world.[6]

Like Arlo Hill under Diana's curse, the world is not ugly although ugliness abounds in it. Nature shuts out from her audience the infernal powers, but she does admit Pluto and Proserpina, dark divinities who partake, nevertheless, of the light. The succession of seasons and months brings with it sweat but also harvest, shivering cold and blazing heat but also the warm fire and the cooling bath. The meaning of the exclusion of the infernal powers is reflected in the descriptions of Night and Death, part of Mutabilitie's procession. Night is not the simple evil to whom Duessa appeals in the Legend of Holinesse. Here she

> covered her uncomely face
> With a blacke veile, and held in hand a mace,
> On top whereof the moon and stars were pight,
> And sleep and darknesse round about did trace

and here she is the mother, not of Falsehood, but of

> the Howres, faire daughters of high Jove,
> . . . the which were all endewed
> With wondrous beauty fit to kindle love　　　　　(vii.44, 45)

Death, too, is no unambiguous horror:

> Death with most grim and griesly visage seene,
> Yet is he nought but parting of the breath;
> Ne ought to see, but like a shade to weene,
> Unbodied, unsoul'd, unheard, unseene.　　　　　(vii.46)

In the context of Nature, labor, night, and death form part of the enormous variety which is the beauty of Mutabilitie.

In the mixture of human life the dark may predominate. When it does, we enter the House of Pride, Acrasia's Bower, Malecasta's castle, the den of Ate, Grantorto's realm, the lair of the Brigants. The contrasting state is presided over by symbolic figures Venus-like or associated with Venus. There is Charissa who hates Cupid's wanton snare but sits in an ivory throne with doves at her feet and playful infants all about her. The task of her servants arises out of the world's evil: they bring rest to the weary, food to the hungry, comfort to the sick, burial to the dead. Alma, epithet of Venus in the Lucretian hymn, maintains the order of her house against difference within and siege without. Venus and Diana reconcile their antagonism, and Venus herself reigns over a temple the gate of which is guarded by Doubt, Delay, and the hideous giant Danger.

Isis (another name for Venus according to Renaissance mythographers) holds the fierce Osiris in check. The Graces who teach men to live together are playfellows of Venus; they disport themselves apart from the haunts of men on the Acidalian mount.

These Venus-figures assert the harmony which this world can achieve, a true concord unlike that perverse agreement of the Bower of Bliss. They join together, yet without destroying, faith and doubt, reason and the passions, virginity and womanliness, law and equity. With the exception, perhaps, of the realm of the Graces, their states are not Eden or the age of gold; darkness is of their essence and they could not exist at all without it. And in a sense Mount Acidale, too, belongs to this category, for although it is purely beautiful it is so only because the ugly is deliberately excluded from it:

> For all that ever was by natures skill
> Devized to work delight, was gathered there,
> And there by her were poured forth at fill,
> As if this to adorne, she all the rest did pill.   (VI.x.5)

But that which Nature devised to work pain is absent. In the Legend of Courtesie the Venus-resolution, available only in a fenced-off paradise, is complemented by that of the Hermit. To the Graces is assigned the positive role of endowing some men with the qualities that make civil society possible, to the Hermit the negative one of teaching how the forces which disrupt it may be dealt with and how the wounds which those forces inevitably inflict may be cured. Together, the Graces and the Hermit correspond to the healing and harmonizing symbols of the other books.

The goddess Nature of the Mutabilitie cantos is a Venus of the kind I have been describing. Much has been written about the tradition from which she derives: she has in her something of Lucretius and Ovid, of Boethius and Chaucer, perhaps also of Jean de Meun and Alain de Lille. Like the resolvers of the other books she combines within herself the sharpest of contraries. Since her face is hidden she may be either man or woman, like the hermaphrodite Venus of the Legend of Friendship. "Some" say that she wears a veil

> To hide the terror of her uncouth hew,
> From mortall eyes that should be sore agrized;
> For that her face did like a Lion shew,
> That eye of wight could not endure to view

but others tell

> that it so beautious was,
> And round about such beames of splendor threw,
> That it the Sunne a thousand times did pass,
> Ne could be seene, but like an image in a glass. (vii.6)

Even within the second alternative the reminiscence of the Medusa story incorporates the terrible with the beautiful.

For the purposes of the Legend of Constancie, the most important quality of Dame Nature is not her encompassing of male and female, or beauty and terror. She is also

> ever young yet full of eld,
> Still mooving, yet unmoved from her sted (vii.13)

She is therefore both growth and decay, which is mutability, and yet she is always young and always old, which is steadfastness—ever moving, never changing. By implication at least the paradox is suggested whenever the theme of the world's decay appears, for the mundane, however mutable and degenerate, must nevertheless be the work of a creator perfect and beyond change. The problem of reconciling these oppositions is met head on by Nature's response to the challenge of the Titaness.

That verdict, which grants dominion to Jove, the constant though mutable, rather than to the appellant, the mutable though constant, is almost painfully terse:

> I well consider all that ye have sayd,
> And find that all things stedfastnes doe hate
> And changed be: yet being rightly wayd

> They are not changed from their first estate;
> But by their change their being doe dilate:
> And turning to themselves at length again,
> Doe worke their owne perfection so by fate:
> Then over them Change doth not rule and raigne;
> But they raigne over change, and doe their states maintaine.
>
> Cease therefore daughter further to aspire,
> And thee content thus to be rul'd by me:
> For thy decay thou seekst by thy desire;
> But time shall come that all shall changed bee,
> And from thenceforth, none no more change shall see.
>
> (vii.58–59)

A victory for Mutabilitie would mean an end to mutability, for when
the time comes that all changes, the poet declares in his own person
in the last stanza of these cantos,

> no more Change shall be,
> But stedfast rest of all things firmely stayd
> Upon the pillours of Eternity,
> That is contrayr to Mutabilitie:
> For, all that moveth, doth in Change delight:
> But thence-forth all shall rest eternally
> With Him that is the God of Sabbaoth hight:
> O! that great Sabbaoth God, grant me that Sabaoths sight.

The word "thence-forth" divides the world in which Mutabilitie is
everywhere from that in which she plays no role at all.

The distinction appears in classical times as an attempt to reconcile
the finity of the mundane with the infinity of its maker and in the
Christian era with the added purpose of accommodating the philosophical conception of a world without beginning or end with the
biblical account of creation and judgment. It is found, for example,
in Book V of Boethius' *Consolation of Philosophy,* and a sixteenth-
century English commentary on that book provides a clear statement
of the idea:

Syth than mesure of mevying is called tyme, then sueth hyt that before the worlde meved ther was no tyme. But God eternally ys, er eny thyng meved; or any tyme were, and shall he after that all mevynges cesseth. For hys beyng is mesured by no mevyng of before and after for all tymes present passed and to come, ben to hym verely present. Ne hys beynge is not mesured by successyon of tymes. For he hathe hys beynge unmesured all at ones, wyche ys called hys eternyte. Therfore is god called Inmensus. But the perdurabelte of the worlde ys mesured by mevyng of the heven, wyche is called tyme and lenger than heven meveth shal ther be no tyme. Than ys yt so that the beyng of God is called eternite. The beyng of thys world ys named perpetuyte. Then ys thys the conceyt of Plato sayng that the worlde hath ever ben, That ys to mene, as longe as any thyng hath meved. And as long as anythyng meveth or any tyme ys, so long it shall endure in suche beynge as it now hathe. And after that al mevyng and al tymes cesseth, the worlde renued shal endure in lyffe interminable.[7]

The world of Mutabilitie, in these terms, is perdurable or perpetual; that of the final Sabbath eternal. It is with the former that the first stanza of Nature's judgment is concerned.

Within the frame of the created world, Nature asserts, all things change yet maintain their "states," reigning over change. The paradox is kin to that which describes Adonis in the Legend of Chastitie:

> All be he subject to mortalitie,
> Yet is eterne in mutabilitie,
> And by succession made perpetuall,
> Transformed oft, and chaunged diverslie

If in these lines Spenser is using words in the sense of the Boethius commentator, the expression "eterne in mutabilitie" is itself a paradoxical way of saying "perpetual." But Nature's pronouncement goes beyond a restatement of the idea that although individuals die species endure. It is concerned rather with the question which she, as judge, must settle, the assignment to Mutabilitie of her proper place in the world.

All things, Nature declares, have a "first estate." Their change
from it is not really a change at all but a fateful dilation of their
"being" which results at last in a return to "themselves," or self-
fulfillment. "Rightly wayd," therefore, mutability is the working out
of what was implicit from the beginning, and it is therefore necessary to constancy, the maintenance of "states." The perpetual whirl-
ing of the wheel in time expresses the nature of the wheel.

The conception has a long history. It is found, in rather rudimen-
tary form, in Boethius, and what Boethius says is endlessly repeated
and commented on throughout the Middle Ages.[8] But a very full
statement appears in Plotinus. The "first estate" of which Nature
speaks corresponds in kind to the philosopher's unmoving unity
which holds change and multiplicity compact within it. From that
unity derives that which attempts to achieve through change and
multiplicity the perfection and fullness of its origin. Plotinus distinguishes between the world of change and its logical antecedent:

Engendered things are in continuous process of acquisition; eliminate
futurity, therefore, and at once they lose their being; if the non-engen-
dered are made amenable to futurity they are thrown down from the seat
of their existence, for, clearly, existence is not theirs by their nature if it
appears only as a being about to be, a becoming, an advancing from stage
to stage.[9]

Such "being" as engendered things are capable of they achieve exactly because they change, because, that is, they are in a state of
continual "acquisition," of "advancing from stage to stage." By means
of extension in time and variation in form they imitate the timeless
and all-inclusive, or as Nature puts it, "by their change their being
doe dilate."

The folly of Faunus and of Mutabilitie is therefore not only an
allusion to Adam's error. The descent from the single perfection of
the first state into multiplicity is also the foolish dilation which
Plotinus describes:

A seed is at rest; the nature-principle within, uncoiling outward, makes way towards what seems to it a large life; but by that partition it loses; it was a unity self-gathered, and now, in going forth from itself, it fritters its unity away; it advances into a weaker greatness.[10]

The parallel between the departure of Adam from Eden and the departure of the Plotinian seed from itself, however, is essentially faulty. If this part of Nature's decree were cast in Christian terms it would necessarily turn upon the sin which was the occasion of the Fall and upon Christ's sacrifice by which alone it becomes possible to conceive of a return to an original state of perfection. Instead, Spenser seeks to reconcile the positions of theologian and philosopher. The loss of the "first estate" he ascribes primarily to folly, a term sufficiently ambiguous for either to accept. And since even a theologian would agree that the Fall was not utter tragedy nor God's curse on Adam devoid of felicity the poet is able to allude to the Fall in a comic episode and to describe the power by which the world came to be cursed as a beautiful woman.

The condition of the world

> which Nature had establisht first
> In good estate, and in meet order ranged   (vi.5)

cannot be retrieved in perdurable time. But the natural process of change, or becoming, reflects that good estate to the extent that the necessarily imperfect can imitate the necessarily perfect. The justice of Artegall is such an imitation of the justice of Astraea; the love of Scudamour and Amoret of the love of the Garden of Adonis. Throughout *The Faerie Queene,* the unending struggles and incomplete victories of the champions of virtue are set against Eden and the age of gold.

Since the only way in which the finite can imitate the infinite is by diversifying and going on, the test of the imitation is its fruitfulness. That is why Nature's audience is so large

That Arlo scarsly could them all containe;
So full they filled every hill and Plaine   (vii.4)

and why, at the wedding of the Thames and the Medway, there are
so many guests that

more eath it were for mortall wight,
To tell the sands, or count the starres on hye,
Or ought more hard, than thinke to reckon right.   (iv.xi.53)

When the Red Cross Knight visits the House of Holinesse, Charissa
has just given birth to another child: "thankt be God, and her en-
crease so evermore" (i.x.16). From Britomart's love will spring
noble deeds and from her loins "Most famous fruits of matrimoniall
bowre" (iii.iii.3). Merlin's words to her prophesy the divine end of
her earthly fecundity:

that Tree,
Whose big embodied braunches shall not lin,
Till they to heavens hight forth stretched bee.   (iii.iii.22)

The very forest which is the setting for the first episode of *The
Faerie Queene* is a symbol of the variety, richness, and beauty of the
world's creatures. Yet here the accent falls upon the other implication of mundane plenitude: however delightful the forest, it "heavens
light did hide."

Such ambiguous and distorted reflections of the paradisal state are
constantly under threat of dissolution into chaos. Mutabilitie's ambition brings the moon to a standstill and fills even the gods with fear

least Chaos broken had his chaine,
And brought againe on them eternall night   (vi.14)

The quarrel among the four knights over the false Florimell is compared to a storm at sea in which the winds

all the world confound with wide uprore
As if in stead thereof they Chaos would restore.   (iv.ix.23)

The task of Ate is to bring the world's fair workmanship to its last
confusion,

> And that great golden chaine quite to divide,
> With which it blessed Concord hath together tide.   (IV.i.30)

Confusion, night, and death are the fruit of the Brigants' lair and of the House of Pride. And mortal power is not great enough to avert the catastrophe.

For Spenser does not conceive of Nature's justification of Mutabilitie as adequate in itself. The precarious balance of the world's state may be self-sustaining to a philosopher; it cannot serve for a Christian. In the first of the last two stanzas of the Cantos of Mutabilitie, Spenser declares that although steadfastness may rule over change in the heavens it is change rather than steadfastness that rules the terrestrial sphere:

> Which makes me loath this state of life so tickle,
> And love of things so vaine to cast away;
> Whose flowring pride, so fading and so fickle,
> Short Time shall soon cut down with his consuming sickle.

At critical points throughout the poem the poet reminds us of human helplessness in the struggle with the dark. Since man is surely incapable of salvation through his own efforts, the note is dominant in the Legend of Holinesse. But it is heard in the other books as well. Not their own strength but God's grace rescues Guyon and Arthur in the Legend of Temperaunce. It saves Florimell from the clutches of the lecherous fisherman. When Amoret is about to be recaptured by Greedy Lust, heaven's help alone can redress her wrong. Arthur cannot overcome the Souldan until he unveils his shield of truth; Talus is of no avail here:

> by heavens high decree
> Justice that day of wrong her self had wroken [b]   (v.viii.44)

And indeed those happy accidents from St. George's fortunate fall into the Well of Life to Calepine's arrival "by chaunce, more then by choice" in time to save Serena from death at the hands of the savages (VI.viii.46) can only be understood as divine intervention.

[b] wroken: revenged.

For none of the books of *The Faerie Queene,* therefore, is a true conclusion possible. The powers of darkness may for a time be held prisoner, seen in their true horror and rendered impotent, but since they are of earth's essence they will again break free and threaten destruction, night, and chaos. Despite that ever-present threat, indeed because of it, the created world remains beautiful, various, and fecund, and man may hope that when his own strength cannot avail to keep it so the grace of God will come to his aid. So much of victory is all that can be expected as long as the Red Cross Knight serves Gloriana and Mutabilitie fulfills her natural function. Beyond, and really beyond the bounds of *The Faerie Queene,* St. George unites forever with Una in that final Sabbath when all things rest upon the pillars of Eternity.

Notes

Prince of Poets

1. The principal facts concerning Spenser's life are assembled by F. I. Carpenter, *A Reference Guide to Edmund Spenser* (Chicago, 1923), D. F. Atkinson, *Edmund Spenser, a Bibliographical Supplement* (Baltimore, 1937), and A. C. Judson, *The Life of Edmund Spenser* (Baltimore, 1945). The reader is referred to these works for documentation not provided by the notes.

2. See Douglas Hamer, "Edmund Spenser's Gown and Shilling," *Review of English Studies*, XXIII (1947), 218–25. Hamer concludes that the gift of the gown and shilling was not made "because of either scholastic or real poverty" (p. 225).

3. Although the identity of the Edmund Spenser who was married on that date remains uncertain, the argument for his being the poet seems to me strong. See Judson, *Life*, pp. 62–63, and Mark Eccles, "Elizabethan Edmund Spensers," *Modern Language Quarterly*, V (1944), 423–27.

4. W. A. Ringler, Jr., in "Spenser, Shakespeare, Honor, and Worship," *Renaissance News*, XIV (1961), 159–61, argues that Spenser originally intended to dedicate the poem to Leicester himself.

5. It is possible that Spenser had been in Ireland before, in 1577, for the speaker who expresses his ideas in *A Vewe of the Present State of Irelande* describes an event of that year as an eyewitness. See Judson, *Life*, p. 46. The poet may have been employed on other government missions even while he was a student at Cambridge. A bill dated October 18, 1569, is signed to one "Edmonde Spencer" as bearer of letters to the Queen from Sir Henry Norris, English ambassador to France at Tours (Carpenter, *Reference Guide*, p. 13). Eccles, *Modern Language Quarterly*, V, 415, is inclined to think the messenger was the poet.

6. See W. B. C. Watkins, "The Plagiarist: Spenser or Marlowe?" *ELH*, II (1944), 249–65. In a letter to the *London Times Literary Supplement*, Jan. 1, 1938 (p. 12), Douglas Bush points out other probable borrowings by Marlowe from Spenser in both parts of *Tamburlaine, Dido,* and *Hero and Leander.* He remarks that Marlowe seems to have drawn particularly from Book i, Cantos vi, vii, and viii. I have not seen Georg Schoeneich, *Der litterarische Einfluss Spensers auf Marlowe* (Halle, 1907).

7. The dedication of *Daphnaida,* an elegy on Lady Douglas Howard who died in August, 1590, is dated from London on New Year's Day, 1591. If this means 1591 as we count the years, Spenser is not likely to have been abroad three days before, as Ponsonby testifies. If it means 1592, as it may in the practice of the time, the date conflicts with the dedication to Ralegh of *Colin Clouts Come Home Againe* from Kilcolman on December 27, 1591. The earlier date is the more likely.

8. Sonnet lxxx of the *Amoretti,* which was entered for publication in 1594, asserts that the poet had by that time completed the writing of six books of *The Faerie Queene.*

9. *The Historie of the Life and Reigne of the Most Renowmed and Victorious Princesse Elizabeth . . . Faithfully Translated into English* (London, 1630), Book IV, p. 135. The statement first appears in the Latin edition of 1615.

10. *Ibid.* Joseph Hall is another contemporary of Spenser's who reports that the poet died of "unbeseeming Care/ And secret want." See "To Camden" and "To William Bedell" in *The Collected Poems of Joseph Hall,* ed. A. Davenport (Liverpool, 1949), pp. 105, 123.

11. The fragmentary official records suggest that the pension was paid regularly. See Herbert Berry and E. K. Timings, "Spenser's Pension," *Review of English Studies,* N.S. XI (1960), 254–59.

12. The Diary of John Manningham (Carpenter, *Reference Guide,* p. 68).

13. Th. Birch, *Memoirs of the Reign of Queen Elizabeth* (1754), I, 131 (Mr. Standen to Anthony Bacon).

14. Contemporary references to the "calling in" are conveniently assembled in the *Works,* VIII, 580 ff. See also Harold Stein, *Studies in Spenser's Complaints* (New York, 1934).

15. Edwin Greenlaw, *Studies in Spenser's Historical Allegory* (Baltimore, 1932), Chapter III *passim.*

16. See the list of works dedicated to Leicester in Eleanor Rosenberg, *Leicester, Patron of Letters* (New York, 1955), pp. 355–62.

17. Dedication of *Colin Clouts Come Home Againe.*

18. Dedicatory sonnet to *The Faerie Queene.*

19. Dedication of *The Ruines of Time.*

20. Dedicatory sonnet to *The Faerie Queene.*

21. *Works,* IX, 6.   22. *Ibid.,* IX, 471.

23. Suggested identifications of "Wrenock" are reviewed by L. S. Friedland, "Spenser's 'Wrenock,' *Shakespeare Association Bulletin,* XVIII (1943), 41–47.

24. According to Roland M. Smith, "Spenser's Scholarly Script and 'Right Writing,' " in *Studies in Honor of T. W. Baldwin* (Urbana, Ill., 1958), "Mulcaster contributed little to the spelling of Spenser" (p. 91).

25. *The Epigrams of Sir John Harington,* ed. N. E. McClure (Philadelphia, 1926), p. 103.

26. H. S. Wilson, in *Gabriel Harvey's Ciceronianus* (first printed 1577), ed. and tr. H. S. Wilson and Clarence A. Forbes (University of Nebraska Studies, November, 1945; Studies in the Humanities No. 4), p. 32.

27. *Letter-Book of Gabriel Harvey,* ed. E. J. L. Scott (Camden Society, 1884), p. 134.

28. Judson, *Life,* p. 53.

29. See *Elizabethan Critical Essays,* ed. G. Gregory Smith (Oxford, 1904), I, 360, n. 9. In matters of spelling, too, Spenser disobeys Harvey's instruction. R. M. Smith, in *Studies in Honor of T. W. Baldwin,* p. 96, quotes Harvey: "Have wee not *Mooneth,* for *Moonthe: sithence,* for *since: whilest,* for *whilste: phantasie* for *phansie: even,* for *evn . . .* and a thousande of the same stampe: wherein corrupte Orthography in the moste, hath been the sole, or principall cause of corrupte *Prosodye* in over many?" Smith points out that Spenser nevertheless continued to write *mooneth, sithens, whilest, fantasy,* and *even.*

30. This is the conclusion of V. K. Whitaker, *The Religious Basis of Spenser's Thought* (Stanford University Publications in Language and Literature, Vol. VII, No. 3, Stanford, Calif., 1950).

31. See *A Vewe of the Present State of Irelande,* in *Works,* Vol. IX, especially ll. 2681 ff. and 5028 ff.

32. *Of the Laws of Ecclesiastical Polity,* Book v (Everyman's Library, 1922), p. 320.

33. *Works,* Vol. IX, ll. 3360 ff.

34. *English Literature in the Sixteenth Century* (Oxford, 1954), pp. 1–65.

35. Tr. E. W. Sutton (Loeb Classical Library, London, 1948), i.viii.33.

36. *Musophilus*, ll. 939–50, in *Poems and A Defence of Ryme*, ed. A. C. Sprague (Cambridge, Mass., 1930).

37. *The Ruines of Time*, ll. 451–53.

Colin Clout

1. The last lines of this Envoy disclaim the ambition to compete with "Tityrus" or with "the Pilgrim that the Ploughman playde a while." I take Tityrus in this context to mean Vergil, although the name is used for Chaucer in the February eclogue and Vergil is specifically "the Romish Tityrus" in *October*. The Plowman-Pilgrim must refer to the Chaucerian (not for Spenser pseudo-Chaucerian) *Plowman's Tale* in which the Plowman does indeed play the Pilgrim for a while. Some scholars understand "Tityrus" to mean Chaucer and the Plowman Langland. A. C. Hamilton, who holds this view, reads Spenser's line as a reference to a Pilgrim (i.e., Langland's Piers) who played the role of a Plowman ("The Visions of *Piers Plowman* and *The Faerie Queene*," in *Form and Convention in the Poetry of Edmund Spenser: Selected Papers from the English Institute*, ed. William Nelson [New York, 1961], pp. 2–3).

2. It is sometimes conjectured that E. K. is Spenser himself, and the idea dies hard. See D. T. Starnes, "Spenser and E. K.," *Studies in Philology*, XLI (1944), 181–200.

3. *Works*, IX, 18.

4. *The Shepherd's Calendar*, ed. W. L. Renwick (London, 1930), p. 173.

5. The woodcuts themselves resemble those in contemporary editions of Vergil's *Bucolics*. See, for example, *Opera Virgiliana* (Lyons, 1529), fols. XVII ff. These cuts are said to reproduce those in the edition of Jean Grüninger, Strasbourg, 1502, and appear in many sixteenth-century editions of Vergil.

6. *The Shepherd's Calendar*, ed. Renwick, p. 167.

7. Other scholars have come to different conclusions about the structure of the poem. A. C. Hamilton ("The Argument of Spenser's *Shepheardes Calender*," *ELH*, XXIII [1956], 171–82) contends that Spenser's argument is "the rejection of the pastoral life for the truly dedicated life in the world" (p. 181). R. A. Durr ("Spenser's Calendar of Christian Time," *ELH*, XXIV [1957], 269–95) proposes that the governing subject of the poem is "the contrast between good and bad shepherds" (p. 270) and asserts that "the only meaningful division of the *Calender* must therefore be that between the flesh and spirit, *amor carnis* and *amor*

spiritus, between love of self and world and love of neighbor and God" (p. 274).

8. L. Spitzer, "Spenser, *Shepheardes Calender, March* ll. 61–114, and the Variorum Edition," *Studies in Philology,* XLVII (1950), 499.

9. General Prologue to *The Canterbury Tales,* ll. 501–4.

10. I use the large term "Protestant" here although I am aware that not all of those who rejected the authority of the Pope also rejected religious practices lacking scriptural warrant. A desire for the purification of the church, however, is not exclusively "Puritan." I prefer to reserve that label to describe the party that wished to alter or supplant the episcopal system.

11. See also L. S. Friedland, "Spenser as Fabulist," *Shakespeare Association Bulletin,* XII (1937), 97 ff., and the same author's "Spenser's Fable of 'The Oake and the Brere,'" *ibid.,* XVI (1941), 52–57, and "A Source for Spenser's 'The Oak and the Brier,'" *Philological Quarterly,* XXXIII (1954), 222–24.

12. P. E. McLane, *Spenser's "Shepheardes Calender"* (Notre Dame, 1961), p. 32.

13. *Ibid.,* pp. 188–234 and *passim.*

14. *An Apology for Poetry,* in *Elizabethan Critical Essays,* ed. G. Gregory Smith (Oxford, 1904), I, 196.

15. See *Works,* VII, 614 ff.

16. W. L. Renwick, *Edmund Spenser* (London, 1925; reprinted 1957), p. 98.

17. Sannazaro's *Arcadia* is suggested as a model for Spenser's use of a variety of metrical schemes by Francesco Viglione, *La Poesia Lirica di Edmondo Spenser* (Genoa, 1937), p. 170.

18. *Colin Clout,* ll. 53–58.

19. *The Collected Poems of Joseph Hall,* ed. A. Davenport (Liverpool, 1949), p. 97. At this time the word *satire* was thought to be derived from *satyr,* so that a rude, uncivilized manner was considered essential to the form.

20. *Collected Poems of Sir Thomas Wyatt,* ed. Kenneth Muir (London, 1949), pp. 187, 192.

The World's Vanity

1. Spenser's delay in publishing an elegy on Sidney, for which he apologizes in his dedication, may have been the result of a concerted delicacy of sentiment among Sidney's friends which led them to "sup-

press rather than to publish their expressions of sorrow." See *Nobilis, or a View of the Life and Death of a Sidney,* ed. and tr. Virgil B. Heltzel and Hoyt H. Hudson (San Marino, Calif., 1940), p. 70 and note, p. 112.

2. *Complaints,* ed. W. L. Renwick (London, 1928), p. 190.

3. See *The Poems of Sir Arthur Gorges,* ed. H. E. Sandison (Oxford, 1953).

4. IV.i.38

5. *The Steel Glass,* in *The Glasse of Government,* ed. J. W. Cunliffe (Cambridge, 1910), p. 150.

6. See D. L. Aguzzi, "Allegory in the Heroic Poetry of the Renaissance" (unpublished dissertation, Columbia University, 1959), pp. 450 ff.

7. *The Education of a Christian Prince,* tr. L. K. Born (New York, 1936), p. 163.

8. *Ibid.,* p. 165.   9. *Ibid.,* p. 164.   10. *Ibid.*   11. *Ibid.,* p. 165.

12. *Colin Clout,* ll. 1113–14.   13. *Ibid.,* ll. 310–12.

14. The *Tale* seems to have been interpreted as an attack upon Burghley by the anonymous author of *A Declaration of the True Causes* (1592) and by Richard Niccols in *Beggars Ape* (written 1607 and published 1627). See Brice Harris, "The Ape in Mother Hubberds Tale," *Huntington Library Quarterly,* IV (1940–41), 191–203, and Harold Stein, *Studies in Spenser's Complaints* (New York, 1934), pp. 79 ff.

15. See Edwin Greenlaw, *Studies in Spenser's Historical Allegory* (Baltimore, 1932), pp. 115 ff.

Love Creating

1. H. H. Hudson, *The Epigram in the English Renaissance* (Princeton, 1947), pp. 2, 4.

2. Thomas Sebillet, *Art Poétique,* quoted by W. F. Patterson, *Three Centuries of French Poetic Theory* (Ann Arbor, Mich., 1935), I, 260.

3. *The Epigrams of Sir John Harington,* ed. N. E. McClure (Philadelphia, 1926), p. 66: "Comparison of the Sonnet, and the Epigram."

4. John Erskine, *The Elizabethan Lyric* (New York, 1903), pp. 153–54.

5. See Louis L. Martz, "The *Amoretti:* 'Most Goodly Temperature,' " in *Form and Convention in the Poetry of Edmund Spenser: Selected Papers from the English Institute* (New York, 1961), pp. 146–68.

6. *Ibid.*

7. Francesco Viglione, *La Poesia Lirica di Edmondo Spenser* (Genoa, 1937), pp. 299–300, remarks on the link between the last of these odes ("So now I languish till he [Cupid] please,/ my pining anguish to ap-

pease") and the last of the sonnets. He concludes, "La quattro odi, dunque, dello Spenser, sono come un anello di congiunzione tra gli *Amoretti* e l'*Epithalamion;* quindi non fuor di luogo, ma come una pausa, un respiro tra le ultime sofferenze e la glorificazione dell'amore, con la gioie delle nozze."

8. See Thomas M. Greene, "Spenser and the Epithalamic Convention," *Comparative Literature,* IX (1957), 215–28, for a discussion of Spenser's deviations from the tradition.

9. By A. K. Hieatt, *Short Time's Endless Monument* (New York, 1960).

10. Professor Hieatt (*Short Time's Endless Monument,* Chapter II, and "The Daughters of Horus: Order in the Stanzas of *Epithalamion,*" in *Form and Convention in the Poetry of Edmund Spenser,* pp. 103–21) argues that the first twelve stanzas of the poem "match" seriatim the last twelve. His comparisons, though ingenious, seem to me strained, and the effect of his thesis is to obscure what I take to be the obvious structure of the poem.

11. For a recent study of these works and others like them see John Charles Nelson, *Renaissance Theory of Love* (New York, 1958).

12. *The Complete Works of Sir Philip Sidney,* ed. A. Feuillerat (Cambridge, 1912–26), I, 246, 250, 251.

13. *Ibid.,* p. 322.

14. Girolamo Benivieni, "Ode of Love," tr. Jefferson Butler Fletcher, *Literature of the Italian Renaissance* (New York, 1934), p. 340.

15. Spenser's account of the celestial hierarchy has puzzled his commentators because it corresponds to none of the usual descriptions (see C. A. Patrides, "Renaissance Thoughts on the Celestial Hierarchy," *Journal of the History of Ideas,* XX [1959], 161). But there is a close analogue to Spenser's list in *Discorsi del Conte Annibal Romei* (Venice, 1585), pp. 6–7, and it may be that both derive from a common source. Romei's categories and Spenser's begin and end in the same very unusual way. The Italian list runs (from lowest to highest): human souls, intelligences (also called the *anima mundi* and nature), seraphs, cherubs, thrones, dominations, powers, principalities, angels, and archangels. Spenser's version reads: human souls, intelligences and ideas, powers and potentates, dominations, cherubs, seraphs, angels, and archangels. Romei's book was translated into English by J. Kepers under the title *The Courtiers Academy* (1598). See the excerpt from this translation in *The Frame of Order,* ed. James Winney (New York, 1957). In a supplementary note ("Renaissance Views on the 'Unconfused Orders Angellick,' " *Journal of the History of Ideas,* XXIII [1962], 265–67) Patrides

refers in passing to Romei's hierarchy, asserting only that Romei "inadvertently reduced the nine orders to eight." But this count ignores the lowest division of the intellectual realm, the human souls and intelligences which appear also in Spenser's list. Perhaps Romei intended angels and archangels to constitute but a single division.

16. *La Vita Nuova,* ii (tr. P. H. Wicksteed, the Temple Classics).

17. In the *Metamorphoses.* See E. R. Curtius, *European Literature and the Latin Middle Ages,* tr. W. R. Trask (New York, 1953), pp. 106 ff.

18. Book ii, Met. 8.

19. *The History of the World* (first printed 1614; London, 1687), i.i.10.

20. See William and Malleville Haller, "The Puritan Art of Love," *Huntington Library Quarterly,* V (1942), 235–72.

21. John Wing, quoted *ibid.,* p. 261.

22. A. O. Lovejoy, *The Great Chain of Being* (Cambridge, Mass., 1936; reprinted New York, 1960), pp. 24 ff.

23. Ralegh, *History of the World,* i.vi.7.

24. Plotinus, *The Enneads,* tr. Stephen MacKenna, 2d ed. revised by B. S. Page (London, 1956), ii.ix.17. With lines 134–61 of the *Hymne in Honour of Beautie* compare Ficino's comment on this book of the second *Ennead:* "Apud nos quidem potest forte, sed raro, in corpore formoso esse anima in praesentia non formosa, quoniam anima, quae ab ipso conceptionis initio formosa fuit, postea paulatim deformis evasit: sed omnino pulchra erat quondam, quando elegit, coepitque pulchrum corpus effingere, sub pulchro sidere rursum atque daemone. Potest quin etiam esse anima pulchra interdum in corpore non formoso: vel quia, quae quondam pulchra non fuit, pulchra tandem evasit: vel quoniam saepe animae pulchrae molienti formosum corpus effingere, impedimentum quoddam ex his, quae circumstant, et quae confluunt contigit, vel contingit. At animae mundi neque accedit quicquam, neque recedit, neque obstat impedimentum. Nihil enim universo tale potest accidere." *Plotini Opera Omna . . . cum Marsilii Ficini Commentariis* (Oxford, 1835), I, 357. Spenser's rejection of the idea that beauty depends upon proportion (*HB,* 75–77) is specifically Plotinian. See *Enneads,* i.vii.1.

25. *Enneads,* vi.vii.33. Compare *Colin Clouts Come Home Againe,* ll. 871–78.

26. *Enneads,* iii.v.1.   27. *Ibid.,* iii.v.7.   28. *Ibid.,* iii.v.1.

29. *Ibid.,* ii.ix.18.   30. *Ibid.,* vi.vii.34.   31. *Ibid.*

That True Glorious Type

1. I have used the edition entitled *P. Virgilii Maronis Opera cum Servii, Donati, et Ascensii commentariis* (Venice, 1542) (cited hereafter as *Virgilii Opera*). Badius' preface to the *Aeneid* is at fols. 101v–102r. On the subject of Vergil's influence on Spenser see Merritt Y. Hughes, *Virgil and Spenser* (Berkeley, 1929).

2. More properly, the line may be rendered: "Or to speak words at once pleasing and useful to life." But Jonson's version suggests the way in which Renaissance writers understood Horace.

3. "Et hic est ordo rerum gestarum, aut quae pro gestis a poeta recitantur, verum alius longe ordo a poeta observatur."

4. Cooper's *Thesaurus,* the standard Latin-English dictionary of Spenser's time, translates *plausibilis:* "Receyved with joye and clappynge of the handes: acceptable: pleasaunte: plausible."

5. *Godfrey of Bulloigne,* tr. Edward Fairfax (first printed 1600; London, 1687), Sig. A 2 (r).

6. Quoted and translated by D. L. Aguzzi, "Allegory in the Heroic Poetry of the Renaissance" (unpublished dissertation, Columbia University, 1959), p. 208. The passage is also cited by Susannah Jane McMurphy, *Spenser's Use of Ariosto for Allegory* (University of Washington Publications, Language and Literature, Vol. II, 1924), p. 15. G. P. Pigna, in *I romanzi* (1554), ascribes a similar method rather to the romance than to the epic: "The romances readily devote themselves to several deeds of several men, but . . . they concern especially one man who should be celebrated over all the others. And thus they agree with the epic in taking a single person, but not so in taking a single action, for they take as many of them as seem to be sufficient. The number is 'sufficient' when they have put the heroes in all those honorable actions which are sought in a perfect knight" (Bernard Weinberg, *A History of Literary Criticism in the Italian Renaissance* [Chicago, 1961], I, 445–46).

7. 1.xxvi.118, tr. E. W. Sutton (Loeb Classical Library, London, 1948). Compare also Cicero's *Orator,* ii.7: "Atque ego in summo oratore fingendo talem informabo qualis fortasse nemo fuit."

8. Everyman's Library edition of Hoby's translation, pp. 16, 29.

9. Christophoro Landino, *Camaldulenses disputationes* (Strasbourg, 1508), Books III and IV.

10. *Poetics,* xv.4 (tr. S. H. Butcher).

11. Dionigi Altanagi, *Ragionamento de la eccelentia et perfettione de la historia* (1559), quoted by Weinberg, *History of Literary Criticism,* I, 458.

12. By the time Spenser came to write the *Amoretti* he may have decided to follow Vergil's example in making ethics the subject of the first six books of his poem and politics the subject of the last six. So he seems to say in Sonnet LXXX when he promises to attempt "that second worke" after resting from his labor on "those six books" he had already written.

13. Ernst H. Kantorowicz, *The King's Two Bodies, a Study in Medieval Political Theology* (Princeton, 1957), p. 42.

14. Quoted *ibid.,* p. 7.

15. When Mercilla is at last forced by "strong constraint" to doom Duessa she suffers "more then needfull naturall remorse" (v.x.4).

16. The case is forcefully presented by J. W. Bennett, *The Evolution of "The Faerie Queene"* (Chicago, 1942; reprinted New York, 1960).

17. *Works,* IX, 82.

18. See T. D. Kendrick, *British Antiquity* (London, 1950), pp. 128 ff.

19. Compare the attitude of Ronsard with respect to his story of Francus as he expresses it in the 1587 preface to the *Françiade,* cited by I. Silver, *Ronsard and the Hellenistic Renaissance in France* (St. Louis, 1961), pp. 145–46.

20. *Elizabethan Critical Essays,* ed. G. Gregory Smith (Oxford, 1904), I, 164.

21. Henry Peacham, *The Garden of Eloquence* (1593), facsimile reproduction (Gainesville, Fla., Scholars' Facsimiles and Reprints, 1954), p. 25.

22. George Puttenham, *The Arte of English Poesie* (first printed 1589), ed. G. D. Willcock and A. Walker (Cambridge, 1936), p. 187.

23. *Godfrey of Bulloigne,* Sig. A 1 (r-v).

24. *Orlando Furioso in English Heroicall Verse* (first printed 1591; London, 1634), pp. 405 ff. Susannah McMurphy (*Spenser's Use of Ariosto,* p. 15) notes that what commentators on the *Orlando Furioso* mean by allegory "is often merely the moral lesson that may be derived from the incidents. The characters are not embodied virtues and vices, neither are their actions symbolic of spiritual experiences; they are often only men and women who offer examples of virtue and vice, prudence or folly, from which the observer may derive profit."

25. It has not been remarked, I think, that the transformation of Malbecco is imitated from that of Daedalion in Ovid's *Metamorphoses,* XI, ll. 338–45:

Effugit ergo omnes, veloxque cupidine leti
Vertice Parnasi potitur. miseratus Apollo,
Cum se Daedalion saxo misisset ab alto,
Fecit avem et subitis pendentem sustulit alis,
Oraque adunca dedit, curvos dedit unguibus hamos,
Virtutem antiquam, maiores corpore vires.
Et nunc accipiter, nulli satis aequus, in omnes
Saevit aves, aliisque dolens fit causa dolendi.

I have previously noted (*Modern Language Notes*, LXVIII [1953], 226–29) that Spenser drew suggestions for the Malbecco story from George Gascoigne's *Adventures of Master F. J.,* and despite the strictures of Waldo McNeir ("Ariosto's Sospetto, Gascoigne's Suspicion, and Spenser's Malbecco," in *Festschrift für Walther Fischer* [Heidelberg, 1959]) the conclusion still seems to me valid.

26. *The Pastime of Pleasure* (1509), ed. W. E. Mead (London, for the Early English Text Society, O.S. No. 173, 1928), pp. 192 ff. The name of Hawes's monster is "malice prevy."

27. *Ibid.*, pp. 129–30.

28. A. C. Hamilton, *The Structure of Allegory in 'The Faerie Queene'* (Oxford, 1961), pp. 59 ff. For the view that the Legend of Holinesse is not a continued allegorical narrative but is organized in terms of "concepts" according to "the arrangement of Christian doctrines customary in Renaissance theological treatises and confessionals" see Virgil K. Whitaker, "The Theological Structure of the Faerie Queene, Book I," in *That Soveraine Light: Essays in Honor of Edmund Spenser, 1552–1952* (Baltimore, 1952).

29. Hamilton, *Structure of Allegory,* pp. 150–52.

30. Northrop Frye, "The Structure of Imagery in 'The Faerie Queene,'" *University of Toronto Quarterly,* XXX (1961), 123.

31. See the excursus entitled "Jest in Earnest in Medieval Literature" in E. R. Curtius, *European Literature and the Latin Middle Ages,* tr. W. R. Trask (New York, 1953), pp. 417–35. On the subject of Spenser's use of humor see also W. B. C. Watkins, *Shakespeare and Spenser* (Princeton, 1950; reprinted Cambridge, Mass., 1961), Note I, and R. O. Evans, "Spenserian Humor: Faerie Queene III and IV," *Neuphilologische Mitteilungen,* LX (1959), 288–99.

32. See the pseudo-Vergilian *Ciris,* ll. 294 ff.

33. See H. G. Lotspeich, *Classical Mythology in the Poetry of Edmund Spenser* (Princeton, 1932), p. 43. Henry Lyte in a curious book entitled *The Light of Britayne* (1588, reprinted "at the Public Press of

Richard and Arthur Taylor," 1814) identifies Britomartis with "Diana of Calydonia sylva" and with Queen Elizabeth, "The bright Britona of Britayne."

34. *Orlando Furioso in English Heroicall Verse,* p. 15.

The Legend of Holinesse: The Cup and the Serpent

1. "To Mr. George Herbert, with one of my seals, of the anchor and Christ."

2. *The Lyfe of Saynt George,* reprinted from Caxton's translation of *The Golden Legend* (Wynken de Worde, 1512) in Alexander Barclay's *The Life of St. George* (Early English Text Society, O.S. 230, 1955), p. 115.

3. See Rosemond Tuve, "Spenser and Some Pictorial Conventions," *Studies in Philology,* XXXVII (1940), 173–75.

4. *The Life of St. George,* p. 112.   5. *Ibid.,* p. 114.

6. Cambridge, for the Parker Society, 1844 (No. 13), pp. 620–40. The general title of the tract is "The Christian Knighte."

7. Part 3, Sec. 4, Mem. 2, Subsec. 3

8. "A Learned and Comfortable Sermon of the Certainty and Perpetuity of Faith in the Elect," in *Of the Laws of Ecclesiastical Polity, Books 1 to 4* (Everyman's Library, 1925), pp. 6–7. Compare also the tract by John Bunyan entitled *The Acceptable Sacrifice; or, The Excellency of a Broken Heart.*

9. "A Learned Discourse of Justification," in *Of the Laws of Ecclesiastical Polity, Books 1 to 4,* p. 48.

10. *Virgilii Opera,* fol. 255r. See also fol. 467r. Christophoro Landino, *Camaldulenses disputationes* (Strasbourg, 1508), Sig. K ii (r), writes: "Ex hoc autem Acheron manat: quae res gaudij privationem denotat." Compare *Paradise Lost,* ii.578: "Sad Acheron of sorrow, black and deep."

11. "A Learned and Comfortable Sermon," in *Of the Laws of Ecclesiastical Polity, Books 1 to 4,* p. 12. Hooker, of course, is thinking of Daniel.

12. The savages who capture Serena in Book vi are also tamed by their idolatrous religion (viii.43).

13. Satan as tempter is often portrayed as woman above and serpent below. Professor Helaine Newstead points out to me the passages in *Piers Plowman* B, xviii, 333–36, and Chaucer's *Man of Law's Tale,* ll. 360–61. See also Hesiod's *Theogony,* ll. 293 ff., and J. M. Steadman,

"Sin, Echidna and the Viper's Brood," *Modern Language Review,* LVI (1961), 62–66.

14. *The Institution of Christian Religion,* tr. Thomas Norton (first printed 1561; London, 1634), 1.3.1.

15. *Of the Laws of Ecclesiastical Polity,* 1.vii.6 (p. 172).

16. iv.24 (tr. P. H. Wicksteed, the Temple Classics).

17. *Godfrey of Bulloigne,* tr. Edward Fairfax (London, 1687), Sig. A 3 (v).

18. *Virgilii Opera,* fol. 124r: "Quam Graeci ὕλην vocant, poetae nominant sylvam, id est elementorum congeriem, unde cuncta procreantur."

19. *Ibid.,* fol. 256r: "Nam per sylvas, tenebras et lustra, significat, in quibus feritas et libido dominatur."

20. *Ibid.,* fol. 124v: "Per sylvam igitur, significatur nobis diversitas influentiarum, in qua difficile est illum aureum ramum, de quo in sexto mentio fiet, inuenire." Fols. 255–56: "ex hac sylva, quae mundi sunt occupationes, in lucem emergamus: opus est aureo ramo, id est sapientia. Nam, ut dicit Seneca epistola ultima, viij libri, Anima in hoc corpore, tanquam in vinculis premitur, nisi adsit sapientia. . . ." "Sylvam, vocant Platonici hylem. et omnium planetarum congeriem, seu influentiam: unde, quia nos sydera, ad varias trahunt affectiones: difficile est, rectam viam semper tenere: aut sylvae, id est corporis passiones virtutem occulunt."

21. Facsimile reprint of 1576 edition (New York, 1947), p. 87.

22. As Upton long ago proposed. "Fra" in "Fradubio" may be the Italian preposition meaning *in* or *among,* although most commentators take it for *brother:* Brother Doubt. Spenser's spelling and the rhythm indicate that the first syllable of Fraelissa's name is to be pronounced "Fræl" rather than "Fra," the whole therefore standing for *frailty, fragilezza* in Italian. The poet hints at the meaning of these names in the lines immediately preceding Fradubio's speech: "fraile men . . . doubtfull eares" (ii.32).

23. *Orlando Furioso in English Heroicall Verse* (London, 1634), p. 47.

24. *The Queen's Majesty's Entertainment at Woodstock,* 1575, ed. A. W. Pollard (Oxford, 1903 and 1910), pp. xxvii–xxviii.

25. Reproduced in E. Wind, *Bellini's Feast of the Gods: A Study in Venetian Humanism* (Cambridge, 1948), Plate 48, and described *ibid.,* p. 18.

26. *Ibid.,* Plate 47.

27. Commentary on the Prophets Haggai and Obadiah (1560), in

The Works of James Pilkington, B. D., Lord Bishop of Durham (Cambridge, for the Parker Society, 1842), pp. 67–68.

28. *De Genesi contra Manichaeos, Patrologia Latina,* XXXIV, 208: "Et ideo ad arborem se dicuntur abscondere, quae erat in medio paradisi, id est ad seipsos, qui in medio rerum infra Deum et supra corpora ordinati erant. Ergo ad seipsos absconderunt se, ut conturbarentur miseris erroribus, relicto lumine veritatis, quod ipsi non erant."

29. Sir Walter Ralegh, *The History of the World* (London, 1687), pp. 37–38.

30. The Latin is quoted by D. W. Robertson, Jr., in "The Doctrine of Charity in Medieval Gardens," *Speculum,* XXVI (1951), 26, from *Patrologia Latina,* CLXXV, 171–72. Robertson cites other examples of the allegory of the tree. Landino interprets similarly the elm tree which stands at the entrance to Vergil's underworld: "In ulmi autem descriptione / idem quod et paulo supra ostenderat: pulcherrimo nunc / ac omnino poetico figmento depingit. Ipsa enim in medio posita: magnum spatium occupat: fructum autem nullum praebet: sed sola umbra nos delectat sic et turpe facinus ea nobis ostendit: quae nihil solidi habeant / et quae cum magna videantur / nihil sint: ut Phrygij Aesopi exemplo relicto corpore umbram sectemur. Quod eo quoque expressius notat cum addat: in singulis frondibus / singula insidere somnia: atque ea quidem vana: Nihil levius: nihil mutabilius est frondibo" (*Camaldulenses disputationes,* Sig. K vi [r]).

31. *The Institution of Christian Religion,* 1.15.8.

32. *Godfrey of Bulloigne,* Sig. A 3 (v).

33. Robertson, *Speculum,* XXVI, 31. Compare also Louis Réau, *Iconographie de l'Art Chrétien* (Paris, 1957), II, Part 2, 483: "Par la vertu vivifiante du Précieux Sang, l'arbre mort auquel le Christ avait été attaché redevient vivant."

34. S. K. Heninger, "The Orgoglio Episode," *ELH,* XXVI (1959), 171–87, points out the imagery associating Orgoglio with earthquake, the material cause of which, according to Gabriel Harvey, is the "great aboundance of wynde . . . fast shut up, and as a man would saye, emprysoned in the Caves, and Dungeons of the Earth" (*Works,* IX, 453).

35. III.3–4, in Macrobius, *Commentary on the Dream of Scipio,* tr. W. H. Stahl (New York, 1952), p. 72.

36. See C. Bowie Millican, "A Friend of Spenser," *London Times Literary Supplement,* August 7, 1937. Salter (1564?–1646) was chaplain to Edmund Sheffield, third Baron Sheffield and first Earl of Mulgrove.

37. Sigs. G 1 (v)–G 2 (r).   38. Sig. G 1 (v).

39. Calvin, *The Institution of Christian Religion,* IV.2.11; Hooker, "A Learned Discourse of Justification, Works, and How the Foundation of Faith Is Overthrown," in *Of the Laws of Ecclesiastical Polity, Books 1 to 4,* pp. 14–75. The "learned discourse" is largely devoted to a defense of Hooker's "mother sentence": "I doubt not but God was merciful to save thousands of our fathers living in popish superstitions, inasmuch as they sinned ignorantly" (p. 71).

The Legend of Temperaunce: Prays-desire and Shamefastnesse

1. William Camden, *Remaines Concerning Britaine* (first printed 1605; London, 1623), p. 65, derives the name Guy "from the French Guide. A guide, leader, or director to other."

2. See A. D. S. Fowler, "The River Guyon," *Modern Language Notes,* LXXV (1960), 289–92.

3. See Susan Snyder, "Guyon the Wrestler," *Renaissance News,* XIV (1961), 249–52.

4. *The "Summa Theologica" of St. Thomas Aquinas,* tr. the Fathers of the English Dominican Province (London, 1914), Part II (first part), Question xxxvii, 4. I am grateful to Miss Susan Snyder for this reference.

5. *Ibid.*

6. Spenser's division is a form of the traditional analysis. Burton summarizes some of the opinions on the subject (*Anatomy of Melancholy,* Part I, Sec. 2, Mem. 3, Subsec. 3): "They [perturbations and passions] are commonly reduced into two inclinations, irascible and concupiscible. The Thomists subdivide them into eleven, six in the coveting, and five in the invading. Aristotle reduceth all to pleasure and pain, Plato to love and hatred, Vives to good and bad. If good, it is present, and then we absolutely joy and love: or to come, and then we desire and hope for it: if evil, we absolutely hate it: if present it is sorrow; if to come, fear. . . . All other passions are subordinate unto these four, or six, as some will: love, joy, desire, hatred, sorrow, fear. The rest, as anger, envy, emulation, pride, jealousy, anxiety, mercy, shame, discontent, despair, ambition, avarice, &c. are reducible unto the first." See Merritt Y. Hughes, "Burton on Spenser," *PMLA,* XLI (1926), 545–67.

7. Professor Craig R. Thompson has pointed out to me the commentary in Erasmus' *Adagia* on "Vini liquorem perdidisti infusa aqua." Erasmus quotes from the Greek Anthology: "Hinc iunctus Nymphis est Bacchus gratus. at ignem/Ardentem capies, hunc nisi miscueris."

Excessive dilution of Bacchus by the Nymphs may be noxious and productive of hangover, Erasmus remarks, citing Aristotle for the idea that water makes wine more subtle and therefore more capable of penetrating the narrow foramina of the brain.

8. *Secular Lyrics of the XIVth and XVth Centuries,* ed. R. H. Robbins (2d ed., Oxford, 1955), p. xxxii. The scribbler is quoting from a translation from Claudian by Sir Thomas Elyot, *The Book of the Governor,* Book II, Sec. I.

9. *Nicomachean Ethics,* tr. W. D. Ross, II.3.

10. *Republic,* tr. F. M. Cornford, III.414.

11. *Nicomachean Ethics,* x.9.   12. Frag. 970.

13. For the contrary view see E. Sirluck, "The Faerie Queene, Book II, and the Nicomachaean Ethics," *Modern Philology,* XLIX (1951–52), 73–100.

14. *Nicomachean Ethics,* III.11.

15. *Ibid.,* IV.9.   16. *Ibid.,* I.10.

17. Harry Berger, Jr., *The Allegorical Temper* (New Haven, 1957, Yale Studies in English Vol. 137), pp. 19 ff.

18. St. Augustine cites Cicero's use of *aegritudo* for sorrow (*The City of God,* tr. M. Dods [New York, 1950], XIV.7).

19. In addition to the studies cited in *Works,* Vol. II, Appendix XI, see Carroll Camden, "The Architecture of Spenser's House of Alma," *Modern Language Notes,* LVIII (1943), 262–65, and Vincent Hopper, "Spenser's House of Temperance," *PMLA,* LV (1940), 958–67.

20. Part of the joke is the echo of Revelation 3:7: "the key of David, which openeth and no man shutteth, and shutteth, and no man openeth."

21. Badius comments on the pseudo-Vergilian *De venere:* "Alma dicitur Venus, ab alendo, quia eius praesidio, alitur omnium animantium genus" (*Virgilii Opera,* fol. 469r). Spenser tells us that Alma feasted Guyon and Arthur (x.77, xi.2).

22. See Carrie Anna Harper, *The Sources of the British Chronicle History in Spenser's Faerie Queene* (Philadelphia, 1910), especially pp. 177 ff.

23. Isabel E. Rathborne, in *The Meaning of Spenser's Fairyland* (New York, 1937), Chapter II, identifies the rulers described in the book which Sir Guyon reads with Osiris, Hercules, Bacchus, and other gods and heroes of antiquity (for her later thoughts on the subject and for the comments of others see the correspondence in *London Times Literary Supplement,* February to July, 1948). Professor Rathborne is led to conclude that Spenser's Fairyland is similar in some respects to the classical land of the dead.

The Legend of Chastitie: Maid and Woman

1. *Orlando Furioso in English Heroicall Verse* (London, 1634), p. 406.

2. Servius, cited by E. R. Curtius, *European Literature and the Latin Middle Ages,* tr. W. R. Trask (New York, 1953), p. 192.

3. *Metamorphoses,* III.155–62, tr. Rolfe Humphries (Bloomington, Ind., 1957), pp. 61–62.

4. My colleague, Professor Maurice Valency, pointed this out to me many years ago. It is suggested in a note by Robert Ellrodt, *Neoplatonism in the Poetry of Spenser* (Geneva, 1960), p. 88. No doubt, this "mount" is the "some-what" that stirs foolish Faunus to laughter when he sees the naked Diana in her secret retreat in the Cantos of Mutabilitie (vi.46).

5. See particularly the articles by J. W. Bennett in *PMLA,* XLVII (1932), 46–80, and *Journal of English and Germanic Philology,* XLI (1942), 53–78 and 486–89, and those by Brents Stirling, *PMLA,* XLIX (1934), 501–38, and *Journal of English and Germanic Philology,* XLI (1942), 482–86. A recent treatment of the subject is to be found in Ellrodt, *Neoplatonism in the Poetry of Spenser,* Chapter IV.

6. Emile Bréhier, *La Philosophie de Plotin* (Paris, 1928), p. 53.

7. *Plotini Opera Omnia . . . cum Marsilii Ficini Commentariis* (Oxford, 1835), I, 237, 241, 549, etc.

8. *Enneads,* III.3.7.

9. *De genesi ad litteram,* lib. v, ed. Josephus Zycha, *Corpus Scriptorum Ecclesiasticorum Latinorum,* XXVIII (1894), 168: "Sicut autem in ipso grano invisibiliter erant omnia simul, quae per tempora in arborem surgerent, ita ipse mundus cogitandus est, cum deus simul omnia creavit, habuisse simul omnia, quae in illo cum illo facta sunt, quando factus est dies, non solum caelum cum sole et luna et sideribus, quorum species manet motu rotabili, et terram et abyssos, quae velut inconstantes motus patiuntur atque inferius adiuncta partem alteram mundo conferunt, sed etiam illa, quae aqua et terra produxit potentialiter atque causaliter, priusquam per temporum moras ita exorerentur, quomodo nobis iam nota sunt in eis operibus, quae deus usque nunc operatur."

10. *Enneads,* II.3.17. 11. *Ibid.,* II.3.11.

12. *Plotini Opera Omnia,* I, 240: "Sic non solicitudine, non labore, sed indefessa facilitate, tum naturalia ab ipsa natura, tum naturae semina ab intelligentia pullulabunt." Compare Spenser:

Ne needs there Gardiner to set, or sow,
  To plant or prune: for of their owne accord
  All things, as they created were, doe grow   (vi.34)

13. *Enneads,* III.7.11.

14. Jean Guitton, *Le Temps et l'Éternité chez Plotin et Saint Augustin* (3d ed., rev.; Paris, 1959), p. 59.

15. *Enneads,* III.7.11.   16. *Ibid.,* II.3.15.

17. Compare Ficino, *Plotini Opera Omnia,* I, 235.

18. *Enneads,* II.1.1.   19. *Ibid.,* v.8.1.

20. Another tradition identifies the cosmic year or great year of the world with the time required for the seven "planets" to return to the position they occupied on the day they were created or with the time which separates two successive conjunctions of all of the planets at the spring equinox. See Pierre Duhem, *Le Système du Monde* (Paris, 1913–59), I, 65–85, 275–96; II, 214–23. Although the period of rotation of the fixed stars is usually given as 36,000 solar years, two of Spenser's contemporaries, Sir John Davies (*Orchestra,* Stanza 35) and Du Bartas (Fourth Day of the First Week) assert that it is between six and seven thousand years.

21. *Plotini Opera Omnia,* II, 995: "Paucas ergo vitarum mutationes in anno mundi magno edere anima tua potest: praesertim cum vitam in terris quidem brevissimam, super terram vero longissimam agat. In anno autem mundi sequente non fit vitarum mutatio, sed eorundem omnino hominum resurrectio." On *Enneads* I.5, Ficino comments (I, 80): "Denique (ut summatim dicam) si ex universo mundi circuitu, quem triginta sex millibus annorum compleri quidam putant: tercentum annis, diverso tamen tempore, animus tanquam exul hic habitet, vicissim tribus saltem annorum millibus patrias sedes colere putant: eosque animos et hic brevius adhuc, et illic longius habitare: qui vel ab initio praestantioribus tum stellis accommodati, tum daemonibus fuerint commendati: vel ipsi efficaciori virtute muniti caduca contempserint, aeterna coluerint."

22. *Enneads,* II.3.13.   23. *Ibid.,* III.5.9.   24. *Ibid.*

25. Christophoro Landino, *Camaldulenses disputationes* (Strasbourg, 1508), Sig. H vi (r–v): "Mater est materia: quia sinum praestat: deus gignit et creat: ac sua quidem vi. Illa autem ex alterius immixtione concipit. Concipit autem infusione spiritus divini / quam animam mundi nominat Trismegistus: Quae res eum mouet / ut deo officium patris tribuat: quoniam infundit. Silvae vero matris: quia a deo con-

cipiat. Animam denique mundi vim seminis habere dicit: quia a deo ipsa inspiretur in silvae gremium."

26. Natalis Comes, *Mythologiae* (Frankfurt, 1581), p. 533.

27. See J. W. Bennett, "Spenser's Garden of Adonis," *PMLA*, XLVII (1937), 48.

28. Facsimile reprint of 1576 edition (New York, 1947), p. 118. See also the passage on pp. 231–32 cited by J. W. Bennett in "Spenser's Garden of Adonis," p. 52.

29. *Pietro Bembo's "Gli Asolani,"* tr. Rudolf B. Gottfried (Bloomington, Ind., 1954), pp. 189–90.

30. Tr. M. Dods (New York, 1950), XIV.24.

31. *Enneads*, III.5.1. 32. *Ibid.*

33. Compare Boccaccio, *Ninfale Fiesolano*, Stanza 304, and the *Decameron*, VIII.4.

34. *Orlando Furioso in English Heroicall Verse*, p. 7.

35. The Chaucerian version, l. 1033.

36. *The Philosophy of Love*, tr. F. Friedeberg-Seeley and Jean H. Barnes (London, 1937), p. 339.

37. Diodorus Siculus, *The Library of History* (Loeb Classical Library), IV.27. Thomas P. Roche, Jr., "The Challenge to Chastity: Britomart at the House of Busyrane," *PMLA*, LXXVI (1961), 340–44, refers to Ovid, *Ars amatoria*, 1.643–58. He also suggests that the name "Busirane" is intended to recall the word "abuse," or "abusion."

38. *House of Fame*, I, ll. 345 ff.

39. *A Fifteenth Century School Book*, ed. William Nelson (Oxford, 1956), p. 56.

The Legend of Friendship: The Hermaphrodite Venus

1. *Parlement of Foules*, ll. 379–81. Theodore Silverstein, in a review of J. A. W. Bennett's *The Parlement of Foules* (*Modern Philology*, LVI [1959], 274) traces the last quoted line to the Pseudo-Aristotelian *De mundo*.

2. "The Legend of Cambel and Triamond in the Faerie Queene," *Studies in Philology*, XXXV (1938), 195–201.

3. *Aeneid*, VIII.563–66, tr. H. R. Fairclough (Loeb Classical Library). Servius' comment (*Virgilii Opera*, fol. 327v) reads: "Hoc autem loco per tres animas magnum et perfectum indicat virum."

4. Badius comments on *De venere*, in *Virgilii Opera*, fol. 468v: "nam

caestus, est zona Veneris: dictus a castitate, qua legitime nubentes
cinguntur."

5. Lines 2304–11.   6. Lines 2341–45.

7. III.1210–11.   8. III.1230–32.

9. See Macrobius, *Commentary on the Dream of Scipio,* tr. W. H.
Stahl (New York, 1952), pp. 186–88. Chaucer refers to the story and
links it with the tradition that the biblical Tubal-Cain invented the art
of music (*The Book of the Duchess,* ll. 1162–69).

The Legend of Justice: The Idol and the Crocodile

1. See Isabel Rathborne, *The Meaning of Spenser's Fairyland* (New
York, 1937), pp. 88–89.

2. *Histories of the Kings of Britain* (Everyman's Library), III.xvii.
Geoffrey (IX.xii) mentions another Arthgal, earl of Warwick, among
the noblemen who paid allegiance to Arthur. Richard Grafton (*Chronicle
at Large* [London, 1809], I, 83) expands this bare reference: "In this
tyme also I finde mencion made of a noble and valiant man called
Arthgall, and he was the first Erle of Warwike, and he was one of the
knightes of the round Table of King Arthure. . . . This Arthgal tooke
a Beare for his beast because the first sillable of his name which is
Arth, in the Britishe speche, and is in English a Beare." Spenser may
have had this Arthgal in mind as an allusion to the Dudley family.

3. For a study of this tradition, see Marjorie Hope Nicolson, *Moun-
tain Gloom and Mountain Glory* (Ithaca, N.Y., 1959), Chapter II.
See also D. C. Allen, "A Note on Spenser's Orology," *Modern Language
Notes,* LXI (1946), 555–56.

4. See James E. Phillips, Jr., "The Background of Spenser's Attitude
toward Women Rulers," *Huntington Library Quarterly,* V (1941–42),
5–32, and "The Woman Ruler in Spenser's Faerie Queene," *ibid.,*
pp. 211–34, and Kerby Neill, "Spenser on the Regiment of Women,"
Studies in Philology, XXXIV (1937), 134–37. Phillips quotes the letter
from Calvin to Bullinger: "Concerning female government, I expressed
myself to this effect, that seeing it was contrary to the legitimate course
of nature, such governments ought to be reckoned among the visitations
of God's anger. But even so, the grace of God sometimes displayed itself
in an extraordinary way, since, as a reproach to the sloth of men, he
raises up women, endowed not after the nature of men, but with a
certain heroic spirit, as is seen in the illustrious example of Deborah."

5. Hooker, *Of the Laws of Ecclesiastical Polity, Books 1 to 4* (Everyman's Library, 1925), I.viii.9 (p. 182).

6. *Natalis Comes Mythologiae* (Frankfurt, 1581), pp. 117 ff.

7. I.i.18–20, 43–46, 65–67.

8. The editors of *Works* elect the 1596 reading "rebellions" in preference to "rebellious" which appears in later editions.

9. *Merchant of Venice*, IV.i.211–12, 217–18.

10. Jean Bodin, *The Six Bookes of a Commonweale,* tr. Richard Knolles, 1606, ed. K. D. McRae (Harvard University Press, 1962), p. 764. See also Aristotle, *Nicomachean Ethics*, V.10.

11. Cited by J. Wilson McCutchan, "Justice and Equity in the English Morality Play," *Journal of the History of Ideas,* XIX (1958), 405–10. The case involved the Earl of Oxford.

12. *Measure for Measure,* II.ii.90; I.iii.22.

13. The association of Geryon with Spain is traditional. Spenser has transferred his three bodies to his own fiction, the son Geryoneo. Wonderful to relate, classical myth gives to Geryon's father, sprung from the blood of Medusa, the name of Chrysaor, Artegall's sword of justice! (Hesiod, *Theogony,* ll. 280 ff.)

14. *Measure for Measure,* III.ii.196–99.

The Legend of Courtesie: The Rose Revealed

1. *Wife of Bath's Tale,* ll. 1125–26.   2. *Ibid.,* ll. 1113–24.

3. *Ibid.,* ll. 1152–58.   4. Fols. 72–73.

5. Compare Dante, *Convivio,* IV.xvi (tr. Wicksteed, the Temple Classics): "I say then, that if we would have regard to the common custom of speech, this word 'nobleness' means the perfection in each thing of its proper nature. Wherefore it is not only predicated of man, but of all other things as well; for a man calls a stone noble, a plant noble, a horse noble, a falcon noble, whenever it appears perfect in its own nature. . . . I say, then, that inasmuch as in those things which are of one species, as are all men, we cannot define their best perfection by essential principles, we must define and know it by the effects they manifest; and so we read in the Gospel of St. Matthew when Christ says: 'Beware of false prophets; by their fruits ye shall know them.' So the straight path leads us to look for this definition (which we are searching for) by way of the fruits; which are moral and intellectual virtues whereof this our nobleness is the seed."

6. For discussions of this difficult passage and the sources of Spenser's treatment of the Graces see De Witt T. Starnes and Ernest William Talbert, *Classical Myth and Legend in Renaissance Dictionaries* (Chapel Hill, N.C., 1955), pp. 50–55, 87–93, and E. Wind, *Pagan Mysteries in the Renaissance* (London, 1958), pp. 33 ff.

7. *As You Like It*, iii.2.

8. See the note by W. L. Renwick summarized in *Works*, VI, 247.

Cantos of Mutabilitie: The Ever-whirling Wheel

1. See Northrop Frye, "The Structure of Imagery in The Faerie Queene," *University of Toronto Quarterly*, XXX (1961), 111.

2. William P. Cumming, "The Influence of Ovid's Metamorphoses on Spenser's Mutabilitie Cantos," *Studies in Philology*, XXVIII (1931), 241–56.

3. 1.156–62, tr. Rolfe Humphries (Bloomington, Ind., 1957), p. 7.

4. *Virgilii Opera*, fol. 286v: "dicti autem sunt Faunus et Fauna a vaticinando, id est fando. Unde et Fatuos dicimus inconsiderate loquentes." Spenser's familiarity with this etymology is made evident by Faunus' self-betrayal through what is certainly inconsiderate utterance (vi.46). Cooper glosses Fauna "idem quod Fatua."

5. *The Utopia of Sir Thomas More*, ed. J. H. Lupton (Oxford, 1895), p. lxxxix.

6. The point is made cogently by Sherman Hawkins, "Mutabilitie and the Cycle of the Months," in *Form and Convention in the Poetry of Edmund Spenser*, ed. William Nelson (New York, 1961), pp. 76–102.

7. John Walton, *Boethius: de Consolatione Philosophiae*, ed. M. Science (London, for The Early English Text Society, O.S. No. 170 [1927, for 1925]), p. 378.

8. See Book IV, Meter 6 and Book III, Meter 2, cited by Brents Stirling in "The Concluding Stanzas of Mutabilitie," *Studies in Philology*, XXX (1933), 193–204.

9. *Enneads*, iii.7.4.   10. *Ibid.*, iii.7.11.

Index